Schools Council
English 16-19 Project

CW01486635

16404

THE TEACHERS' CENTRE
WORCESTER STREET
MIDDLESBROUGH
CLEVELAND TS1 4NT

Education 16-19:
The Role of English
and Communication

Schools Council English 16–19 Project
The Project has written and produced a series of booklets on aspects of
English teaching, 16–19. These can be ordered from;
Schools Council English 16–19 Project
Bretton Hall College of Higher Education,
Wakefield, West Yorkshire WF4 4LG
(Not available from Macmillan Education)

Project Booklet Series

1   English in the New Sixth: Approaches to the First Year
2   Opportunities for Writing at 17+
3   Developing Active Comprehension
4   Exploring a new A Level: Communication Studies
5   Extending the Possibilities of English at 16–17
6   New Directions in General and Communication Studies
7   Introductory Handbook to Communication Studies
8   A New Tradition in A Level Literature
9   Students Articulating their Response to Literature
10 A Foundation Course in Communication

Schools Council
English 16-19 Project

Education 16-19:
The Role of English
and Communication

John Dixon
with
John Brown
Dorothy Barnes

Macmillan Education

© Schools Council Publications 1979

All rights reserved. No part of this publication
may be reproduced or transmitted, in any form
or by any means, electronic, mechanical,
photocopying, recording or otherwise without
the prior permission of the publishers.

First published 1979

ISBN 0 333 27005 3   Boards
ISBN 0 333 27006 1   Limp

Published by
MACMILLAN EDUCATION LIMITED
Houndmills Basingstoke Hampshire RG21 2XS
and London
Associated companies in Delhi Dublin
Hong Kong Johannesburg Lagos Melbourne
New York Singapore and Tokyo

Typesetting by
Parkway Group London and Abingdon
Printed in Great Britain by
Redwood Burn Ltd
Trowbridge and Esher

Contents

Preface   viii

Introduction: The work and aims of the English 16–19
    Project, 1975–1978.   xi

Part 1: The Underlying Demand for Change

1.1 Changes in the demand for full-time education beyond the
         leaving age: an analysis of the massive changes during the
         generation 1951–76 and implications for the next generation.   1

1.2 Achievement trends and the accusation of declining standards:
         refutation of criticisms from employers and academics in the
         light of research evidence.   4

1.3 A changed understanding of language: a review of criticisms
         1951–76 of existing syllabuses and examinations in English
         in the light of a better theoretical understanding.   12

1.4 Changing definitions of the role of English within the curricu-
         lum: a discussion of the place within English studies of oral
         language, drama and language in contemporary media, and
         of the relationship between English and communication.   18

1.5 Policy needed for a new generation at 16–19: the grounds for
         revising past systems of assessment designed for small minorities,
         for bridging the gap between academic and vocational educa-
         tion, and for offering general as well as specialist courses at
         16–19 with specific implications for English.   22

Part 2: The Main Paths ahead in English and Communication

2.1 Branching routes in English beyond the fifth form: a discussion
         of the scope of syllabuses available, the level and forms of
         qualification needed, and the routes between qualifications
         at 17+ and 18+.   33

2.2 Qualifications and education: a review of the historical evidence that English has been badly examined, but that some recent assessment methods have positive effects on teaching and learning.   40

2.3 The 18+ tail that wags the dog: introducing an analysis of new opportunities made available during the project and the overall range necessary at 18+, especially as A level is the target for the largest single group of full-time students.   43

2.4 The potential of literature at 18+: a review of teachers' aims, the difficulties they face in realising these, given the traditional examination, the qualities they wish to see recognised and the major experiment now taking place.   45

2.5 The potential of communication studies: the aims of students on the new A level course, the interpretation of the syllabus in practice and the directions such syllabuses may take in future.   70

2.6 Continuing English to A level: the common ground already established, some fundamental aims and objectives, the way to provide for flexibility, and in conclusion an anthology suggesting a range of writing that might be included.   88

2.7 Language studies to 18+: an analysis of the directions that language study may take and of developments in progress, including the new optional paper at A level.   104

2.8 Choice and scope from 16+: the FE contribution, defining the uses of language 'to get things done', and drawing on examples from joint workshops and linked departments.   109

2.9 Where schools and FE meet: the contrast between uses of language leading to success or failure in action, and uses leading to better understanding, with a critique of the effect in FE of demanding syllabuses based on lists of objectives.   116

2.10 A bridge from school to community and work: recent developments in one-year sixth form courses and the links with FE these make possible.   121

2.11 The criteria for one-year courses: the majority need for an intermediate level of qualification at 17/18+, and thus for 'foundation courses' with a choice of orientation.   128
Finally a note on N & F.   132

Part 3: The Need for Local and National Support

THREE LEVELS OF CO-ORDINATION

3.1 At the local and departmental level: the need to co-ordinate
the choices on offer at 16 and establish positive links between
academic and vocational work.   133

3.2 At the national level: the current need for an agency to review
16–19 curricular provision as a whole, and to establish a new
balance between specialist and general education and a new
relation between academic or vocational preparation on the
one hand and social and personal education on the other.   137

A POLICY FOR CURRICULUM AND EXAMINATIONS DEVELOPMENT

3.3 Examining a student's work in English: positive ways in which
the boards are learning to adapt the mass examination system
and to take into account the quality and range of work
students actually achieve.   141

3.4 The changing role of the boards: a discussion of the boards'
role in curriculum development.   145

3.5 Introducing new subjects: the interlocking roles of teachers
and the boards, with special reference to the project's joint
experience with the AEB in introducing the new A level in
communication studies.   148

3.6 Changes in traditional subjects and methods of assessment:
the teacher's task and the supporting agencies needed,
drawing on the project's experience with alternative A levels
in literature.   152

3.7 Teachers' roles in syllabus and examination design: a discussion of opportunities and difficulties experienced by the
boards.   157

3.8 Co-ordinating developments in course, syllabus and examination the need for national discussion where there are serious
conflicts in practice and policy, with special reference to
English.   163

3.9 The immediate tasks ahead.   166

Appendix: Notes, sources, acknowledgements.   169

Preface

The English 16–19 Project and this report on it inevitably raise questions that go beyond the teaching of a single subject. To begin with, English cannot be regarded as a 'subject' in quite the same sense as mathematics, physics or geography. Academics have sometimes tried to reduce it to the study of literature alone; vocationalists to the study of business transactions. Yet the essence of English is language, and language is the most important form of communication between human beings. Certainly it is not the only form of communication today, nor is communication the only function of language. Nevertheless, for older adolescents coming to terms with themselves and their new social roles, this aspect of language should be an essential element of any curriculum. Whether we start from the needs of a society dominated by endemic change, or from the personal needs of the people who make up society, we arrive at the same conclusion.

Secondly, there is an illusory simplicity in employing the phrase '16–19' to denote a stage of education. It masks wide divisions and discrepancies. Although most parts of Britain offer a unified system up to the age of 16, at that point comprehensive provision comes to a sharp and decisive end. Young people find themselves set on widely diverging paths — or even on no very clear path at all. In contrast with most European countries, the majority of 16 to 19-year-olds are receiving neither continued education nor much training beyond an elementary induction to their job.

Nevertheless, concern for the 16–19 age group is being fed from three different sources — the increased numbers staying on in education beyond the statutory leaving age; a growing anxiety in industry and commerce about the quality of its workforce; and more recently the substantial rise in the number of the young unemployed.

At 16 many young people are intuitively aware of their unreadiness for the adult world of work. They choose, therefore, to stay on in education either in sixth forms or in further education colleges. They pursue a variety of courses, many of them designed for other types of student with different perspectives. For this group of young people their courses perform the function of sustaining them through the final stages of adolescence and leading them into adulthood. The so-called 'new sixth' and its less easily discernible but no less real parallel in further education produce the anomalies that give rise to the first source of concern.

The second source is the discovery by commerce and industry that, with over 40 per cent staying on in full-time education, their recruits at 16 have no longer the same range of attainments or background as their predecessors of twenty, thirty or forty years ago. At the same time the range of tasks they are now required to perform has been transformed. Employers now require a better educated and more realistically trained workforce drawn from the ranks of those who in the past would have left school at 14. Today they are required to show qualities of flexibility and adaptability in meeting the challenge of the late twentieth century, not only in the factory with increasingly automated production lines but in the office with its word processors and desk-top computers.

The third and most recent source of concern is the prolonged unemployment or irregular employment of large numbers of young people, a depressing phenomenon that Britain shares with other industrialised countries in the West.

Separate solutions have been sought for these separate anxieties. To meet the anomalies of extended sixth forms, new types of examination — CEE and N & F — are being explored. In technical and commercial education, new course systems are being elaborated, such as those of the technician and business education councils. For the unemployed, the Youth Opportunities Programme has been created. A beginning has even been made with the unified vocational preparation programmes to redeem ancient promises and to meet the needs of that large group in employment who at present receive neither continued education nor training. Each development is discrete and relates only to its own group of 16–19s.

From such different strands, how can we weave the web of a common programme?

The report offers eloquent testimony on how far current provision still falls short. No doubt many teachers bend existing curricula to meet the real needs of their students, but such practices are inadequate. The situation calls for a unified structure of education and training for the whole age group, including those who fall outside present provision. Within that structure there is a need for a range of curricular pathways that express the divergent vocational routes of individuals but contain a central core that speaks to the common need of the older adolescent.

In the sixties English teachers in secondary education discovered the personal and creative uses of languages and built curricula around them. In the late seventies we have proceeded to identify the social uses of language and are beginning to use them as central curricular elements. In a society multi-ethnic in composition, participative in its administrative style, and increasingly dominated by the media of mass communication, we neglect at our peril these two aspects of the education of our young people.

Against this background the Schools Council English 16–19 Project has been working with teachers throughout England and Wales. It has mapped the full spectrum of formal education; it has sought common ground; it has identified new initiatives designed to meet the central problem. It has not confined itself to description or diagnosis. In the workshop conferences it has run and the groups that have recurrently grown out of them, in the range of its publications, the programme of dissemination, it has attempted to seize on those seminal strands that are working to unify and transform the present *ad hoc* provision into a coherent curricular pattern.

In the report the project team offers signposts for new courses and indicates how they may be developed and assessed. This work must now be taken forward by others. Teachers and advisers carry a major responsibility, but so do all those others involved in education — politicians and administrators, parents, governors and employers. Nor can those concerned with industrial training and the continuing education of young workers stand aloof. Professional educators and laymen alike need to appreciate the message of this report. As Chairman of the Project Consultative Committee, I warmly commend it to them.

29 November 1978   F. D. FLOWER

Introduction

This report is the product of three years' joint work and discussion with groups of teachers. It is an attempt by the three of us on the project team to describe, on behalf of those teachers, what we have learnt.

When the project started in September 1975, we each came to it with particular expectations. Dorothy Barnes, head of department at a large comprehensive school in Leeds, was one of a pioneer group of Yorkshire teachers. During the sixties they had successfully proved with the JMB that a folder of course work could be made an effective basis for O-level language assessment; by 1975 many of them were asking whether both the course and the examination in A-level literature could not be strengthened by a similar approach. John Brown's comprehensive lay outside Brighton and drew on a working-class housing estate as well as a wider area. His department had already tried to design courses better suited than A level to some of the students staying on beyond the fifth form, and at the same time had used oral and dramatic work to broaden the value of A-level literature itself. John Dixon had recently been organising workshops with teachers in England and Canada, aiming to clarify the ways language is actually used in the service of imagination, feeling and thought. The power and resource of those workshop groups suggested an exciting and still untapped potential in English teaching. For our first year and a half we were additionally strengthened when Margaret Gill, an Australian colleague studying on an Imperial Research Fellowship, joined our team. Her practical experience as a teacher in the reform of the school-leaving examination in Victoria and her research interest in strategies of curriculum development were to be of decisive importance.

We had a sense of elation, therefore, in facing the tasks that had been outlined for us at a Schools Council delegate conference at York the previous year. With a surprising degree of accord, the teachers represented there had proposed a general broadening of English syllabuses beyond the age of 16, the design if possible of a 'common core' suited to a very broad range of students, the development of a range of options at A level, and the introduction of course work alongside examination scripts as the basis for assessment in English. It was made clear that, with 'the evident acute shortage of trained English teachers', special support would be needed to allow groups to meet, discuss and plan such new work, and that the DES scheme proposed by Mrs Thatcher for a major expansion of in-service education would help to prevent teachers feeling — as they often had — 'thwarted for lack of time, money and support'.

That was Easter 1974. By the time the project had got under way, Europe had lurched into an economic depression and nearly 100,000 school leavers were headed straight for the dole. Education budgets were cut. Newly trained teachers were among those facing unemployment. And to twist the knife deeper, the media and people with political influence were looking round for scapegoats, not in the economic system, but in the social services and the schools.

It was not a good time, in 1975–6, to be talking about the future. We might have expected many teachers to be content to sit tight, and let the storm pass over. This would not have been unreasonable; after all, it had been clear from earlier regional conferences that education 16–19 was developing very unevenly across the country. 'The national picture is complex — and confusing — for a number of reasons: the varying proportions of the age group staying on in full-time education after the Fifth; the varying impact of secondary reorganisation; the varying relationships between schools and FE colleges; the sharp contrasts between vocational demands and higher education demands. . . .' These difficulties were already acknowledged in the project proposal. In addition, by 1976 education as a whole was on the defensive — at the DES and in the examining boards, as well as in schools and colleges. It was a hard time for any teacher to assert the need for new opportunities, or to argue the case for more valid standards, in English 16–19. Indeed, before the end of our first year we knew of six or seven frustrated groups who had had alternative A-level proposals turned down.

Nevertheless, some teachers persevered, with the encouragement of their English advisers, and so successfully that by the end of 1976 the project was negotiating on behalf of local groups a national experiment in A-level literature, and was planning support for a new A level in communication studies, which had been independently designed by a northern group of teachers. Both set up a challenge to teachers to design new courses, in the first case to broaden the range of reading and writing, and in the second to allow for productive and receptive work in other media as well. This was not the whole answer at 18+, but it was certainly a breakthrough. It set the team two important tasks: first, to find the most effective methods of helping the teachers concerned to explore and define the new courses these syllabuses made possible; and secondly, to clarify the relationship between English and communication. This set us on the road for the main practical work of our last two years, and a central part of the present report.

We already knew, of course, that for some sections of the teaching profession the very title of our project was a misnomer. In further education, work on spoken and written language was increasingly being incorporated into communication courses — or, more radically, into communication elements within a unified vocational course. For some teachers this entailed a new concentration on basic skills; for others, an imaginative extension of liberal studies.

It was immediate help in defining these courses that FE teachers needed, especially when the new Technician Education Council (TEC) called for a particularly rigid statement of communication objectives. We had no wish to add to the divisions between schools and FE — rather the contrary. Indeed, as the project developed, we increasingly realised the need for an integrated policy at 16–19, covering both academic and vocational interests. So, after a preliminary seminar with the Association for Liberal Education, we committed ourselves in 1976–7 to working with two regional groups of FE teachers, one in Lancashire, the other in London and the South-East, in order to clarify with them the role of language in communication, and to understand more fully the relationship between the two subjects, English and communication. As it happened, two tertiary colleges were represented in the Lancashire group, and they served as a steady reminder to us that in the longer term the institutional gap at 16–19 has to be bridged.

From 1976, then, we were in effect a project in English and communication. Readers from either side will see the results in this report. We hope that whatever their current commitment, to English or to communication, teachers will actively consider what students at 16–19 are gaining from both subjects. We have tried not to hide the differences, but to concentrate positively on what both sides are trying to achieve.

Ideally, we should have brought both of them together, in the definition of courses for the growing number of students staying for a year beyond the fifth form. This was not possible. Indeed, reviewing the brief given us in 1974, we recognise that it is the students staying to 17+ who have gained least from our work. There are two main reasons for this. First, no national decision was — or has yet been — taken on the pilot CEE courses specially designed for students in schools. Secondly, the relationship between these one-year courses and the mainstream qualifications, whether academic or vocational, has yet to be adequately defined.

It did seem in 1976 that a very important part of our task would be to co-ordinate the enthusiastic development work for which the pilot CEEs had been the vehicle in many different regions — the East Anglican, Welsh, Southern, Metropolitan and Midlands especially — and to help a widening circle of teachers to reap the benefits. In fact, we had a series of regional seminars planned, but these were abandoned in mid-1976 as we came to realise that, with continuing postponement of national recognition, only individual, pioneering schools were likely to persevere and, though it was a fight against the odds for them, they had least need of our practical help. At the same time, as we prepared case studies based on their work and produced the booklets that accompany this report, we were ironically aware that many of the teachers we discussed the material with had little doubt that this represented exactly the sort of challenge they had been hoping to offer their own one-year students.

This relative failure over one-year courses did have a positive outcome. With the help of our Australian colleague, Margeret Gill, acting as an informal evaluator, it led us to consider much more critically the forces that assist, deflect or inhibit teachers — or schools and colleges — who currently feel the need to reshape elements of the 16–19 curriculum in the interests of new groups of students. We looked again at the effects of segregating education post-16 into academic or vocational wings. We considered the role of different boards, positively and negatively, in fostering teachers' initiatives and taking course work of value into account. Looking back over the twenty-five years the three of us had been teaching, it seemed that the national system for education 16–19 had never fully adjusted to what was actually happening in the more advanced schools, colleges and LEAs.

Thus, in 1977, as we discussed the provision for students in the inner city, in newly developing tertiary colleges, in areas with a strong immigrant population, or in localities with strong school–FE links, we could see why some teachers — a minority at present? — were held back by the lack of a broad English qualification at 18+. It was easier to understand, in the light of our analysis, why a system that had served roughly 5 per cent of 16 to 19-year-olds reasonably well was already beginning to fail when 30 per cent or more were staying on full-time. Did this not mean that a new effort was needed to weld the best of the school and FE traditions, and that LEAs were going to have to prepare the way for the majority to stay in education — more flexibly organised and more imaginatively co-ordinated by schools and FE?

If we were at all near the truth, it was not sufficient to write a report addressed solely to teachers of English and communication. We had to start by placing the challenges now facing them — and many other colleagues? — in a historical perspective, showing heads, principals and advisers the reasons why a decade of curriculum development at 16–19 may now be a necessity, because of the changes schools and colleges themselves have helped to produce within a generation. We had to explain to people outside English departments how the very notion of using language effectively has undergone a critical change during that period, so that the standards of 1951 or 1964 are no longer acceptable. This is the audience we had in mind for Part 1 of our report.

In Part 2 we report the new developments we have observed in the work of teachers of English and communication, trying to interpret the value of one side to the other, to show where manifest progress has been made, and to indicate the places that still call for much active, constructive work, despite our best efforts.

Finally, in Part 3, we turn to the structures that will enable or resist the development of a curriculum adapted to a new generation of students. If teachers and students are to continue to produce new work of quality — as they have continued to do through a national depression — they will need co-ordinated support from their LEA, the examining boards, the national councils for education and the DES. Drawing directly on our experience as a project team, we have tried to show some of the key points where this support may be critical for education 16–19 in the next decade.

Acknowledgements

The author and publishers wish to thank the following who have kindly given permission for the use of copyright material:

Dr Frances Stevens for extracts from *English & Examinations* published by Hutchinson Publishing Group;

The Times for an extract by Murray Bailey, from the *Times Educational Supplement* 9 June 1978.

Every effort has been made to trace copyright holders, but if any have inadvertently been overlooked the publishers will be pleased to make the necessary arrangements at the first opportunity.

PART ONE

The Underlying Demand for Change

1.1 Changes in the Demand for Full-Time Education beyond the Leaving Age

At present [1959] only 12 per cent of the 17-year-old age group . . . get full-time education; we think that by 1980 half should.

Roughly speaking the stage of the journey that lies immediately ahead of us was accomplished in America in the twenty years between 1920 and 1940, during which the proportion of 17-year-olds who stayed at school . . . rose . . . to 51 per cent.

(Crowther Report, 1959)

In education 16–19 certain radical changes have already occurred, are continuing, and — if there is the will — could be consolidated for the next generation. We are concerned in this introductory part with educational changes over the past generation, from 1951 to 1976, and their lessons for the next generation from 1976 to 2001. In terms of a teacher's lifetime the span of a generation is not all that long. Many of today's heads and senior staff, many senior administrators and advisers, had already started teaching by 1951. That is the period of their early, formative experiences of education. What transformations have they lived through already?

To begin with we will restrict ourselves to one elementary change: the numbers and demand for full-time education 16–19. The young teachers of 1951 felt themselves in at the beginning of an era. The slogan was 'secondary education for all'. The school-leaving age had recently been raised to 15, grammar school education had finally been made free, and the remaining all-age 'elementary' schools were rapidly being replaced by new 'secondary moderns'. That year over 90,000 pupils stayed on to 16, almost all of them to take the new GCE 'Ordinary level' examination, specially designed for them. The vast majority of 16-year-olds, however — 460,000 of them — had already left school.

This is the first contrast. A generation ago fewer than one in six were staying on in education to 16; by 1976 only about one in six had *left* school before completing the fifth year in secondary education.

The key effect is on the function of the school-leaving examinations. GCE O level was designed for the 91,000 who stayed on to 16 to take it in 1951; by 1976 it was being used by 456,000 of the same age group — the majority of 16-year-olds.

1

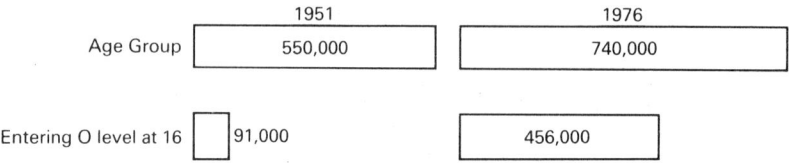

What had happened to the function of assessment at 16+? A generation earlier the system was designed as a competitive examination for a small minority, with pass/fail results. By 1976 it manifestly had to be adapted to assess the levels of achievement of the majority of the age group. This adaptation, and the changes it implies in the conception of assessment, have still to be carried through, as we shall see in section 1.5.

Let us turn next to those who stayed on into the sixth form, or in full-time further education. In 1951 there were about 34,000 aged 17 in sixth forms and a further 6,000 full-time students of the same age in FE. It was a select group; for every one who stayed in education there were twelve already at work. How do the 1976 figures compare?

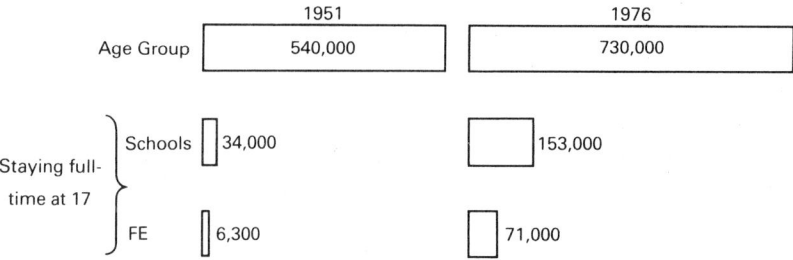

It is a very different story. Consider first the place of FE colleges in full-time education 16–19. Going back a generation, the numbers were small and in no way comparable with sixth forms; by 1976 the colleges were attracting about a third of the students at 17+. How significant is this trend for the future?

Secondly, consider the total number staying to 17+, roughly 220,000 students. This was no longer a tiny majority of the age group. What changes were needed in the courses and qualifications?

In 1951, for example, 13,000 students entered for English literature, one of the most popular subjects in the new 'Advanced level' GCE. A generation later 66,000 were entering, a fivefold increase. If this were simply industrial output, there would be no doubt about the achievement of the system over a generation. But in education success is more complex: are syllabuses and qualifications designed for 2 or 3 per cent of an age group likely to be equally appropriate for five times that proportion? And suppose the increase in candidates continues?

Teachers in 1951 did hope for changes. They were not satisfied with standards. Indeed the following year a national inquiry was set up into 'Early Leaving'. In a national survey of the LEA grammar schools it was found that well over a third of these selected pupils were either leaving without taking O level at all, or were achieving between nil and two passes. At the same time, in the schools' view many pupils suited to an A-level course in two or more subjects were leaving school before 17. When they were asked to estimate how big an increase in the number of boys and girls following Advanced courses would be justified, the schools replied 'about a half and two-thirds respectively'. Perhaps teachers have always erred on the side of caution?

By 1963–4, halfway through the generation, teachers could afford to laugh at the timidity of their hopes — and fears — in 1951. It looked as though the 20 per cent selected for grammar school *could*, after all, benefit from the kind of syllabuses and curriculum in operation at 16, and perhaps half that proportion from the A-level curriculum and syllabuses. However, the powers that be were much less confident about the remaining 80 per cent of students. As they designed the new CSE system that year they hoped (explicitly) that a further 20 per cent of the age group would benefit from its overall curriculum, and perhaps 40 per cent in all from CSE syllabuses in a single subject such as English. Actually, it was already known that all 16-year-olds would be in school by the early 1970s, but it was simply not foreseen that within ten years over 75 per cent of the age group would be entering for CSE or GCE examinations in English.

To sum up: so far we have looked simply — and crudely — at the numbers and broad targets of students 16–19 over a generation. These figures in themselves indicate changes on a massive scale. Equally revealing are the changing assumptions about the numbers likely to benefit by staying on in full-time education: a generation ago a fivefold increase in O- and A-level candidates was unthinkable, and yet it has happened. There are almost certainly similar underestimates today of the generation ahead and its potential aspirations. Worldwide economic depression, unemployment among teachers, and personal contact with thousands of school leavers without jobs has not been a natural source of optimism in the mid-seventies.

So much for numbers; what about targets? These figures also remind us that the original purposes of GCE O and A levels were very different from those of today. O level is already an examination for the majority; A level will follow in the next two decades. Are the traditional syllabuses and papers adequate for the new task?

And, finally, did the O-level and A-level boards preserve standards as the number of candidates increased fivefold, or has more simply meant worse? Many teachers are still confused and subdued by the attacks on educational standards launched by powerful pressure groups in the last few years. What are the achievements of the period 1951–76, and what grounds do they offer for serious judgements — not slogans — about the potential of full-time education for a majority at 17+ and beyond?

1.2   Achievement Trends and the Accusation of Declining Standards

Samuel Pepys was already at the Admiralty before he learned the multiplication table.   (Crowther Report, 1959)

We were impressed by the huge increase in children leaving school with GCE or CSE awards.

We were particularly concerned at the very low level of competence of some unqualified and barely qualified leavers especially in view of the disappearance of many unskilled jobs. There also seemed to be inadequacies amongst craft apprentices.

We were encouraged, however, at the many positive comments about good standards, especially of those entering higher education.

The increasing success level . . . in terms of formal leaving qualifications during the past generation represents a notable achievement by all those parties concerned with education.

(*The Attainments of the School Leaver*, 1977)

For confident generalisations about 'standards', the best qualifications seem to be ignorance of sampling and statistics, unconciousness of bias and a rather unscrupulous use of language. It may not be possible to avoid all of these, but at least one should try, even if the result is that nothing definite can be said about the change in *standards* 1951–76. So the reader is warned that little in this section will merit banner headline treatment.

Criticism of standards achieved at 16–19 comes from two sides: first, from employers, personnel and training officers; secondly, from academics, including (according to the *TES*) a majority of primary and secondary teachers, but not heads. Their grounds for criticism are different and need separate consideration. In both cases we shall focus on English.

Naturally, comments from industry, commerce and public services are not based on nationally representative samples. Thus, although we have met several local firms that could point over ten years, say, to a decline in the average scores on tests they set apprentices on entrance, there are several alternative explanations for this fact, and we know of no nationwide survey that would justify generalising beyond a small locality. In this sense, then, there is no hard evidence to be sifted, weighed and interpreted. Instead, we are mainly concerned with 'impressionistic' evidence. Occasionally this is demonstrably ill-balanced and biased; at times it is grounded on very naive ideas about competence in spoken and written English. Nevertheless, impressionistic evidence should not be dismissed out of hand. Throughout the project's three years we have met well-based and constructive criticism of the difficulties that young workers in a given firm, local industry, or organisation have faced in coping with the language demands of the job. These have come from FE teachers of day-release classes as well as personnel officers. They may not prove a *decline* in standards, but they do indicate a shortfall that English teachers need to take account of.

In some ways it would be plausible to *expect* a relative decline in the English standards achieved by 16-year-old school leavers. A generation ago, as we have seen, over 80 per cent of the age group were looking for jobs at school-leaving age. By 1976 on average only 60 per cent left immediately to look for a job, and it seems reasonable to assume that many of the 40 per cent who stayed on in full-time education would have better qualifications in English. As the proportion staying on continues to increase, the *relative* standard of those recruited to industry at 16 is very likely to fall.

There may also be a second factor at work: the demand from employers for qualifications has produced a rapid increase in the proportion of the age group entered for English language at O level. Thus, we have seen that over 60 per cent of 16-year-olds entered for GCE in 1976, and — though an official breakdown into subject entries is not available — we can surmise that a large proportion of them took English. For those who take a 'traditional' view of standards this may seem a very good thing. But there are other ways of looking at it.

In 1964 a national committee under Sir James Lockwood, Master of Birkbeck College, London, announced that they had 'considered most seriously whether we should advise the cessation of these [English language] examinations for educational reasons' and 'have come very near to that conclusion'. Their eight major criticisms of the examination began with the problem that 'the weaker candidates are often intensively coached so that they can scrape through . . . [and] we are confident that this is no way to develop their powers of expression'. In fact in O-level English 'the results do not depend sufficiently upon ability to use the language'.

There is, then, a history in GCE English of coaching for very restricted uses of language, with little relation to everyday needs, as the Lockwood Report also pointed out. It is conceivable, to say the least, that some of the young workers who cannot follow instructional booklets and so on have been grinding through largely inappropriate courses in the fifth form, ironically enough in order to meet the increasing demands for traditional qualifications. Perhaps it is not so surprising, therefore, that in a survey of thirty-three major firms in the Bradford area a few years ago, John Mitchell found that nineteen considered O-level language 'an adequate preparation for industrial written communications', and fourteen considered it was not. 'Significantly the greatest dissatisfaction was in engineering firms . . . [which] were also shown to be the firms making greatest calls upon their staff in written communication.' It is easy enough for teachers to check this possible effect, simply by looking at the bottom 50 per cent of their English language 'mock' papers; but it will be harder for them to escape from the Catch-22 situation which makes those students, their parents and the potential employers conspire to defeat common sense. This remains one of the urgent problems to be solved in the English component of a new system of 16+ assessment.

So far we have considered reasons why some employers may be justified in feeling that English standards at 16 are low, or conceivably falling in a given locality. Both these reasons, we note, are compatible with a national rise in overall standards in English at 16, and to some extent may be backwash effects of the drive to achieve higher qualifications 16–19.

There are also less justified grounds for employers' criticisms. Perhaps the most important are the results of internal tests used by larger firms to check on their entrants' maths and English. So far as actual use of language on the job is concerned, these tests may have serious defects. In fact we have yet to meet one constructed specifically for that purpose. What we have met are general screening tests with multiple choice answers. For most employers these are of little value — much less than a selected folder of English written work plus an interview. The worst examples to date seemed to have been standardised efficiently enough, but on an academic sixth form population: thus young engineering apprentices in a major national undertaking were being tested on their recognition of 'captious', 'succulent', 'scabbard' and other irrelevant material.

It is incumbent on heads, principals and those responsible for English to explain to industry (and others) that, over the past decade or so, our ability to analyse the actual ways language is used to communicate in everyday life has made a giant step forward; that this has revealed how illusory many past 'psychometric' tests of language were; and that a further decade's patient joint study is needed if workers who face heavy demands on language are to benefit. (We shall be commenting later in the report on some pioneering work by Coventry LEA in collaboration with the local engineering industry.) Meanwhile, common sense should be enough to alert employers who look critically at them to the limitations of most of the screening tests available.

There is a parallel way in which some employers in commerce or public administration expect too much of an English examination. For particular jobs they may have very specific demands; for instance, for 100 per cent accuracy in spelling and punctuation. This is not something that can be attested by a single grade in English. Such a grade represents an amalgam of different kinds of competence in written English (GCE) or in spoken and written English (most CSE). There will be a given weighting for spelling and punctuation, but this is not overriding, so the top grade will not attest to 100 per cent accuracy. And similarly with the ability to answer calls on the phone, prepare letters to individual clients, produce summaries and reports . . . In fact, in the Bradford survey, firms ranked 'inability to express ideas', 'poor presentation' and 'inability to marshal facts' as the worst failings in written reports; spelling was ranked fifth. These are much broader types of competence. The more selective and specialised the language demand, the less likelihood that competence in it will be guaranteed by what is explicitly intended to be a 'general' certificate in 'education', with social and personal aspects of English to be taken into account as well as vocational.

To sum up: in the main, what employers are offering is impressionistic rather than hard evidence. Their internal tests of English tend to assume fairly unsophisticated notions about language, and in a few cases we have met are so misleading it would be better not to use them. However, public examinations may suffer from similar defects, and the backwash effects on the large number of candidates struggling to get a higher GCE grade at 16 could well be helping to produce the relative incompetence in English that employers complain of.

It is not difficult to broaden the kinds of language sampled in 16+ assessment, and some public examinations have already done so. In addition there has been successful experiment over the last decade, by both GCE and CSE boards, in designing methods of assessment that *encourage* less able candidates at 16 to master certain basic uses of English. It is no longer necessary to persist with styles of examination designed merely to show that a certain percentage of candidates were failures in sophisticated and specialised uses of language, and there is good evidence to support employers' impressions that broader vocational — and social — purposes were not taken into account in past examinations of English and are still relatively neglected.

Academic Self-Doubt and Criticism

As recently as September 1977 the *TES* reported that of a representative sample of teachers 58 per cent in independent schools, 36 per cent in secondary schools and 25 per cent of heads believed 'standards of pupil attainment over the past five years have fallen'. The original question was brief and open to several interpretations, we note. Nevertheless, this is a curious position for any profession to take about its work. What grounds can there be?

The schools and universities are responsible for the two main systems of assessment at 16+ and 18+; in this case, then, impressionistic evidence from individual teachers, examiners or schools is inadequate and has to be tested against the hard evidence of national standards offered by the examination boards. (There are standards in academic *argument*, too, and these ought to be upheld.) The question therefore is: what evidence exists and how is it to be interpreted without bias?

It is important at the outset to recognise a fundamental difficulty in discussing 'standards' in English. Complex uses of language of the kinds demanded at 16–19 are not reducible in the main to right or wrong answers. What we are finally depending on for the assessment of written work, reading, spoken English or listening are subjective judgements of individual examiners. The efforts made by teachers and boards to reduce the effect of individual differences of judgement have never been more scrupulous and systematic than they are today. Nevertheless, the inherent difficulty remains and cannot be overcome. Research units in the examination boards are fully aware of this: it is time parents, students and many teachers were too.

What are the chances that, given a different paper and different markers, the individual student would get the same grade? Until this question is answered, the problem of 'maintaining' standards in English cannot be understood. Fortunately there is hard evidence. In a complex piece of research by E. A. Hewitt, published by the NUJMB in 1967, a subsample of 1,960 students were asked to sit two different JMB papers in O-level English language and two independent groups of markers were used. Most of these candidates were prepared for the first paper, which counted as their substantive entry, and schools were informed that if the individual candidate's result was much improved on the second attempt the first attempt would be 're-scrutinised'.

The three JMB papers included in the overall experiment (A, B and C) were 'closely similar in layout'. Thus, any differences in results can be attributed to one of three factors: differences in detailed content, differences in marking or differences in individual performance on the day. The researcher points out that part of the difference may be caused by 'reduced motivation' in the second examination. There is some evidence to support this: where paper A was taken first and paper C second the number of passes fell (from 211 to 151), but where paper C was taken first and A second, passes again fell (from 179 to 102). Part of this discrepancy could well be caused by 'reduced motivation'; part, perhaps, by unfamiliarity with the second paper.

If the 'reduced motivation' hypothesis is accepted, however, and applied to the rest of the results, they are all the more surprising. Thus, where A was taken first and B second, overall results tended to improve (from 363 passes to 455); when C was taken first and B second, overall results were almost exactly even (158 passes became 156 passes); and — not surprisingly — where B was taken first results fell heavily on the second examination in both cases (from 408 passes to 137). On this evidence B seems to have been considerably the easiest paper in content, marking, or both.

So far we have considered how the overall results differed, but ideally what we should like to know is how each individual fared: it is not much comfort to know that the same *number* of students passed in Papers C and B if in fact most of the individuals who passed on C failed on B, and vice versa. What is needed is a measure of the difference between the two awards for each individual. *At the time the experiment took place*, the marks on each paper were normally grouped by the board into *nine* 'grades'; Mr Hewitt used these to calculate how the difference between the two awards affected each individual. The following table shows this for all the JMB papers.

Rounded percentage of pupils whose awards **differed** *by the number of 'grades' indicated*

0	1	2	3	4	5	6 or More	Total Candidates
17%	29%	20%	14%	9%	6%	3%	1960

Thus for about two-thirds of the results the difference was not more than two 'grades' (of the nine then in use), and for the remaining third the difference was three 'grades' or more.

Hewitt notes that 'the correlation between the two sets of examination results varies widely from school to school' but that 'the correlation between school estimates and either of the two examinations is of the same order of magnitude as the correlation between examinations'.

This piece of research, and many others on the same lines, indicate the irreducible difficulty of maintaining standards in the same year between one group of English examiners and another. It was carried out on GCE O-level language. Since 1965, of course, a growing number of candidates have actually been entered each year for two examinations in English — CSE and GCE. As the CSE grade 1 is equivalent to the former pass at O level, this has enabled a running comparison to be made of the relative chances of either or both being awarded. There is a myth abroad that CSE is a more lenient exam: 'if GCE is beyond you, CSE will oblige. They are *reasonable*; they pass 95% of the entry,' wrote an English professor in 1969. The innuendo on 'reasonable' and 'pass' is typical of the lack of intellectual rigour in this debate. What was the evidence, if he had chosen to wait for it?

The relation of CSE grade 1 and GCE O-level grades A–C (the former pass level) has been extensively investigated by several different methods. Desmond Nuttall of NFER, using an aptitude test as a scaling device, found that 'in 1968, the CSE boards as a whole awarded fewer grade ones than would appear to have been deserved in English, mathematics, geography, French and general science. . . . This pattern of severity at grade 1 has appeared consistently in earlier years.' He notes that this method of analysis is 'not completely satisfactory'. An alternative approach was adopted for

English in 1973 in research reported by Terry Brown of the Durham Institute of Education. In this case 926 London or Oxford GCE candidates also sat the Northern CSE English *language*, and similarly 267 Northern CSE candidates also sat the London or Oxford O-level English *language*. The 'results of all three experimental examinations . . . as well as discussions between teachers and representatives of the three Boards' suggest 'that the CSE Grade 1 is more difficult to achieve than a GCE pass'. A third approach was adopted by P. E. Roe, Secretary to the Yorkshire CSE Board: in 1973 and 1975 centres entering for the board's exams were asked for the results of candidates double-entered in CSE and GCE. In 1973,

    1404   awarded O-level pass and CSE grade 1
     560   awarded O-level pass but *not* CSE grade 1
     451   *not* awarded O-level pass but gained CSE grade 1

In 1975 the figures were roughly reversed:

    1090   awarded similar grades in both
     509   awarded O-level pass but not CSE grade 1
     622   not awarded O-level pass but gained CSE grade 1

Thus, 'if one adds the figures for 1973 and 1975 the number obtaining O-level grade C or higher . . . is virtually the same as the number achieving CSE grade 1'. Actually in English, though the subsample was small, once again the CSE standards appeared more severe than GCE.

If anything, then, English CSE examiners tended at first to be more severe in awarding grade 1 than GCE examiners in awarding a pass, and it was some years before the two examinations became roughly comparable at this level. On this evidence there is no justification for relating any decline in standards to the introduction of CSE; rather the contrary.

The main case that remains is that the level for awarding a GCE O- and A-level 'pass' has declined over the years. 'Many more children are staying on at school and taking these examinations, in which the same approximate percentage always pass. The standards are not objective.' Despite the recurrent appeal to objectivity, no evidence has ever been adduced to justify this kind of assertion. Generally it is implied that somehow a fixed pass rate is imposed on the boards, either by the former Secondary Schools Examinations Council or by its successor, the Schools Council. But this is known to be false. For instance, in 1969 the Secretary of the JMB published a very clear and fair description of what occurs when the chief examiners, having satisfied themselves that marking to a common standard has been achieved, sit down with the Secretary and his staff to consider what should be the minimum mark for a pass in the subject. It is worth quoting in full.

    In addition to their own views on the standard of work as seen in the scripts which they themselves have marked, the chief examiners receive detailed reports from each member of the marking panel. They are also provided by the Secretary with statistical information about the way in which the marks in the subject as a whole run in the year under review as compared with previous years. If the distribution of marks is significantly different from that of previous years they must establish on the evidence available to them whether there has been an improvement (or deterioration) in the quality of the entry or whether the question paper, despite all the efforts made at the preparatory stage, has proved to be easier (or more demanding) than the corresponding paper set in the previous year.

If the pass level were decided simply on a percentage basis, the presence of the chief examiner, his judgements and the reports from his marking panel would all be irrelevant; there would be no point in discussing whether the entry had improved or deteriorated, and whether the paper was more demanding or easier. To any fair-minded onlooker it will be obvious — in the light of earlier evidence — that these are extremely difficult questions to answer, calling as they must for the experienced, but in the last resort subjective, judgements of the examining panel. Nevertheless, the attempt is made, and it is on this basis that the pass levels for the year are decided.

It is tempting for some teachers, nevertheless, to deduce that as more and more students have been put in for the examination, the standard has declined. It is especially tempting for those who fervently believed in 1951 or 1965 that only 20 per cent were suited to a grammar school education — that there is, in effect, a limited pool of ability. This hypothesis is extremely difficult to prove. For those who continue to believe it, there seems to be only one way of establishing that — contrary to *their subjective expectations* — standards have remained steady, or risen during the generation. This would be to ask examiners in the seventies to re-mark papers from the sixties, without knowing the earlier grades awarded.

A minor argument remains. Just as it is argued, despite the evidence to the contrary, that a statistical proportion *have* to be passed in GCE, so it is said that either the Secondary Schools Examinations Council or alternatively the Schools Council insisted that 'the number of candidates in each grade does not fall below a certain minimum proportion of the total entry, whatever the marks given'.

This statement is false: statistics for 1977 show that in English language, for instance, the percentage of candidates who were awarded a grade C or better ranged from 67.8 per cent in Northern Ireland and 66.4 per cent in Oxford and Cambridge to 56.4 per cent in Southern and 45.9 per cent in the Associated Examining Board. The reasons for these differences are not relevant to our present argument, but the fact that they exist, and to such a degree, indicates again the lack of intellectual standards among some of the most widely publicised critics of educational achievements over the past generation.

To sum up: there are no 'objective' standards by which English can be assessed; the best that can be offered is a trained 'subjective' judgement. Individual judgements of a student's work in English will inevitably vary, sometimes considerably, as the research evidence shows. Nevertheless, the machinery set up by GCE and CSE boards aims to generate and maintain from year to year a common sense of standards among examiners.

As regards English at 16–19 the most widely publicised criticisms can be demonstrated to be evasively worded, misleading, unsupported by evidence and, in major respects, false. This does not imply that English 16–19 or the GCE and CSE examinations are above criticism, but it suggests that in planning for the new generation English teachers ought to have some confidence in their past achievements.

These are indicated by the following table.

	Passes awarded at O and A levels (all ages)		
	O Level		A Level
	language	literature	
1951	67,000	52,000	9,900
1976	269,000	146,000	46,000

1.3 A Changed Understanding of Language

Our chief concern . . . is to emphasise the escalating demands for a higher level of literacy and oral communication. . . . The only solution is for future cohorts of school leavers to be better able to read, write, and talk about their work and other aspects of their lives.   *(The Attainments of the*
School Leaver, 1977)

. . . people listen best when they have to take some action upon the information received . . .
. . . reading should satisfy some purpose on the part of the reader . . .
Pupils should learn how to organise their reading, firstly by being able to locate, evaluate and select the material they need, and secondly by applying organised study methods to the material itself.   (Bullock Report, 1975)

To speak or write clearly and precisely one needs more than technical skills. It will often be necessary to assess the needs, knowledge and situation of the recipient.
                                  (Cleveland Schools/Industry Working Paper, 1976–7)

On the evidence, it seems possible — even probable — that over a generation there has been a four- or fivefold increase in the proportion achieving standards once designed for a small minority. How has this been achieved? It must surely have made unusual demands on English teachers.

To answer this question we must consider changes of a more subtle kind than the number of passes in an examination. These have run alongside the changes in numbers and achievement, supporting them and stimulated by them. The first has affected almost all teachers of English in the last decade or more, indirectly through the books and materials they use, or directly in the course of active efforts to continue their professional education. It is a change of a most fundamental kind, a powerful new understanding of 'language for life' — of the ways language is used for better or worse in personal, social and vocational activity.

Thus, for many of the teachers of English and communication we have met and worked with during the project — and these add up to thousands overall — it is rather ironic to be talking defensively of 'keeping up the standards' of 1951 or 1963. These are manifestly not good enough. The restricted range of writing, reading and — if it is included at all — spoken English they called for was demonstrably a handicap to good English teaching in 1976.

For the sake of non-specialists, for parents and employers, this new professional understanding of English and its role in communication needs clear explanation. We shall be content in this section to sketch how, in the light of it, old 'standards' are being critically revised and their limitations recognised among examiners as well as teachers.

The 1951 GCE model of English was concerned with the student as writer and reader and we shall look closely at three major elements:

(a) the *essay*, as evidence of uses of writing;
(b) the *literary essay*, as evidence of appreciative understanding and enjoyment of books;
(c) *comprehension* and *précis*, as evidence of the uses of reading other than literature.

In the traditional English examination each indicates a vital part of the subject, while illustrating a severely limited way of sampling it.

Thus in the 1951-style examination, the essay normally served as a representative sample of all the original writing that might be expected of a 16-year-old. It has become clear that this sample is restricted in four respects: topic, time, 'audience' and purpose. The topic is always set by the examiner; thus a student's ability to define and write on a topic of his or her own is not assessed. In selecting a short list of topics, the examiners too are under heavy constraints. Each topic ought to appeal to the majority of 16-year-olds; there is no room for minority interests. No specialised knowledge, personal experience or interest must be assumed, therefore. No preparation time with reference to books or other materials must be expected. In the hour or less allowed, there is no time for drafting and little for revision — indeed, none if the candidate is slower than average in the mechanics of handwriting. In effect, a student is assessed on the ability to write for about an hour on a popular set topic which can be handled without more than a few moments for reflection, reference, drafting or revision. These are hardly appropriate conditions for any kind of writing, whether imaginative or informative. Do they produce the kind of writing that English teachers and examiners in 1979 wish to sample, or feel they ought to assess?

Many kinds of writing require personal initiative, discussion, reading, interviewing, time for reflection, selection and synthesis of material, drafting and redrafting, at times with a known 'audience' in mind, whose criticisms of the finished work or a late draft may be useful to the writer. Work that involves some or all of these activities is more likely to generate a sense of standards in the student of 16+, so that self-criticism and revision (in an editorial role) become an important part of the work.

The topic and time restrictions are particularly severe in traditional 'literature' papers. In order to ensure that a student is assessed on a range of texts, essays must be written on three, four or five of them in three hours or less. Each essay is concerned with a major work of literature, but in the examination the student is not allowed to work from the text itself; this has to be discussed from memory. Under these circumstances, knowing that answers will be prepared, the examiner must try to find the one or perhaps two questions on each text that will stimulate the majority of candidates, not reward them for second-hand opinions, not demand too detailed a recall of the text, and not require more than thirty to sixty minutes for a reasonable answer. Common sense tells us it is too much to expect. Indeed, these conditions are precisely the opposite to those the same examiners, as teachers of literature, would normally want to encourage 16 to 19-year-olds to work in. By this age students, in consultation with their teacher, should be taking some responsibility for selecting texts to study. They will be expected to take time to reflect after reading a text, and while the experience is still fresh ('carried alive into the heart by passion', as the poet hopes) to select some part or aspect that calls for a sensitive, thoughtful scrutiny. This may be discussed, or pondered on alone, with notes, jottings and further close reading. The time taken for writing and the style and scope of completed 'essays' may vary a good deal, but whenever a major work is looked at as a whole, several hours will be needed, time possibly for more than one draft, and the final version may extend to several thousand words. This is the kind of care and concern — the standard to be expected — if reading literature is to become 'a criticism of life'.

Returning to the 'original' essay: there were less obvious — and probably unconscious — restrictions in the traditional 1951 model. Who is the student writing for? And for what purpose? If much writing is essentially a means of communicating between people, who are the students of 16–19 learning to communicate with? It may be simply with examiners. But it could include the teacher and other interested adults; some of their peer group; younger and older people; familiar 'audiences'; and even a wider public. We realise today that learning to write (or speak) after a certain stage involves learning how to adapt content, tone and presentation to a range of 'audiences', taking into account their age and experience, their background knowledge, their possible motives for reading and listening and their expectations. On different occasions the reader (or audience) may want to be informed, advised, persuaded, convinced . . . and entertained. Student writers have to learn how each of these functions affects the organisation, selection and tone of what they have to say.

Turning from writing to reading ought to mean looking at what we have just said, but from the reader's point of view. What in fact does the traditional examination model offer?

There are one or perhaps two passages followed by a series of questions largely concerned with the meaning of words, phrases, and idioms — 'literal comprehension', as Bullock puts it. More recently some boards have turned these into multiple choice questions (a further restriction on the student's use of language). In addition most have now cut out the 1951 follow-up question requiring a summary 'in not more than a third of the original words'.

The question that must be asked is: how close is this to the way we read and study articles, reports, minutes, letters . . . books that we intend to *use* in everyday life? On reflection it seems that, like the writer, readers study with purposes in mind, and these seem to fall into three main groups:

(a) with recipes, instructional booklets, guides . . . we expect to be able to follow and carry out the instructions — to act on what we read;

(b) with articles on social and political issues, appeals, propaganda, advertising . . . we read critically to make up our minds on an issue, or to spot the flaws in an opponent, to build up a case, or reach a decision;

(c) with informational handouts, brochures, news reports, articles, business letters . . . we read to find out things we need to know, or feel it important to be informed about, and sometimes to sift ideas we can use or need for further purposes (like replying to the letter).

These three main functions — regulative, persuasive and informative — call on different abilities in the reader, none of them required in the standard model, surprisingly enough.

At least in the précis, there was somewhere embedded the idea that we study in order to *use* what we have read with such care. Unfortunately, once more there was no sense of the further 'audience', who might need or use the summary, nor of the function they might be expecting it to serve. Why should further readers wish the length to be reduced? Did they simply require a list of points, or a flow diagram? Or would a paragraph be better, given the nature of the material and their needs? Should quotation of key phrases be incorporated in the summary, to give clear indications of the way the original writer (or speaker) wanted to put things? These are the kind of questions that are faced in real life when notes, memoranda, minutes and other forms of summary have to be produced. A formula like 'reduce to one-third' is largely irrelevant.

Précis was founded, in a confused way, on an important requirement for the advanced student: the ability to perceive the structure and organisation of a longer piece of writing or speech, and to put that analytic ability to use in reports for a further 'audience'. So little of this notion survived in the ossified exercises of the fifties that this fundamental element in English studies has been largely dropped, instead of being adapted and related again to social, academic and vocational demands. (We shall see later how it is beginning to creep back under the heading of communication.)

To sum up so far: by 1976 the 1951 methods of sampling and assessing language competence were known to be open to severe criticism. The model of language they assumed lacked the most elementary features, purpose and 'audience'. Several of the constraints accepted in the examination papers ran contrary to common sense. There was no conception of the range of language that needed to be sampled, either within writing or within reading. What was true of the examination was no doubt also true of much English teaching at this level. By 1964, when the Lockwood Committee reported and CSE English was being designed, professional awareness of these weaknesses was much stronger, and beginning to develop a theoretical base. Andrew Wilkinson's *Spoken English: Some Aspects of Oracy*, which came out the same year, conveniently marks a new effort to study language in use, and on this foundation to reconstruct the assessment of English at 16–19.

Since 1964 there have been new approaches not only in the areas of language indicated in the 1951 model, but also in those omitted. Since the latter had often been neglected in their own formal education, this has meant a major effort by English teachers to extend their professional competence as well as their understanding. This is our second theme.

The principal omission in the 1951 model was speech. As CSE was set up, efforts were made to include oral language in all English syllabuses and generally in the system of assessment too. Several boards set up large-scale in-service programmes with the LEAs to enable teachers to gain greater experience and expertise. It is probably time to sift the best of that work to date.

On one wing, oral language runs parallel with written. Alongside 'writing for a given audience and purpose' there should be 'speaking to a given audience for a given purpose'; alongside 'reading for certain uses', 'listening or viewing . . .'. And since we are actually in the last quarter of the century of radio and television, 'speaking' may include an illustrated talk, a tape and slide presentation or a videotape programme. These are among the forms that will be met, and perhaps expected of the advanced student, in life outside school.

In addition, there is another wing to oral language: its use not in monologue but in 'dialogue'. Consultations, committee meetings, working parties, discussion groups, interviews, telephone conversations, form a natural part of many people's working and social lives, and are increasingly used in the 'classroom' as a method of teaching and learning. Learning to play a constructive and collaborative role in such dialogue is a fairly fundamental human demand. What a student needs to learn varies according to the size of the group, on the one hand, and its formality and the type of task, on the other. Thus, within a larger, formal group with a pre-set agenda, such as a committee, there will be specialised roles to learn, such as chairman and secretary. Within smaller, informal groupings with more open-ended tasks it will be important for each member to recognise his or her share of responsibility for making progress, and to understand what helps and hinders that process. Thus there is a strong element of social education in dialogue, interwoven with the language demands of the specific task in hand.

As with written language, oral monologue and dialogue serve a wide range of purposes: some of these emphasise the process (sharing experience, exploring ideas, turning over pros and cons, for example), others the end-product (planning, reaching decisions, coming to conclusions, resolving a dispute). Of course, in a given session the discussion may serve several purposes in turn.

Currently, most oral work probably goes on much as writing did in 1951, without any clear theoretical perception of the key factors involved. But even by 1976 there were pioneering departments — and boards — actively engaged in making more explicit the range of purposes, roles and constraints to be taken into account. Over the next generation it seems highly likely that the clarity of aims — and with that the value — of the oral aspect of English teaching will grow in much the same way as the written aspect did between 1951 and 1976.

In common-sense terms, then, these are some of the main questions and ideas about 'standards' in English that have been developing over the past twenty-five years. Many of them are supported in depth by research investigations; all could be refined beyond the brief summary we offer here. Taken together, they offer a critique, on the one hand, of the implicit assumptions accepted in GCE syllabuses and papers a generation ago and, on the other, of many of our methods and aims in the English classrooms of the fifties. At the same time, it should be recognised that several GCE, CSE and vocational examination boards have fostered — and are fostering today — experimental work, seeking to realise these new conceptions of standards in English; and that the main ideas we have described have been worked ı the classroom by pioneering departments and groups of teachers.

We shall see in detail later the reformed kinds of assessment that this experimental work has made possible in English.

1.4 Changing Definitions of the Role of English within the Curriculum

Oral work is, we are convinced, the foundation upon which proficiency in the writing of English must be based.

The writing of plays in school is a form of English Composition, and a very valuable and practical form. . . . A class that has composed and acted its own plays is in a much better position to read other plays. . . . (Newbolt Report, 1921)

Ideally, then, we would recommend that in the secondary school drama should be an essential part of work in English while at the same time having scope as an activity in its own right.

One of the most powerful sources of vivid experience is the general output programmes of television, particularly documentaries and drama.

Television is now part of our culture and therefore a legitimate study for schools.

Two issues remain, each of fundamental importance to the curriculum 16–19 and the role English is to play in it. Both concern major facets of oral language: first, its use in drama, role play and simulation; and secondly, the study of it in the main media of communication and culture today, especially television and radio.

Over the last generation, 1951–76, a series of outstanding teachers have demonstrated (particularly through the new medium of television) that drama, role play and simulation offer an extremely powerful extension of the ways of learning and teaching — notably within English, but also in the wide range of subjects that call for understanding of social, cultural, histori-cal or vocational issues. 'Try to get inside someone else's way of thinking and feeling, and then stand back to consider what you have found out in that act': this is what modern drama asks the student to do. And it has been found that, with such a basic human propensity, students 16–19 of a very wide range of academic attainment have a surprising potential for learning in this way.

Currently the place of drama in the curriculum, like the place of media studies, is both a structural and an intellectual problem for the school or college. At one pole, drama is highly verbal (thus, much role play and simulation); at the other it relies on different modes of communication — movement, gesture and silence (and thus, mime). Similarly, on the one side drama is part of the arts, but on the other it has become a very practical way of investigating, trying out, understanding, and coming to terms with the way people actually behave.

Thus, setting aside for the moment the structural problems, it is evident that no English teachers who are professionally equipped to do so could omit a strong drama element in their work week by week. By 1976 this included dramatic improvisation, role play and simulations, as well as the more traditional English work in theatre. Equally, by 1976 drama was being assessed as an element in English at 16+ and as a separate subject qualification at CSE and A level. Both developments seem right.

The relation between media studies and English is similar but even more complex. With drama there was a tradition going back fifty years or more for the outstanding English department to make some form of drama a keystone of its work. What has changed between 1951 and 1976 is our professional understanding of the enormous potential range of dramatic work and of its contribution to learning. With the media, especially television, development in their range and uses has taken place outside the school or college; it is only gradually that teachers have come to realise the enormous power of these new institutions in the cultural and social life of Britain.

However, by 1963–4 there were already some pioneering English departments in schools, and general studies departments in FE, who were taking a serious interest in television, film and radio. From an English point of view, these media offered a powerful and influential range of uses of spoken language — imaginative, informative and persuasive. Television drama was already the main form in which most secondary pupils encountered fiction, and during the sixties there were some inspired ventures during adult viewing-time into the presentation of literature, and on radio into the celebration of an oral tradition in story telling. Similarly the media offered the best, and worst, of documentary reporting, depth interviewing, illustrated talks, forums for the discussion and analysis of major social issues. There was much to criticise and much to learn.

From a detached standpoint, this was a welcome phase but unlikely to offer a final answer. Language does play a vital role — perhaps often a dominant one — in the media, but, as with drama, non-verbal signals are continually being used by the people involved, and in television and film the changing visual image offers a new and equally important mode of communication. It is precisely this complex interweaving of verbal, visual, kinetic and musical communication that makes the 'audiovisual' media so powerful in impact, dangerous in use and difficult to perfect. But to consider them only as media of 'communication' is not enough: the media — so called — are becoming key institutions for the formation and discussion of contemporary culture and society. Their power to educate opinions, beliefs, attitudes and assumptions — for better or worse — must be given equal weight with the schools and colleges. An invitation to study 'the media' is therefore a challenge to combine two ranges of interest: the first in interwoven modes of communication, and the second in the discussion and scrutiny of contemporary culture and society. By 1976 there was still no clear national position about the place of either in the 16–19 curriculum — nor for that matter in higher education.

However, though we have little evidence of changes in schools beyond the position established in the sixties, in FE there have been major changes in policy and practice. General studies teachers have been actively redefining their first-year work in technical education in terms of communication and life 'skills', and now see communication (in a variety of media) as a basic part of their responsibility. Currently, new integrated courses are being planned in business education, and a communication approach has already been adopted in the national objectives for the English element. Moreover, in 1976 it was a group of FE teachers who gained recognition for a new A level in 'communication studies', with the media as one of the four main elements.

Thus in 1978 there are conflicting definitions of the curriculum in the two main sectors of full-time education. Vocational FE departments have moved decisively to communication and, given the existence and uses of mixed media in the actual working world, it is difficult to see how they could do otherwise. There is still a debate going on about the place in FE general studies of a critical scrutiny of contemporary culture and society.

In schools (and thus in the academic departments of FE) the examination curriculum is still generally defined in 1951 terms. Thus, beyond 16, drama and media studies tend to be seen as extensions of English and examined as such in the experimental CEE. Drama and communication studies did exist at A level by 1976, but they were so new that their relationship to English remained *ad hoc* and peculiar to the few individual schools or colleges involved.

Historically, there are ironic echoes of the position only a century ago when English literature and the other 'modern' subjects were knocking on university doors, seeking for recognition, and still being regarded as soft options in the public schools by the dominant 'classics' side. Communication and media studies are meeting a similar reception, though this time it tends to be professors of English literature who pour scorn on the pretensions of these upstart crows.

Whatever the outcome of that struggle it seems impossible for English teachers to deny their interest in language in the media, or to refrain from a cultural critique of those products of the media in which language plays the dominant role. If the new A level in communication studies offers English teachers the opportunity to work alongside colleagues with other specialist contributions, so much the better: this joint work could then inform the study of communication and culture in the media within their own department.

In the longer term, there are deeper issues to face. The 1951 curriculum and its predecessors earlier in the century were based on single subjects and oriented to university honours courses in them — or, for a small minority, to vocational qualifications. By 1976–7 there were already signs that for some 16–19 students an alternative path might be opening up. Thus the Business Education Council opted in principle for courses that integrated four 'elements', and, by rejecting the idea of four isolated subjects, hoped to stimulate a stronger practical emphasis. Other vocational boards were similarly interested in integrated courses, especially where the students had the benefit of work experience and could see for themselves what was relevant to it.

Meanwhile, on the school side, pilot CEE work had given some schools an opportunity to consider one-year courses for students not oriented to higher education; in a few cases this led to proposals for courses organised in four or five 'fields', each wider than the conventional subject. Thus, tentatively on the academic side, and positively on the vocational, the idea that all students should study three to five isolated subjects has begun to be challenged. It is easy to see why teachers whose qualifications include experience in industry, commerce, administration or social service may be happier to adapt to this alternative than the honours degree specialist. However, if the majority are staying in education to 18 or 19 by the end of the century, it could well be that a curriculum developed essentially in 1918 or earlier will be neither adequate nor appropriate to all of them.

To sum up: between 1951 and 1976 certain aspects of drama and of contemporary media of communication were integrated into the teaching of English by many departments, including some of the best. Beyond 16 this work has met with no encouragement or recognition in the traditional English examination, though it has been included in experimental CEE options. Meanwhile in the vocational courses beyond 16 there has been a radical change since 1963–4: the curriculum has been redefined and competence in spoken and written language is becoming the major element in communication syllabuses and courses. Thus at 16–19 a conflict has developed in the definition of the curriculum.

There are two issues, therefore. First, how broad — or narrow — should 'subjects' be at 17+ and 18+? In choosing the broadest definition, FE vocational departments have offered overall coverage of communicative competence, in language and other modes. In effect they have rejected a specialist approach to the same domain via English, graphics, and so on. This allows — as they wish to do — for some integration of the communication element into an overall technical or business 'course'. The academic curriculum in schools and FE is based on single subjects. The second, supplementary question is: should the number of specialist subjects at 17+ and 18+ be extended to include drama, language studies and media studies alongside English literature, or should provision be made beyond 16 for more general subjects — English, communication studies — and specialist options be allowed for within them? By 1976 the CEE and GCE boards seemed to be opting for the latter alternative, but nationally provision was patchy and inconsistent. Some long-term thinking about the 16–19 curriculum seems badly needed.

1.5   Policy Needed for a New Generation at 16–19

We have seen, in the last twenty-five years, a period of change unparalleled in any period of peace . . .

It would be surprising if the curriculum in all schools had managed to keep pace with these developments.   (*The Attainments of the School Leaver*, 1977)

The conclusion is inevitable that the curriculum of the Sixth Form cannot be drawn up with the needs of only future university students in mind.

. . . it seems that on educational grounds we shall need a much greater elasticity in the shape of Sixth Form courses . . .   (Crowther Report, 1959)

In four sections we have tried to summarise some of the essential changes that have been struggled for and achieved over a generation. Taken together these demonstrate three or four major issues that must be resolved if teachers are to work and plan effectively for the generation that began in 1976 and that carries us through to the opening of the twenty-first century. Most of the staff who will be teaching them in 2001 are already in the schools and colleges. Will the framework for their teaching, and the professional support they need, be adequate to the task ahead?

Probably not. Not, that is, unless certain pressing issues are faced nationally first. We have selected here the three that may be overriding, first for schools and colleges as a whole, and secondly for teachers of English and comunication.

(a) Qualifications for a Majority
At present the desire for a qualification is probably the strongest single drive behind education at 16–19. In English, for instance, over 75 per cent of the age group entered for a public examination at 16 by the mid-seventies. And there is no reason why the trend should stop there. In certain LEAs the majority of these students are already staying for at least one year beyond the fifth form, looking for further qualifications. Within a decade, they may be staying for two.

The existing system of qualifications was designed for small minorities. The universities, or advanced FE, or certain professions needed a preliminary means of sifting applicants for admission: awarding a pass or fail over a *group* of subjects, as in the old School Certificate, was an elementary way of meeting their requirements. O-level GCE offered a more flexible range of information about a student's relative success or failure in anything from one to a dozen subjects. Because they were catering for minorities, both examination systems could make certain assumptions, some as obvious as the pass/fail level, others much more easy to miss. These assumptions, so familiar today that many teachers and examiners are scarcely aware of them, radically affect the design of the instruments used for assessment and the 'results' desired. It becomes difficult to conceive of any alternative.

The notion of an alternative system of qualification, specifically designed for the majority of the age group at 16, did not reach the agenda until the seventies. Currently the proposals are best developed, and the issues most clearly discussed, not in English but in modern languages.

In French, let us say, it was not difficult for experienced teachers to put together an O-level paper for the one student in six who used to stay on at grammar school, and to be reasonably fair — given the usual constraints — in awarding higher or lower grades of pass. The standard represented by those grades, though in some sense arbitrary, was adjusted, consciously or not, to meet university matriculation requirements. These requirements in themselves were not absolute (and indeed the overall demand has been raised considerably over the period 1951–76). Nevertheless, they focused in the main on proficiency in reading French for certain purposes, and to a lesser degree in writing it for a more restricted range. The 'qualification' that resulted was mainly an indication that a student had made reasonable progress in reading the language, and in further studies might become proficient enough to draw on French scholarship in the original.

So much for those who passed. For those who failed, no prognostication was offered and it was unnecessary to design the paper in such a way that their *achievement* was defined.

There are three factors worth noting in this system of qualification: first, the restricted group of likely users of the qualification, and the relative similarity of interests assumed; secondly, the restricted range of competence in the language that satisfied their requirements; thirdly, given that sufficient numbers passed, the assumption that the actual achievements of those who failed need not be considered, and thus could be set aside in designing the paper.

It is the change in these three key factors that poses the essential problems in designing a system of assessment for the majority.

Thus the French teachers of 1976 had a much more difficult task in hand. Let us look at the first factor. There were still academic users who would put the reading of literary and scholarly French first. There were others, especially in commerce and administration, who might require equal competence in the spoken and written language, not for scholarly but for business purposes. There were the students themselves, for whom the most relevant target might be using French for social and leisure purposes in visits abroad. And there were combinations of all three.

This plurality of uses for the qualification leads, as we have indicated, to an expansion of the overall range of competences to be surveyed — the second factor. Spoken uses of the language for a range of purposes and contexts; a wider range of listening and reading, for a variety of purposes; a variety of written tasks, some elementary, some more complex: all of these call for extensions and modifications of the traditional assessment methods.

Finally, there is the third factor. There may be students whose French — like Churchill's Common Entrance Latin — is nil. But for the rest, the challenge in 1976 was to produce not negative evidence, showing they had failed in complex tasks with which others succeeded, but positive evidence of the tasks they were capable of undertaking with competence.

Thus modern language teachers had produced by the mid-seventies a system for assessing the *achievements* of 16+ students across the whole range of ability in the subject, and of indicating by a *profile*, not a single grade, the extent of each individual's competence in the four main aspects of language: speaking, listening, writing and reading.

We have deliberately considered a foreign language first; a more restricted and examinable range of skills is to be expected, and yet throughout there are strong parallels with English. If anything, the range of user interest in English is even wider, and the need to indicate positive achievements more compelling when students are working in their first language. Can a parallel system be designed in English for assessing the achievements of the majority?

To some degree it is already being developed. Thus the Assessment of Performance Unit in English is currently being designed to monitor a cross-section of 15-year-olds' work. For the assessment of 'achievement in writing' it is recommended that eight kinds of writing should be sampled, and these have been defined in the light of recent gains in our understanding of language in use. Thus, for instance, they should vary from one in which the writer 'has complete control' to one in which 'both the subject matter and the manner' of handling it are laid down — the remaining six falling between these two poles. It is proposed that the sample should be drawn partly from the student's course work over the year, and partly from writing specially set, both in normal classroom conditions and in test conditions.

The aim will be to supply 'not a single score but a matrix of scores . . . [which] could then be grouped and selected according to the information required'. The profile should therefore show both relative achievement in 'different tasks and contexts', and variations according to the different criteria used in assessment. Thus 'if someone wanted to know the accuracy in spelling and punctuation' of students working under given conditions, 'this information could be abstracted'.

For writing, then, the APU has already been asked to sample positive achievement in English across a range of purposes, and to offer a very detailed matrix of scores rather than a single-grade 'result'. Whatever teachers' apprehensions about the APU itself — and the possible abuses it is open to — the briefing paper on writing will certainly reward careful, critical readers. Few of the current 16–19 examinations in English will stand up to the same scrutiny of their intellectual basis. It is a notable first attempt to consider how, in English, standards of achievement over a whole age group might be sampled.

At 16+ there is already practical experience in several CSE and GCE boards of sampling on lines that approach the APU in stringency. Over the decade 1966–76 regional groups of English teachers in consultation with external moderators have now learned how jointly to define a sample of written and, in some cases, oral course work to represent a student's achievements over the year. Thus tapes, videotapes and folders of written work are actually available, illustrating different levels in the handling of the main aspects of English. In this respect there is strong experience of selecting positive evidence of an individual student's work in language for something close to the whole 16+ age group.

What remains to be done in English? The final step that would help student, employer and further/higher education alike would be to select 'case studies' from the videotapes and folders already available at the different grade levels of CSE and GCE, and on this evidence to define what differences were demonstrable in the range of English handled with confidence, and the kinds of sensitivity and control evinced in the use of language. In the light of such a description, borne out by case study 'illustrations', it should be possible to give grades in English substantive meaning, so that they became genuine standards for the majority to strive for, and serviceable indicators of achievement to a wide variety of potential 'users'.

It seems, then, that the most urgent task today is to devise a system of assessment at 16–19 that offers the incentive of positive and demonstrable qualifications to the majority of the age group.

(b) Academic and Vocational Definitions of Education
There is, however, a second, interlocking question: qualifications for what? When the number staying on beyond 15 was small, it was convenient to offer two quite distinct alternatives in continuing education: one on academic courses in grammar schools, the other on vocational courses in FE colleges. At the time it seemed reasonable enough that, for the small minority involved, university boards should effectively lay down the academic route to higher education as the one alternative and boards with employer representation should define the other in terms of educational routes to certain specialised careers in industry or business.

It is time we looked closely at the assumptions behind these decisions of a generation ago. First, it seems to have been assumed at the time that it was possible and desirable for all students at 15 (or 16) to select either the academic or the vocational path — and thus it seemed reasonable to hive off the two groups in separate institutions. Secondly (it followed that) links between academic and vocational interests in 16–19 courses were neither possible nor desirable. And thirdly, it seemed to be expected, implicitly or explicitly, that universities and employers would temper their demands for specialist academic or vocational preparation with a common concern for a student's general education — to equip him or her for active rather than passive roles in a complex industrial civilisation.

Each of these assumptions needs reconsidering in the light of experience a generation later, and also of the massive expansion in the number seeking education beyond 16.

Is it possible or desirable for all the students now staying beyond 16 to make an immediate choice between an exclusively academic or an exclusively vocational course? Of course, if students are given no choice in the matter it is difficult to say what they desire. And this is still the position in many schools. In FE, however, where major changes have been made over the generation, it is normal to offer a choice between academic courses, vocational courses, or *both*. Thus there is one source of evidence. Rather surprisingly, the annual statistics published by the DES entirely ignore this fact. However, a recent NFER survey, based on a large if not fully representative sample, suggests that at 16–18 the majority of full-time students on vocational courses were also studying certain subjects for GCE O or A level. (The actual figures show over 70 per cent on one-year and over 50 per cent on two-year vocational courses taking GCE courses in addition.)

This must be treated as a crude indication, but at least it throws doubt on the idea that by 1976 students beyond 16 did not desire to keep some of their options open, if they were able to.

On the school side, there were uneasy feelings nationally by 1976 that education for work deserved better recognition that it had had. Indeed, as we shall see, some of the most interesting work in one-year English courses beyond the fifth form had allowed for a combination of academic, vocational and personal interests. Some schools were active alongside FE colleges in pioneering the new City and Guilds Foundation courses for community care, business and other major areas of work. Linked courses between schools and colleges had developed, especially during the seventies. And in certain LEAs the gap between academic and vocational institutions had been ended by bringing both into a tertiary college.

There are signs, then, that the idea of linking academic and vocational interests beyond 16 is no longer ruled out, and in some schools — though possibly a minority as yet — is being actively explored.

This was the case with one-year courses; with the two-year courses to A level, the position in 1976 was largely unchanged from 1951. Most A-level syllabuses — including those in English — were still oriented to university honours degree courses, and there was growing uneasiness about this. Although entry to higher education had increased, Britain by then actually ranked in the bottom three or four in Europe in terms of HE places available for the 18+ age group. In subjects such as English, moreover, the number of students annually entering honours degree courses in the subject (c. 2600) was actually under 4 per cent of A-level candidates (66,000).

Reviewing the position in 1977, the English Steering Group set up to commission and vet N & F proposals — with forceful representatives from university English departments — had this to say:

> English A Level attracts the largest number of candidates, and probably the widest range of ability, backgrounds, interests, and ambitions of any A Level subject. . . . In devising the briefs . . . we had in mind three main categories of students. The smallest group intend to proceed to an honours degree course in, or including, English. The next and much larger group, though aiming at higher education in a form other than single-subject English honours, nevertheless wish to study English in the sixth form both for personal growth and as a preparation for the next stage in their education. By far the largest group taking English are those who aim to go directly to employment or professional training at the end of their courses.
>
>   Clearly, the range of options between syllabuses should attempt to satisfy all three populations, and the range of options within syllabuses must allow for the needs of individuals . . . By no means all students know at the start of their sixth form course what they will want to do in two years time. For these, the syllabus structure ideally should allow for a gradual narrowing of choice, rather than impose a once-for-all decision. For others, an early decision to specialise should be possible.
>
>   . . . We consider that the future for the examining of English at 18+ *under whatever national overall structure* (our italics) is likely to move towards greater diversity of choice.

It has been authoritatively recognised in English, then, that the range of alternatives for two-year students who want an advanced qualification needs to be extended, so that some courses are available that allow for both broad academic and broad vocational interests. As the most popular subject at A level and the most widely desired qualification at 16–19, English is naturally among the first to face these problems, but they will be met increasingly at 18+ in all the main subjects as the proportion wishing to stay on rises. This calls for a major effort in curriculum development.

As it is made, and different user interests are consulted, the third assumption made in 1951 will be tested: how far are university specialists and representative employers able to temper their demands with a concern for a student's general education? How interested or willing are they, for instance, to see students of 16–19 learning to take on active roles in the cultural, social and political life of their society?

There are three possible answers in the light of past and current experiences.

(i) HE and employer representatives may treat education beyond 17 entirely as a preparation for specific academic courses or specific kinds of job, and make their syllabus demands accordingly.

(ii) These representatives may recognise the need for more than vocational or academic preparation, but play a passive role in the discussion of any further definition of educational aims and syllabus construction.

(iii) These representatives may take an active role in the definition of aims and in the integration of social and personal education with the vocational and academic.

In the subsection that follows we shall try to demonstrate some of the consequences of each of these lines of action.

(c) General Education and Specialist Preparation

There is no doubt, particularly given hindsight, that certain students stay on voluntarily at 16 with a clear ambition — to become a doctor, a secretary, an engineer, a social worker — or simply to study medicine, maths, sociology or English for a degree. Some of those who leave at 16 find that work experience gives them a new confidence when they take FE day-release courses, and they become committed to their vocational studies as they never were at school. Thus at 16+ there are students who want to specialise and who demonstrably benefit from doing so.

This argues that for some students a course beyond 16 that is manifestly a preparation for a specific career or higher education course is an educational advantage. Such students have become an ideal stereotype and we British rather enjoy looking back nostalgically today to Nelson, Pitt and those captains of industry who specialised young, fought their way to the top, and in doing so built the Empire.

However, daydreams apart, there also exist at 16+ two other and possibly much larger groups of students: first, those who at 16+ know exactly what they want to do, but by 17 or 18 have changed their minds; and secondly, those who feel uncertain of their future at 16+, either because they have a secure sense of the wide range of things they might do well, or because they are currently unsure whether there is anything they will really do well enough. Thus, as teachers from schools and FE put it to us in a recent conference, courses are needed beyond 16 to help such students discover and 'define a commitment' — whether academic or vocational.

What should an advanced syllabus for such students aim to do? It must encourage but not pre-empt decisions. It must define and relate forms of competence in English, for instance, that would be valuable in higher education, in a vocation, and also in social and personal life. And it must allow for individual students or small groups, as their commitment becomes clearer, to select differentiated tasks, some of them directly related to an academic or vocational future.

As a project team we have searched for any schools or colleges already operating such courses in English, and have found that some indeed do exist, but only for the first year beyond 16, for reasons that will become clear as we survey the English A-level syllabuses currently available. Nevertheless, these teachers, working to some degree against the grain of the 18+ examinations ahead or exploiting the greater freedom of CEE, have indicated fairly clearly how the broader aims we have outlined may be interpreted in practice.

Their English courses include some or all of the following elements:

(a) not only the reading and discussion of literature, some chosen by the teachers, some by students, and the writing of poetry, short stories and other imaginative work;

(b) but also 'attachment' for a number of periods to a local community group, or firm, or social service, or similar organisation in order to observe, assist under guidance, study and build up a report based on the experience gained;

(c) not only 'cultural' studies, based on literature, broadcasts and theatre visits that illustrate the roots of the multi-cultural society in which the students live;

(d) but also the study of 'personal and social issues', based partly on direct experience and contact with people from outside school (listening, discussing, interviewing) and partly on a close analytic study of media reports and documentary material;

(e) not only the selection and carrying through of longer individual 'depth study essays' or group reports based on one or more of the classwork elements above;

(f) but also detailed preparation of students, during all the above work, for taking responsibility in the organisation of visits, interviews and investigations; in the preparation and presentation of reports to the class (or a wider audience) and in chairing the ensuing discussion; in the collection, analysis and sifting of material for depth studies, and in drafting and redrafting major pieces of written or taped work;

(g) and, finally, 'language studies', to support the work in (f) especially, so that students are more consciously aware of the factors that may help or impede their communication with other people for various purposes.

There are a large group of schools, colleges and LEA English advisers who believe that courses *broadly* on these lines would have much to offer a wide range of students at A level, and currently the possibility of framing appropriate syllabuses and methods of assessment is being actively discussed with the boards.

How will the syllabuses and objectives differ from those of 1951? First, they will include the explicit demand for certain 'study skills' — and particularly those concerned with observing and reporting, seeking and collating information, defining and carrying through an investigation or other major task, and analysing language in a range of media. Secondly, they will be explicit about the 'social skills' that may be needed in writing letters or phoning to organise visits, working in particular kinds of attachment, interviewing, chairing discussions and presenting group reports, and working effectively as a member of a team. And thirdly, they will allow for differences of emphasis.

Some of the drive we have observed in such courses comes from personal and social interests; some from academic or vocational. There is a balance to be kept between these interests, or pressures, if the certificate awarded is genuinely to testify to a course that is 'general' not specialist, and an 'education' rather than training.

Thus, it seems possible from the evidence available in one of the major subjects — English — to envisage *some* advanced courses that will offer students an opportunity to define a commitment between 16 and 19, rather than assume a single-minded specialist ambition at 16+. Some of the elements for such courses may already be clear enough, through experience in CEE experiments, or through conscientious efforts to keep the first year of an A-level course as broad as possible — even if much of the work goes beyond current syllabus demands and gets no recognition at 18+. Carried through for one or two years beyond the fifth form, work on these lines will offer an important general contribution either to further academic study, or to a career, or both.

The investigation of such syllabuses is an urgent task. And here we must return to the question of the role of the university or industrial representative within the boards. It would be a pity if they were to see themselves simply as spokesmen for the specialist demands of a specific industry or honours degree. This would effectively limit their contribution to the design of syllabuses for the 'fixed ambition' student. In the design of more flexible syllabuses that are already demanded in a central subject like English, and will increasingly be needed elsewhere in the curriculum, higher education and 'industrial' advice *is* essential, but the questions to be asked are not, for example, about requirements for an English honours degree, but about the fundamental uses of language required by many forms of advanced study (academic or vocational) and the contribution that a broader understanding and control of language can make in many kinds of career.

These are not questions for the academic or industrial 'specialist' at all: that a broader understanding and control of language can make in many kinds of career.

These are not questions for the academic or industrial 'specialists' at all; they are best answered by people with an interest ranging beyond the particular degree course or firm in which they are working. Equally, advice about the actual language demands in study or work cannot at present be authoritative; few higher education or industrial representatives have studied the question, nor for that matter have many teachers. Many local schools–industry conferences have been held in 1975–8, and the project has been in contact with several joint working parties, notably in Coventry and Cleveland. English and communication specialists have much to offer and gain from a detailed analysis of language demands at work, especially in jobs that favour the candidate with higher qualifications. So an important beginning has been made; but those who have begun feel they have not yet reached a stage much beyond enlightened common sense. So the best contributions from vocational or HE representatives in curricular discussions will come from those with an active interest and an openness to new inquiry.

What, it might be asked, is the role of school and college representatives in these discussions? Essentially, they have two tasks: the first is to ensure that in the framing of English syllabuses, for instance, the social and personal uses of language — so much of the language 'for life' — are not forgotten. English teachers have been powerful advocates for this cause over the generation 1951–76. The second, in which they have been less active and successful overall, is to seek for a synthesis between the diverse, and sometimes conflicting, demands of language for study, for work and for life in the wider society.

To sum up: there are rational grounds for expecting systems of assessment designed for small minorities to be inadequate and ill-equipped to offer qualifications for the majority of an age group. What users (including the students) need is evidence of positive achievements at a sequence of levels that probably amount to developmental stages. With 375,000–750,000 students to be assessed, the potential users are so varied that they must inevitably benefit more from a 'profile' than from a single grade.

Already in 1976 a system for the majority at 16+ was overdue; it may even be introduced a decade too late. The strain and harassment this causes among students and teachers has to be realised. By 1976 40 per cent of the age group were already staying on full-time to 17+. Provision for those who left after one year was still makeshift or 'experimental'. Finally, 25 per cent of the age group were staying on for a full-time course to 18+. It is not

THE TEACHERS' CENTRE
WORCESTER STREET
MIDDLESBROUGH
CLEVELAND TS1 4NT

certain how soon that, too, will become a majority demand: it might be within two decades, it could be in one. There have been other times in which Britain did 'too little, too late'. Is this to happen again?

The design problems are not simple. Questions include much more than the kinds of material to be sampled, and the methods of assessing and publishing 'results'. They raise fundamental issues about the curriculum. What is the relationship to be between vocational and academic studies at 16–19? What range of alternatives may be needed, if students without a fixed ambition at 16 are to get the right chances? Where students had an alternative in 1976, the majority chose a mixed vocational and academic course to 17 or 18+. But in most cases they had no such alternative. Where the opportunity was available beyond 16+, some teachers of English, for instance, were indeed designing courses that allowed for a range of special interests to develop within a broad overall frame. But without provision for a broad English A level on these lines, they had perforce to stop short at the end of one year and demand a specialist commitment from that point on.

These are matters not simply for small groups of teachers, schools and colleges, struggling against the grain, but for a national policy for a new generation.

*   *   *   *

In the remainder of this report we shall attempt to answer three questions that follow from our thesis in Part 1.

Part 2

Taking English and communication 16–19 as a key curriculum element, what are the main paths ahead that are already being marked out by an active minority of schools, colleges and examining bodies?

Part 3

What co-ordination is needed, in English and communication as in other subjects, if the educational strands that answer social, academic and vocational demands are to be woven together instead of remaining separate and unrelated?

What agencies are needed to support teachers, and in particular what are the roles of examining bodies, if the challenge of a curriculum for the majority is to be met?

PART TWO

The Main Paths ahead in English and Communication

2.1 Branching Routes in English beyond the Fifth Form

In this section we turn from general issues in education 16–19 to a specific curriculum area, English and communication. How are teachers in this area responding to the challenge of a new generation? In particular, what lessons can be learnt, positively and negatively, from the work the English 16–19 Project has assisted and stimulated over its three-year period?

Each subject will undoubtedly face problems of its own. A timetable slot labelled English, geography, maths . . . gives a spurious similarity to the familiar academic subjects: they are not, alas, well-bounded little rectangular blocks, neatly fitting together to cover 'the curriculum'. Nevertheless, English and communication, taken together, have important affinities with the arts, with modern languages, with social studies, and — more indirectly — with all subjects that rely on language for rational thinking, the organisation of ideas and their effective presentation. It could well be, therefore, that by describing the position as we see it in English and communication we can help those with a broader interest in the challenge to the 16–19 curriculum to see some underlying issues that cross several subject fields. We have tried to keep them in mind as well as the English or communication specialist.

The first question, we feel, is how to lay out and chart the routes beyond 16+ that have traditionally been available, have recently emerged, or are currently at the planning stage, under active discussion. To begin with we want something quite elementary, even crude; there will be opportunities as the section develops to refine this initial map. We start then by considering the actual uses of language *demanded in the various qualifying exams* at 16–19: is the qualification in effect saying this student has mastered a fairly specialised use of language, appropriate to a specific course in HE or a specific vocation, on the one hand, or rather, is it indicating a fairly broad mastery of language in which social, personal, vocational and academic purposes overlap? Thus we can use one dimension of the chart to show how specialised or general the major qualifications are, the more specialist being towards the edges, the more integrated towards the middle of the page.

SPECIALISED *ACADEMIC* . . INTEGRATED PURPOSES . . SPECIALISED *VOCATIONAL*
    PURPOSES   including *SOCIAL* and *PERSONAL*   PURPOSES

◄ ··················   ·················· ►

To get a historical perspective, we should start from the 1951 provision for 'English' 16–19. As we have seen, this was dominated by GCE O level, which divided English into a separate language and literature qualification. How general or specialist were these qualifications? At the time, they were probably intended to be fairly broad, but, as we have seen from the 1964 Lockwood Report and from the more recent analysis in section 1.3, in fact both were asking for oddly specialised uses of written English, with little direct relation to social or vocational life — or to academic studies, for that matter.

What English routes were open beyond 16? The primary one was English literature at A level, which attracted roughly 10,000 students. Again, we must ask, how general or specialised were the uses of language demanded in the final examinations, and the answer is, rather specialised. This may seem surprising, considering how broad the reading and discussion of literature often is — and we shall return to this point in depth. For the moment, it seems fair to say that the written English on which the qualification was based was entirely literary-critical and subject to severe constraints. On the vocational side the numbers studying English were much smaller and the main examination either offered strictly business tasks or — perhaps surprisingly — followed the dominant style of the O-level language paper.

Thus a generation ago, English at 16 was effectively — if unconsciously — a narrow qualification, and the two main alternatives on offer beyond 16 were effectively specialist qualifications for further academic studies or vocational tasks. The centre of our page was largely blank.

By 1963–4 two significant changes had started. First, at 16+ the new CSE English syllabuses and examination were being prepared. They tended in the majority of cases to differ from O level in three respects. First, they did not separate language and literature, and in some cases called explicitly for an 'integrated' approach to English. Secondly, they included an assessment of spoken as well as written English: in some cases this was quite broadly conceived, in others it was as narrow as O-level (written) language. And thirdly, both in the written papers and in the provision for samples of course work, they demanded a wider range of language uses. This range was still implicit in many cases, and where it was explicit the emphasis was often on personal and imaginative uses of language — because of recent new achievements in teaching this aspect of English. Thus, while CSE English was demonstrably broader than either O-level qualification, the range of language use demanded was not yet discussed in an explicit or systematic way.

The other major change afoot was in further education, where the 1957 provision for a general or liberal studies element in technical courses had stimulated much new thinking about 'language in education'. Fred Flower's book on the subject, published in 1966, indicates many parallels between the ideas, and the actual courses, in schools and FE during the mid-sixties. General studies naturally placed a strong emphasis on social awareness and language use. The work was not publicly assessed, however, so that the strength of the language element in general studies depended on individual colleges or teachers. As with O level the main vocational English examinations remained largely unchanged at that period.

This was broadly the national position, then, till the early seventies. Change when it came has come in a rush, much of it since 1975, when our project began. For simplicity we will turn aside from the historical perspective to ask what has occurred to alter the map — quite radically — over the last five or six years. To begin with we will be content with a quite summary answer, and will focus on the blank central area.

First let us look at 17+. The pilot CEE examinations gave regional groups of English teachers and boards an opportunity to review the design of CSE English and consider the provision needed a year beyond it. In most cases the boards decided to keep an integrated core of English, with branching assignments, or optional sections, that allowed for a choice among further literature, drama and theatre, media or film, and language studies, for example. Some syllabuses included an element — or option — in vocational English/communication, for the first time. The systems of assessment, with their strong emphasis on folders of course work, called for writing for a wider range of purposes and audiences, in some cases explicitly indicating the range to be covered.

Thus at 17+ the minority of schools who have taken up CEE English are edging further into the middle of the map. This movement, and its implications, call for closer study.

At 18+ there was a dramatic change in opportunities when a new A level in communication studies was set up at the end of the project's first year. Looking for the moment crudely and simply at the potential language demands in the final assessment, there are three elements to consider. The first — surprisingly enough — is a traditional essay paper with all the usual constraints, and no indication so far of purpose or audience, other than the examiner. The second and third take a much sounder view of communication. Paper II consists of a case study, which calls on the students first to study and master several pieces of written (or optionally, graphic) material on a given topic, and secondly to analyse and reorganise it selectively on behalf of a given audience. Paper III consists of a course work project, one of the options being a 4000-word written report, booklet or other study, designed for a specific audience, and possibly tried out with them and revised in the light of their response.

Again, a closer scrutiny will follow later. For the moment the significant point is that social uses of language are given a central place in the project and case study, and indeed among the topics for some of the essays in Paper I. Thus, a shade ironically perhaps, it is not in English but *within* its close relative, communication studies, that students have had the first major opportunity to gain a qualification that allows for the study and use of language across the middle of our map. However, there is one severe implicit limitation: the imaginative and personal uses of language are largely ignored.

Both at 17+ and at 18+, then, there have been important extensions to the 'academic' qualifications on offer, and teachers exploiting these opportunities have, as we shall see, begun to design courses with a less specialist basis. What has happened meanwhile to the 'vocational' qualifications: have they in effect broadened out into the central area? Currently this is in doubt. Since 1975 there have been sweeping reforms in the syllabuses for technical and business studies, directed by the two new national councils, the TEC and the BEC. In the main the new 'communication' elements are much better integrated into the vocational course. At their best they are based on an acute analysis of the language and social 'skills' demanded in different jobs, and are likely therefore to offer a better vocational preparation than in the past.

However, in what was probably the premier vocational qualification in English, the National level in business studies, the current guidelines and national syllabuses do appear to assume that the contexts for mastering the use of language will be almost entirely vocational. Similarly, in the TEC guidelines the original emphasis on the 'personal and social' element in education seems to have been largely submerged in the demand for communication skills directly needed on the job.

It is in the lower level courses, ironically, that the current emphasis shifts from 'vocational' to 'social and life skills'. With the young unemployed, or with students not able to cope with the first level of standard vocational courses, the emphasis, as we shall see, shifts to 'a language for life' — to encouraging social awareness, confidence, and the ability to cope with day-by-day demands on language. The fact that this concern exists in FE is of major importance for the longer term, but at present the pressures on FE teachers of communication run in the opposite direction, we believe. We shall look at these conflicting trends more closely later.

For the moment, let us take stock of the progress so far in redesigning qualifications in English and communication to meet the needs of the majority at 17+ and beyond. What is the current state of our chart, and what questions does it raise? We have tried to indicate the range and restrictions in a simple way on p. 37.

Starting at 16 we must ask whether the English qualifications available offer a foundation in language on which can be built confident participation in social life; personal understanding and awareness; and the ability to take

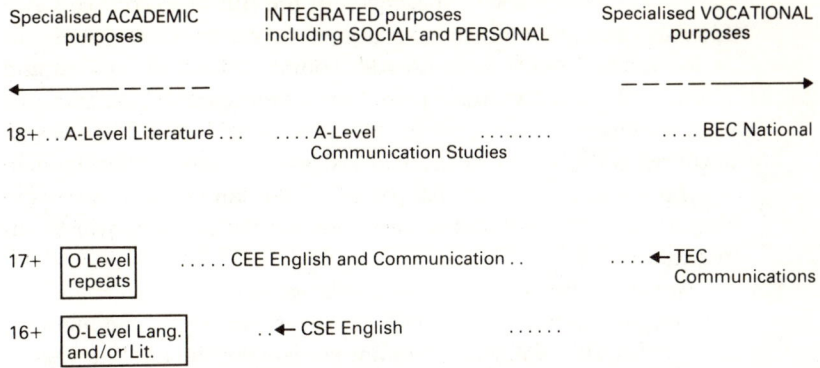

LANGUAGE USES DEMANDED IN EXAMS

Specialised ACADEMIC purposes	INTEGRATED purposes including SOCIAL and PERSONAL	Specialised VOCATIONAL purposes

18+ . . A-Level Literature . . .   . A-Level   . . . . BEC National
                                    Communication Studies

17+ [O Level repeats]   . . . . . CEE English and Communication . .   . . . ←TEC
                                                                            Communications

16+ [O-Level Lang. and/or Lit.]   . . ←CSE English   . . . . . .

on specialist language demands, whether in further academic/vocational studies or directly on the job. This is a tall order. Still, common sense is enough to tell non-specialists as well as English teachers that current English qualifications at 16+ were designed for the 40 per cent who stay on, not the 60 per cent who leave. Yet by 1976 a large minority taking them were leavers.

For those who do stay on, there is a further series of questions.

(a) *Are the current English qualifications at 16 effectively related to the develping rane of courses beyond 16+?*
The facts are quite clear. The main qualification for which the majority of the age group are entering (probably over 60 per cent) is O-level English language. This qualification excludes spoken English and literature: effectively, therefore, it covers about a third of the field. In content alone it is a specialised examination, and traditional examining methods reduce the range of language sampled still further, as we have seen.

English syllabuses that include spoken English and literature are available at 16+, and methods of extending the range of language sampled have been thoroughly tested over the past twelve years. Moreover, methods of certification have been developed at 16+ that do allow for a 'general' qualification — in this case in English — plus 'additional', more specialised aspects such as addirional literature, drama and media studies. Dual certification is normally used. These facts need to be carefully weighed in the design of a new 16+ system.

(b) *Are the qualifications at 17+ all assuming a specialist academic/vocational student or are some allowing for specialist interests to develop from a broader base in the year beyond the fifth form?*

In the major recognised qualifications (O level, A/O level, and the vocational courses of TEC, BEC, C & G) a student is assumed to have made the choice to specialise. In the still-unrecognised CEE, English and communication syllabuses vary across the regions, but in the main provide for a broader course in English (spoken and written). Beyond that, some permit branching specialist assignments, others demand a choice from a range of specialised options in addition to the 'core'. Vocational assignments and options figure in several syllabuses. A national pattern of this kind is badly needed in English at 17+. Without it, provision for the majority will be inadequate.

(c) *Are the qualifications at 18+ making similar assumptions?*

The major qualification at 18+ is A-level literature: the numbers entering in 1976 (66,000) were not far short of the total number of 17+ full-timers in vocational education (71,000). This A level is still normally oriented to an honours English course. One board (AEB) has extended the range of language samples in one syllabus, and another (London) is about to introduce an optional paper in 'language studies'. However, for a large majority the qualification is a specialist one.

Provision for more general uses of language has come not in English but in the related area of communication studies. This calls for a broad range of social uses, and allows for branching assignments based on vocational or academic interests. As a general qualification this A level has already been accepted by many universities and higher education institutions; at the same time, its vocational potential is being recognised by many firms and organisations. Thus a first step has been made in producing a course to 18+ that allows students to 'define a commitment' and includes a strong language element.

For the moment, however, the communication framework and the demands this sets up on teaching and resources are confining the course to a handful of schools; it is the FE and tertiary colleges that are likely to make it widely available over the next ten years. Not surprisingly, therefore, at a 1978 delegate conference with over fifty LEAs, the project team found that the main demand was for a broad English A level to be set up alongside existing courses.

In reviewing the answer to these three questions, then, it seems that progress has indeed been made, especially in the mid-seventies, to meeting the needs of students at 16+, 17+ and 18+. But at all ages, the majority have not been affected by the new developments in English and communication. Nor is there any sense of national urgency in tackling the difficult task of shaping a system fit for the majority. This negative attitude has had its effects not only in slowing progress at each level but also in failing to connect one level with another.

At 16+ two systems of qualification have been allowed to develop in competition with each other. The thousands of candidates double-entered in GCE and CSE indicate one of the results of this decision. It seems likely that much of the extra work this involves for students, teachers and examiners is waste; the time and money could be invested with advantage in better methods of assessment and better syllabuses. Are the decisions at 17+ and 18+ going to be as shortsighted?

In terms of our two-dimensional chart, things may currently look hopeful for English and communication. But there is a third dimension to be taken into account. Suppose a student opts for a one-year English course to CEE (or O-level language), but finds at the end of a year that she or he has developed unexpectedly well — either in the general core, or in vocational or academic options, or in both. Ideally, teachers would like to see a lot of one-year students do precisely that. What happens next? If the student now wants to stay on for a second year, there is probably a difficult choice to face. CEE English is unrelated to A-level literature, and both are unrelated to communication elements in vocational courses. Currently no bridges exist between the three. It is all a snakes-and-ladders game, in which the most likely option is to go back one year — 'you should have been better at 16+; then we would have known'.

What options could be offered in a more rational world? It is not necessary to make the bridge direct from a broad first-year course in English to the second year of such highly specialised courses as A-level literature or Ordinary National business studies. What are needed instead are two-year courses that are less specialised and that offer a qualifying standard equal to A level or the ON Diploma. But let us recall that within a generation it is the majority of the age group who will in all probability be staying on in full-time education. Even if half of them by then are continuing in full-time study after 18, the levels of qualification ought to be indicating positive achievements rather than relative failure to cope with language tasks fitted to those destined for HE or a specific profession.

Our revised chart of the routes available, then, ought to take three things into account:

(a) The scope of the English and communication syllabuses available. These should allow for both general and specialist interests to be harnessed between 16 and 19.
(b) The level and form of qualifications available. At 17+ and 18+, as at 16+, an increasing range in the level of achievement in English is to be expected, as the number staying on shifts from a minority to a

larger and larger majority. High achievers may leave at 17+, low achievers stay on to 18: both groups need a system that allows their positive achievements in English to be recognised and indicates how specialised or broad these have been.

(c) The routes from one qualification level to the next. One-year courses that reach a dead end at 17+, without a route through to a two-year qualification, are necessarily wasteful. Thus the best of CEE's pilot work needs to be related to new two-year courses and to qualifications at A level; similarly with the best of O-level experiments over the past decade.

2.2 Qualifications and Education

There must be some readers at this point — especially among English teachers — who have been waiting impatiently for the discussion of numbers, syllabuses and qualifications to end and 'the real thing' to begin: a description of the actual quality of work in English that is being achieved by students and teachers. In the three years of the project we have learnt a good deal impressionistically about attitudes to examinations, qualifications and their role in education.

Perhaps English teachers as a group are unrepresentatively sceptical; perhaps not. Certainly teachers with very diverse positions about the aims of secondary education or English teaching sometimes turn out to be curiously united in their view of examinations. 'About two terms beforehand, you say to the sixth, "Right, that's the end of the educational part of the course: now let's look at the question papers. Take this essay: Donne is a scholar, not a poet. Discuss . . . A term from now I want you to spot immediately this is a 2:3 essay. Two paragraphs showing he is to a degree a scholar at times, and three showing that in these three respects he transcends the mere scholar. You're going to recognise the type of essay expected as soon as you've read the question. Because you've no time for more than five or six paragraphs. And every paragraph will have one, or at the most two, well-chosen supporting quotations. You're going to learn to play a game, and together we're going to beat the examiner at it".'

This parody, or epitome, may draw on two or three schools of thought, but the unifying quality is the worldly cynicism about examinations, and thus about qualifications.

Teachers who adopt this line may see no need to change the system, or no hope of doing so. There are qualifications, and there is education. Do not confuse the two.

We are not immune to worldly wisdom, especially if the teacher is genuinely trapped without a choice. But we cannot forget that there are other English teachers who are working in systems of assessment they respect, have struggled to improve, and continue to analyse critically each year. Worldly Wiseman's readiness to play the game may be perpetuating that dichotomy between education and qualification he can afford to regard so sceptically.

Moreover there is almost certainly an element of naivety or self-deceit in the sceptical teacher's story that a big chunk of the course can be kept undefiled by the exam for which he has no professional respect. Mind-forged manacles do not click on and off; finally, as it were, the physical constraints are removed, but one still moves as if they were there. We have had excellent evidence of this in the past three years. Thus, even groups of teachers who have struggled to win acceptance for course work (and project team members) can analyse in one session the limitations they want to transcend in traditional examination questions, and in the next session feed them back into suggested course work titles.

Wherever an examination betrays the aims of education, that kind of feedback is almost certain to happen. And, conversely, we have evidence to suggest that where a system of assessment fosters those aims, the feedback is equally important positively.

We reject, therefore, the notion that in their classrooms the teachers are free, if they choose, to set aside the constraints of anti-educational 'qualifications'. Besides, it is in the interests of all concerned — employers and HE as well as teachers and students — to ensure that qualifications testify to things of real value, and that the massive investment of time and money they demand is not wasted on a game.

There will be sceptics of a different kind who will say this is impossible. Qualifications to them are a kind of sham currency, used to reward those students who accommodate to the school system and, in general, to reject those who will not. They enable bureaucratic minds to think in terms of B B B instead of asking what the real qualities needed for higher education are. They relate only to the examinable, and in English that means often enough missing the essence. They put the focus on external end products, and not the internal processes of education: how you got to your conclusion does not count.

In calling this critique utopian we intend neither to sneer nor totally to dismiss the case. In fact, with regard to English examinations, most of these criticisms have been made and accepted nationally. In 1921, when the current system was effectively set up, one of the foremost opponents of the examining of literature was the headmaster of Eton, who 'feared that examination might tend to spoil the teaching'. By 1943, when the system had been running for a generation, a national committee under Sir Cyril Norwood stated: 'the time has passed when such guidance and direction of their work as teachers need can best be given by an external examination . . . the [School Certificate] examination in its present form is having a cramping effect upon the minds of teachers and pupils. *On this our evidence leaves no room for doubt"* (our italics). They went on: "In the study of great literature . . . too much attention has been paid to aspects which are of secondary importance, and the higher values have been obscured. . . . The practice of essay writing . . . has had a harmful influence on the power to write naturally and effectively . . ." As we have seen, twenty years later, in 1964, a national committee under Sir James Lockwood seriously considered abolishing O-level English language on educational grounds.

These are comments on the 'qualifications' that gained the vast majority of us in English teaching entry to college and university. It would be surprising if their cramping effects, their obscuring of higher values and their harmful influences, were not still having repercussions in English teaching today. How can those who have accommodated to such a system in the past rescue themselves now? It looks a vicious circle.

Or does it? The very existence of these — and many more — explicit criticisms, coming from what must surely count as bureaucratic representatives of the state, suggests to us not a monolithic 'system' but a meeting ground of conflicting interests, beliefs and pressures. *External* exams tend to 'make uniform the pattern of teaching . . . Once laid down they take a deal of altering': thus the Crowther Report in 1959. Five years later a new system of examining was laid down at 16+ which not only aimed to allow higher 'internal' standards to be asserted (through mode III), but provided for moderation of an internal element in almost every mode I English assessment. Ten years further on, the CEE English panels have consistently carried this provision a step further. Even the conservative GCE boards had almost all mounted at least *one* experimental syllabus in English with a strong internal element.

After three years' work with committed groups of teachers across the country we are less prone to underestimate the effort and struggle that is needed to clarify, select (and reject) 'internal' values, at this stage of educational development in the country. For the majority of teachers we have met, the best opportunity to do this consistently and without parochial restriction has come through meetings to discuss new syllabuses, modes of assessment and examples of course work.

Certainly, it is a minority of English teachers at present who either have or care to use such opportunities. We believe it should be the majority. Otherwise, a teacher may go through his or her career without any critical scrutiny and discussion of the way he or she assesses students' work, the implicit or explicit criteria to use and the fundamental understanding of language that is required. And yet English teachers' judgements are affecting students every day of the week, not just in a final qualification.

We reject, then, not the utopian dream, but the failure to make an adequate historical analysis. Like Worldly Wiseman, the utopian critic is tempted to assume an innocent English teacher, but in his view this Snow

White falls an easy prey to her evil step-mothers, the boards and the educational establishment. In fact, by any measure, the internal responsibility of the English department, or better of the local consortium of departments, has increased and is increasing, if we take a historical perspective. And there is no Snow White; the current struggle is between better and worse views of our education *and* qualification in English, among teachers and among examiners.

Believing this, we have made no effort to cover up existing criticisms of the teaching and assessment of English. The historical evidence is that in the main English has been badly examined at 16–19 and that bad examinations have encouraged and rewarded bad teaching. If nothing had changed over a generation, there would be reason to despair. Our experience as a project team is that things are changing, and, as might be predicted, there is a steady interplay between changes in the evidence invited or encouraged for a given qualification, and changes in teaching and learning English. It is this interplay, this interaction between the two, that calls for careful description and analysis.

2.3   The 18+ Tail that Wags the Dog

In reviewing and selectively analysing the interplay between qualifications, teaching, and learning English and communication, we shall begin not at 16 but at 18+. What counts as English at 18 critically affects all that goes on earlier. And, conversely, an English syllabus that leads to a 17+ qualification, however intrinsically valuable, will be seen as second best if it does not enable a student to continue through to an A level.

We intend therefore to use the next five sections to consider current and potential provision at 18+, and then to move back to consider the routes that lead through from 16, and the lessons to be learnt from recent work on them. Our main concern throughout will be the need to provide for the majority of the age group as well as minorities, and to escape from the assumption that all courses should be oriented towards academic or vocational specialisms.

It is an indication of the intellectual muddle at this level that we have to begin with problems of definition. There are several alternative ways of drawing up syllabuses for the two broad areas we have been calling English and communication, and also for the specialist elements within them, in particular literature and language. To avoid confusion we shall begin by using the syllabus requirements of existing A levels (or A-level elements) to map out and provisionally define these four major areas. This will avoid initial ambiguity, we hope, and allow for alternative definitions to be discussed as each of the four is considered in depth.

Literature is perhaps least in need of definition, though non-specialists may need reminding that, in addition to poetry, drama and prose fictions, syllabuses will often include autobiographical and other documentary prose, collections of essays, letters and speeches. This is a straight development from O-level syllabuses. However, the one syllabus element in language at A level is not: the requirement is for the analysis of selected speech and writing (including literature), drawing on various elementary linguistic concepts. To mark the distinction we intend to call this 'language studies' — using the second word to indicate that conceptual analysis is expected.

Currently, the one existing English (language and literature) syllabus at A level contains literature, plus the study of the press, radio and television, and live speech. In addition it calls for a variety of original writing and the production of reports, summaries and similar functional prose. This definition of English (though not the overall weightings) is similar to that developed in CSE syllabuses in the 1960s; however, it places less emphasis on speech. It includes literature and, as we have indicated on the diagram, might well be extended to include an element of language studies. Thus, by comparison with literature or language studies, English is an over-arching syllabus, covering a very much broader range of writing and considerably broader range of reading, listening and viewing.

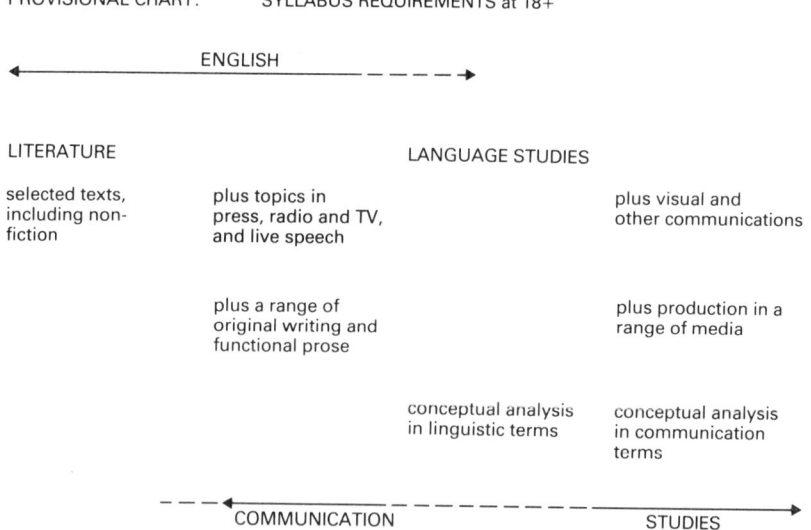

PROVISIONAL CHART: SYLLABUS REQUIREMENTS at 18+

Communication studies, as defined in the current A level, covers a wider area still. The live speech and language of the media are central things to study, but the visual and other non-verbal modes of communication are given equal importance. Similarly students may produce work in sound tape and video, and their written projects may include an important graphics element. The 'studies' part of the title again indicates that a conceptual analysis is expected, drawing on models of the processes of communication, and on research into producers, media and audiences. (In addition a historical dimension is included.) Though there is an overlap, the relationship with language studies is not yet clear, as we indicate by the dotted line, and literature is not specifically included in the existing syllabus — a point we will take up later.

Our chart, then, is not critical or normative, but a provisional working definition of the areas occupied by each of the four existing types of syllabuses. We hope it serves to make clear the current overlap between English and communication, and perhaps to raise some questions about the possible relationship of these four areas.

Such a chart by no means exhausts the curriculum subjects or areas that overlap with English. Two obvious examples are drama, which was recognised in a separate A level in 1974, and media studies, still unrecognised as a subject at this level. The essential reason for omitting them was not simply our own limited competence to discuss them, but the desire to focus as sharply as we could on the central problem of offering some students — and maybe the majority in future years — a less specialist choice and, with it, the opportunity between 16 and 19 of 'defining a commitment'.

2.4   The Potential of Literature at 18+

To begin then with Shakespeare: he was the man who of all modern and perhaps ancient poets had the largest and most comprehensive soul . . .

. . . he seems to have known the world by intuition, to have looked through human nature at one glance . . .

. . . his works may be considered as a map of life, a faithful miniature of human transactions, and he that has read Shakespeare with attention will find little new in the crowded world.

Lear: we wish we could pass the play over, and say nothing about it. All that we can say must fall far short of the subject; or even of what we ourselves conceive of it.

****

In Literature far more than in anything else the range of the examiner tends to be incommensurate with that of the best teacher. The latter will be constantly experimenting, and clearly he should be invited to do so. Many teachers set great store by the cultivation of original work on the part of pupils, or by dramatic performance. It would be a misfortune should the examination system rule such work out of court: the examiner should accordingly apply himself to the problem of how to test it without doing it injury. He too will be constantly experimenting . . .

... there is still great possibility of fresh achievement in the art of examining.
(Newbolt Report, 1921)

English literature is currently the most popular subject at A level, yet during the first year of our project not a month passed without a local group of teachers contacting us because they were dissatisfied with the examination syllabus. Cleveland, West Yorkshire, South Yorkshire, Derbyshire, Nottinghamshire, Hertfordshire, Inner London, Merton, Avon, Devon, Glamorgan, Clwyd . . . all had groups with serious criticisms to make.

To understand the force of those criticisms, one must look not simply at syllabuses but at underlying aims. Why study literature? What aims are teachers seeking to realise with their 16–19 students? In most literature syllabuses the focus is exclusively on the texts: there is no analysis of what students will be learning if the course is to be successful. We believe, as a result of our work, that a much more careful analysis of aims is needed: we shall start therefore with a summary of those expressed by a cross-section of teachers (from schools and colleges, from the state and private sector) who joined a national workshop organised by the project team.

In studying literature — reading, listening or viewing with particular care and commitment — they hoped to 'widen understanding of the human state'. As students are taken inside the thoughts of people and observe them in action, they can reach 'an increased understanding of themselves and others' and 'a better understanding of their place in the world'. They can 'gain in depth of thought' and in the 'desire to know more'. In consequence they will be encouraged 'to observe people and things more closely', to develop 'awareness . . . of their own experience and that of others' and to 'appreciate the complexities of life'. Faced with those complexities, the reader may become a sadder and a wiser man or woman, with more 'tolerance of the plurality of existence'.

The encounter with literature, then, is seen as a 'meeting of minds' which modifies our 'personal understanding' of the world we meet through the writer's mediation, and our awareness of the world we live in.

Aims such as these express the fundamental, human purposes in studying literature, we take it. They remind us that in order to 'meet' another mind, readers have to summon from their own experience the subtleties, complexities and pluralities that will bring the words on the page to life. To 'appreciate mature ideas and feelings maturely expressed', they have in some ways to make them *their own*. Thus, as students turn to their own world, they may be more sharply aware of it, and of potentialities in themselves and others that they have not realised before.

'Teaching' literature involves helping students to make the best of such encounters. Within our cross-section this led to three further aims. First, to give students 'more confidence in their approach to previously unknown texts'. Each text (or record) carries with it the writer's personal and cultural assumptions. To 'approach books . . . written in an unfamiliar style' demands some effort of 'understanding and sympathy'. Teachers aim to broaden the range of writers a student can meet with heightened expectations, and to give 'some ideas of the ways *into* any book' that seems alien or puzzling. More than that, they aim for an active tolerance, which senses qualities in 'literature they do not greatly care for as well as that which they do enjoy' and perhaps is able 'to realise *why* this is so'.

This increasing ability to entertain visions of life and perspectives on it that are initially alien, confusing or antipathetic depends on the people we learn to respect and our feeling for the language they use. This leads to the second subordinate aim: 'a training to read carefully and thoroughly', 'with sensitivity to emotion and tone' and an 'understanding of literature as a concrete presentation of ideas'. Teachers were aiming beyond this, too, for an appreciation of 'the elements of all kinds of written language', 'not simply the literary', and a greater awareness of the 'importance of language' in ordinary living.

The third aim depends on both the others: it concerns discrimination and judgement. In encountering new minds, a student can 'develop a feeling for the kinds of values they represent'. Maybe 16 to 18-year-olds will begin to 'use a growing critical faculty on what they read or see', and 'rely on their own judgement in matters of criticism'. There were mixed feelings about realising this aim under present conditions, and we shall return to them later.

These three subsidiary aims — meeting with confidence; listening, viewing or reading with care; and learning to consider the values represented — all affect the quality and range of the encounter with literature. Equally it is worth noting that each of them affects our everyday encounters with people, and especially the accounts we give each other of important experiences in our lives.

In the aims we have summarised up to this point, then, teachers are concerned with the relationship between the written text and the perspective on human experience that it offers. The complex language of the text is valued because it renders some aspect of experience with new penetration and insight; the vision of the writer, because it disturbs, challenges and at times inspires. And, in some way, a relationship can be set up between this imaginary experience, the actual experiences of daily life and the language used to construe them both.

They seem ideal aims. But when we asked the teachers to discriminate between aims they felt they could realise and those that were currently beyond realisation (for whatever reason), they placed the aims we have discussed so far in the first category. It will be obvious already then that such teachers are setting very high targets for any system of assessment. If reading and listening to literature is indeed a fundamental human activity, we do not see how this could be otherwise.

However, while many of the aims expressed concerned literature for the 'common reader', some suggested an element of specialist study, first in terms of 'the craft of writing' and secondly in terms of historical analysis.

In reading literature, an awareness of craft may 'enable one's appreciation to be deepened'. To understand from the inside the process of composition — perhaps through studying successive drafts — can lead to a greater 'awareness of the relationship of form to content'. And as literature changes under the pressure of 'general movements and their conventions' so the prevailing forms and the techniques they call for change. Even the word 'craft' itself is most at home in an age of deliberate, very consciously constructed forms; at the other pole one might discuss the notion of 'organic shaping' and intuitive choice.

'Perhaps the quickest way to understand the elements of what a novelist is doing is not to read, but to write; to make your own experiment with the dangers and difficulties of words', as Virginia Woolf once said in talking to a school. In this way what might otherwise seem a largely external, clinical study of craft can be animated with a practitioner's interest and admiration. Young writers can realise, from the weight of the decisions in their own writing, what force might be intended by a shift in lineation or rhythm, the movement into a new stanza pattern, the thematic resonances of an opening scene and its images, the significant 'sense of an ending'. However, for many of our cross-section 'the full use of imagination in practical writing or drama' remained an unrealised aim in current conditions — a point we shall return to later. Thus, in general it was a narrower consideration of craft that was being realised.

The remaining major aims were to study 'texts in the context of their time and cultural background'. Initially, this demands some grounding in Elizabethan (or Chaucerian) language, and ideally the ability not simply to make sense of what is lost or archaic in modern English, but to pick up the contemporary implications, attitudes and feelings implicit in a given phrase, within a given context. This in turn depends like most language learning on a wide range of encounters with Elizabethan language *in use*, preferably on the stage, where intonation and action will reinforce the interpretation. Perhaps there is a gradient here that begins with the enthusiastic reader (or play-goer) intuitively picking up and enjoying the Elizabethan idiom, and ends with the scholarly specialist, able to define contrasts and shifts in meaning within the period (as Empson did for 'honest'). With Chaucer's language — especially when one considers the lack of weight in some of the tales regularly selected — it seems that scholarly and specialist interest has already been assumed.

In addition to the language of text, there is of course the cultural background that fed and sustained the imaginative work, and especially the literature. There was some uncertainty in our sample about the feasibility of introducing students to this by 18+. Perhaps in part the explanation is that such studies have a choice of starting point. Looking out from a given text, they may help to place its conventions, assumptions and stance by building up a richer sense of contemporary ideas, feelings and attitudes — and even simply by living for a day in contemporary costume and sets, as one school reported to us. There is in addition the desire to stand back from the texts and study the way 'cultural, social and economic pressures influence writers . . . and writers one another' so that one discovers on the one hand literature's connections with politics or religion, and on the other its interplay with painting, music and the arts. Thus the student is taking the first steps to an understanding of the historical role of a given writer in culture and society. It will be obvious that to some degree both starting points — and especially the second — move beyond literature to the imaginative and scholarly demands of history: to that extent, by comparison with our first group of aims, they seem less a matter for the 'common reader' than for the committed specialist.

The balance between general and specialist intersts is the heart of the problem of defining examination syllabuses at 18+, we believe. If the mode of assessment is entirely designed in the interests of the scholarly preparation of the 4 per cent who go on to read honours English, they and the remaining 96 per cent stand to suffer from the relative inattention to broader humanistic possibilities in the course. Let us turn then from aims such as have been expressed here to the major issues they raise for the examining of literature at this level.

If reading literature is indeed to be a meeting of minds, who is the student to meet? This is a crucial question. A literature course at 16–19 offers each student the opportunity to take a major step in defining his or her own culture. Ideally, therefore, we assume students will be reading and studying some texts they themselves have suggested, individually or collectively, and others that their teachers have similarly suggested. If all the texts for study are selected by teachers, the student is left with the cultural choice of acquiescence or rejection. If some of the texts for discussion are self-selected, students have a positive, adult role. They may discover in the process that some of their proposals turn out to be less good than they seemed at first. Equally, they may find that others are very rewarding, for the teachers as well as their peers. As a result, the teachers, too, are in a significantly different position in making further suggestions; there is a sense of reciprocity, of challenging and being challenged, of a mutual response to enthusiasms and discoveries.

When our project began, most established syllabuses at 18+ ignored or ruled out this process, whether intentionally or not. The main papers in all but the Cambridge board assumed the study of up to a dozen texts externally set. There was no attempt to include in the assessment a student's ability to study equally closely a group of texts chosen personally, in consultation with teachers.

The main reason for setting a group of texts externally is clear enough. When a large number of students answer the same question on the same text it is possible to make quite refined distinctions in placing them in rank order and grading them. However, it sets up three major problems. First, in practice boards try to offer as generous a choice as possible, especially in the 'period' papers, and thus for any given text there may finally be only a small and rather unrepresentative group of answers. Consequently refined distinctions are sometimes ruled out; indeed, it has even been found that occasionally the marks for a given text may be 'negatively discriminating' — rewarding otherwise low scorers, and penalising otherwise high scorers.

The second problem is that of all mass examinations: no given text (and no set question) will be equally appealing to all students. The text may be good enough, but there will be many others equally good that one or other student would have preferred to study. If very fine discriminations are needed — as they are in A-level literature, where the mark range of the middle grades may be as narrow as 3 or 4 per cent — the difference in appeal could be crucial.

The third problem is more complex and fundamental. If the texts for study are determined externally this will have serious consequences for the kind of learning that goes on, and the aims that can be fulfilled. It is as if the student were given a cultural chaperone who decided which minds it was proper to meet. The chaperone's choice may be excellent, but one thing is certain: the students have no scope for learning to choose. They may well learn that texts chosen for them have a great deal to offer, but they will never learn this way how little or much there might be in the texts they themselves would choose.

To understand the importance of this point we must recall that after 18+ very few indeed of the 66,000 candidates will have any further intensive course in literature. The two-year course is their major opportunity to apply 'a growing critical faculty [to] what they read and see' and thus to develop personal preferences founded, if not 'on reason and taste', at least on some close reading and discussion. Not surprisingly, these were among the aims that teachers in our sample felt they could not realise at present.

We must remember too that at 16 and 17 many students are naturally at an early stage in forming their tastes in adult literature. Compared with the reader of 40 or 50 they have a different experience and approach. To be specific: if they are invited to suggest a topic for a longer personal essay, they may opt — as Rodrick did — for 'Fable and its Use in Golding, Bradbury and Science Fiction'. Why? 'I've chosen this because it's closest to the sort of book I'm interested in . . . timeless stories which have morals. I'm not very impressed with things where you have to go back to the period when they were written . . . I'll probably use Golding, *Lord of the Rings,* and Moorcock's *Jewel in the Skull* . . .'. This is an expression of actual taste at 17. Golding, Tolkien and Moorcock are not the group of writers the board would (or should) offer, but the question is rather: what opportunities for learning can be foreseen in the preparation for such an essay? The notion of timeless, mythic fables seems powerful enough. What additional texts might be worth suggesting to this student (an avid reader)? How can the study help him realise differences in quality among these writers — the relative derivativeness of Moorcock, perhaps? Maybe that helps to suggest *who* else might be read. What discoveries might be made through reading such fables, and considering closely some episodes that evoke their moral stance? What is so compelling to this 17-year-old in the visions they offer?

Questions such as these, running through the teacher's mind, reflect we hope the complex mixture of challenge and respect that is needed in approaching each student who cares about what he or she reads. If Rodrick is to learn to define his own cultural choice, he needs such opportunities to consider where he stands and what he actually cares deeply about. The process of working on a long essay will modify his initial perceptions — and possibly those of the teacher too.

We shall be looking in detail at a form of examination syllabus that recognises work such as this, while equally allowing the board to set some texts for all students and the individual department to add to the range, drawing on its general knowledge of the group of students joining the course. Before doing so, however, let us consider the other major issue that arises from the aims we have been surveying.

In fact, it follows directly from the questions raised by Rodrick. These moral fables and the vision of life they offer should bring new insight into people, and challenge or extend the student's sense of the way they live. How is that new understanding to be articulated? What varieties of writing may need to be encouraged, or offered as alternatives, if this fundamental purpose is to be fully realised?

It must be said that the established examination paper offers a poor guide, not because examiners have failed to experiment with the variety of questions set, but simply because of the constraints they, like the candidates, labour under. If the examination is to assess a student's reading of each of nine or ten texts, then that number of questions must be squeezed into three-hour papers: thus on average forty to sixty minutes will be available. If the question is to be answered without reference to the text, there are further constraints. If it is to be equally appealing and accessible to several thousand candidates, it must be based on very general assumptions about their interests and background.

For the teacher none of these constraints apply. Yet the established forms of question set in examination papers inevitably exert a powerful influence on writing during the course. This was clearly foreseen by the English Association, when the 18+ examination system was set up in 1918: 'since the style of question set determines the method of teaching, examining bodies usurp functions which properly belong to the school'. For this reason, they believed, 'purely external examinations in English Literature, in which there is no direct contact between the Examiner and the teacher, cannot be approved'.

It is significant that during the seventies four boards have set up experiments at A level which re-establish that direct contact between English teacher and examiner, and add a selection of written course work to the evidence to be examined. Not surprisingly, one of the main questions they have faced is what kinds of writing are to be encouraged by the course and the experimental exam. This is a task which deserves much more systematic study nationally, we believe.

If the broader humanistic aims of a literature course are to be taken seriously, the potential value of a much wider range of writing may need to be recognised.

Many groups of teachers have discussed the underlying issues with the project team over the past three years and all this section can offer is a sketch of the ideas they have suggested and the practical experiments they have carried out. Nevertheless, some general directions are already clear. Thus, after students have responded with all their resources to an imaginative text or presentation, they need to call on many forms of language in order to express and distill the significance the experience has had for them. One of the main ways a teacher can help is by indicating the range of forms available at different stages, to articulate different aspects of the experience.

Thus, immediately after the first encounter with an original mind and its vision of human action and suffering, it is often important *not* to have to organise a polished statement to a wider audience, but to have time to ponder, to let the imagination dwell on the experience-in-words still acting on it. The demand for a prescribed form like the 'essay' may well be obstructive; students need the opportunity to use their writing as a medium for reflection and discovery, for finding out what already exists to be developed and articulated. We have observed several recent experiments to encourage students to use writing in such ways. Here is one example from a student's initial 'Notes and Ideas' on William Blake.

A Poison Tree
In this poem, the protagonist (the 'I' in the poem) deliberately nurses his grievance or resentment against 'my foe'. It is a deliberate nurturing of his anger but not with the obvious intention of killing (i.e. it's not to say that he went into the

situation with that notion in mind); the point is that the murder of the foe is a consequence of his anger.

The first verse explains the circumstances of the action. 'I was angry with my friend: I told my wrath, my wrath did end' meaning that he told his friend that he was angry with him — so his anger evaporated. But, 'I was angry with my foe: I told it not, my wrath did grow'. He didn't tell his foe he was angry and consequently his anger grew because he didn't give voice to it.

Blake here then is particularly aware of the importance of 'airing one's grievances'. The fact that the consequences are so serious for the foe only serves to bring home this fact more forcefully. Blake was aware also that there was something humanly compelling about a nurtured and nursed brooding.

There is nothing profound about the first two lines — but there is something lively and strangely attractive about the rest of the poem — it is very insidious. The foe is avaricious, comes into the garden at night with the intention of taking what is not his — the apple. The motive for the deed is that the apple is bright. In fact there is an ironic contrast between the apple being so bright, a product of something as murky and underhand as stored anger.

While on the subject of the tempting qualities of the bright apple, it is worth raising the question of whether there is meant to be an allusion with the Garden of Eden here. In my mind, there could well be because the fourth verse seems to have a similar theme as the biblical story of the tempting object which, when taken, bodes misfortune for the recipient.

As the poem progresses, we notice a separation between the man and his anger which becomes a tangible object — a tree which bears fruit. This perhaps explains the apparent aloofness the person feels when recounting that *'I see my foe outstretched beneath the tree'* when he awakes in the morning. It is a terribly chilling tone as though the death is nothing to do with him.

During the middle stanzas, he becomes obsessed with waiting for the apple to blossom. It becomes an over-anxious task for him to get it to grow.

> 'I water'd it in fears,
> Night & morning with my tears;
> And I sunned it with smiles,
> And with soft deceitful wiles.'

'Deceitful' suggesting the insidious nature of it all. Indeed there is a perverse self-indulgence in the middle two verses, even though the foe is present throughout.

There is a sense of discovery about the poem. It is not just the killing but it is the state of mind he is left with at the close; his whole life has been taken up with this. Thus he is relieved when he can *see* the result of his 'labours' — the use of 'glad' (1. 15) shows this — *'In the morning glad I see'*. There is something wholesome and innocent about the word 'glad' even though it is strange that he should feel glad — but then he has done something — it is his work which he has slaved at with his 'tears', his 'smiles' and his 'soft deceitful wiles'.

The relief is shown in the last two lines which are much more reposed and calm. There is an uneasy confidence about these lines, the way they are spoken — one gets the feeling that he might even let it happen again.

To go back a line, if I may: 'When the night had veil'd the pole', the 'pole' being either the pole star or the tree trunk, there is a feeling that the night becomes an active agent in the deed. After 'pole' there is an assured break before the frighteningly revealing final two lines.   Richard

We notice first, perhaps, the direct way a discovery is set down — that a grievance or resentment may be deliberately nursed, and with what consequences. It seems an important perception, but despite the writer's evident ability with language, the second sentence already suggests there is something about it he finds difficult to articulate. It is only after a crabwise return to the opening verse that the writer moves back to a deeper realisation that 'there was something humanly compelling about a nurtured and nursed brooding'.

Realising this seems a source of confidence, for immediately afterwards he says something for the first time about his own response to this encounter: 'nothing profound' at first, but 'something lively and strangely attractive' — 'insidious' even — as the experience developed. The very juxtaposition of lively/attractive/insidious suggests a complexity to be grappled with, but once again the writer postpones any direct struggle with it. Is he perhaps implicitly searching for what stirred the mixed feelings that lie behind those words, as he turns to the signficance of the apple and its brightness?

When he does return, much later, it is with a different emphasis. He has discovered meanwhile, in meditating on 'the apparent aloofness the person feels', a 'terribly chilling tone'. This affects his whole interpretation, taking him back to reconsider the over-anxiety with which the apple is nurtured: it *is* compelling, yes, but as a form of 'perverse self-indulgence'.

For the rest of his note he moves to 'the state of mind [the protagonist] is left with at the close'. It is a passage where the student is remarkably open to Blake's perceptions, to the force of 'glad' in 'the frighteningly revealing final two lines'. Only a very daring imagination, we feel, could admit what he is free enough to say here: 'something wholesome and innocent' . . . 'much more reposed [*sic*] and calm'. This perception too is frightening in its human revelations . . .

Such notes, we hope, leave one in little doubt about the human value on this occasion of reading Blake's poem with care. Nevertheless, if we are right, their organisation is not that of a rhetorically finished product: rather, we suggest, they offer evidence of a mind in the act of searching, criss-crossing the field of the experience with a drive to penetrate complexities in response, linking the moments of discovery with earlier, obscurer feelings and perceptions, and recurrently remoulding the felt significance of the experience, especially where the shaping force of the language is consciously felt.

It seems a very important enterprise, and the sudden switches in attention seem the mark of an active, engaged imagination, not an erring one. If so, this raises a crucial question. In the light of such notes what are we to make of the possible demands when examination candidates are asked to read an unseen poem *for the first time* and to write on it? Manifestly, in comparison with course work, some sense of constraint is unavoidable. With an unknown audience to take into account — and a judge at that — a subtle form of censorship is likely to be exerted; sentences and even paragraphs in the notes above could sound too naive to be left in. But, more important, other avoidable constraints are sometimes added. There may be explicit demands for structure; a well-worn formula, for instance, like 'Compare and contrast the following'. Equally there may be no release from the implicit under-standing that what is said ought to be rhetorically organised into as polished a product as time will allow (for an imaginary and non-existent wider audience). The above example should serve as a reminder that even linguistically able students need freedom for the imagination to work in the *early* stages of encountering a new poem. Rhetorical demands, or the call for explicit attention to 'diction', 'imagery', and so on, seem likely to push the reader into regarding the poem as a linguistic object, rather than an imaginative encounter. The effects of the wording of such examination questions need further analysis.

In general, it is very hard, particularly one imagines for the university don who knows only 4 per cent of the current candidates, not to understimate the difficulties 16–19 students face in trying to keep the imaginative exper-ience of the text alive while also trying to articulate what it has meant to them. Even in course work — with a reading or presentation freshly in mind; the text available; the time pressure relaxed; an understanding, known reader in view — it very often happens at the opening of an essay that the early formulations use language in ways that are sharply different from those that follow as the writer warms to the enterprise. Consider the following two extracts from a response to the scene where Lear, having found Kent in the stocks and searched out Gloucester himself, is told that Regan and Cornwall 'deny to speak' with him. Are there any observable differences in the use of language here?

(a) In this passage we see Lear in a great rage because Regan and Cornwall have refused to see him straightaway. He thinks that their reasons are merely excuses. 'Mere fetches,
    The images of revolt and flying-off.
    Fetch me a better answer.'
Gloucester tries to smooth things over but only succeeds in further provoking Lear, who refuses to consider the character of the Duke, but feels individuality should be subordinate to social status and duty. He even seems to resent Cornwall's reputation for being 'fiery' and unmovable. He perhaps feels fieryness is only for Kings, and Cornwall is becoming too arrogant . . .
    The excuse of illness is very welcome to Lear, because it accounts for, and

therefore eliminates, the insult to his sovereignty. He can comfort himself with the reflection that if Regan and Cornwall were in good health they would never behave in this manner.

'Infirmity doth still neglect all office
Whereto our health is bound.'

However this solace is false, and he soon realises this as he remembers that Kent is in the stocks.

'Death on my state! Wherefore should he sit here?'

If the Duke has put Kent in the stocks he cannot be unwell. This naturally raises Lear's temper again, to an even higher pitch than before with the insult to his messenger he has just remembered . . .

(b)   Lear acts rather like a hurt animal. He is highly touchy and panicky. He needs comfort, but Gloucester is not the person to give it to him. His hysterical manner and violent changes of mood are the first stage in his slide towards insanity. Gloucester is rather naive, in that he sees nothing amiss and cannot understand why Lear is so unreasonable. He is polite and proper, though gives the impression of being bewildered, and out of his depth. On the other hand, the Fool is shrewd and rather bitter, and perfectly comprehends the situation, and its implications.

It is becoming obvious that Regan and Cornwall do not respect Lear as they should. Their rejection of him is not only inevitable — it is planned. Callous natured, they feel nothing for him, but want him out of the way. They feel themselves superior to him, for he is old and weak, and rather foolish, and naive in his ignorance of their true natures and feelings. His daughters scorn Lear, and are revulsed by his demands for filial affection.

The tone of the opening passage seems detached:

'we see Lear in a great rage'
'he thinks that their reasons are mere excuses'
'[he] refuses to consider the character of the Duke'
'he perhaps feels fieryness is only for kings'

Lear is observed at a great distance, as it were; some obvious things about his behaviour are noted, his thoughts are briefly considered, there is a tentative comment on his attitudes. From language such as this we might well gather that the imagination is still running cold and the writer is struggling to say things without, as yet, feeling any active engagement with the experience.

By the middle of the essay and passage (b), a change seems to have taken place.

'Lear acts rather like a hurt animal'
'He is highly touchy and panicky'
'He needs comfort . . .'

The movement into imagery is significant; there is more human understanding to be expressed now. The sentence rhythms suggest a writer who is
actually moved to comment by his growing comprehensions of the action as
it is seen and felt — not only by Lear but by Gloucester and the Fool. The
student recovers perhaps from his first dismissive judgement on Gloucester
to realise that beneath the polite proper surface there may be a kind of
naivety and bewilderment — a man 'out of his depth'. By comparison the
Fool 'perfectly comprehends' what is now becoming obvious to the concerned onlooker.

Thus, although the language is more general, less close to the detail of the
action for the moment, it nevertheless serves to draw together a felt understanding of this episode as a whole. As it happens, this writer does return to
moment-by-moment experience towards the end of this essay, recognising
now the wildness of Lear's curses, the desperation in his appeal to Gloucester,
the frustration as well as the fury in his response — 'Dost thou understand
me man?' It is indeed a scene that keeps on challenging the imagination.

Teachers learn to discount — even in course work essays — some of the
things that are said, as the writer gets under way with the task and struggles
to recover an involvement with the experience. Equally, for readers fresh
from the text the emotional force of a scene such as this may set up very
different problems if they are asked to articulate what was felt and understood, as we shall see later. It is rarely easy both to keep the imaginative
encounter vividly alive and to articulate adequately what one has found
there of human action and suffering.

This natural fact makes the job of examiners setting a traditional three-
hour essay paper doubly difficult. They know the students will be without
the text; will have to turn from one text to another, three or four times in the
session; will have to be asked an unseen question; will have to produce a
rounded essay, organised on the spot in answer to it. Under these additional
pressures, what results are to be expected from any but the most well-
adapted candidates? What evidence of the quality of reading and response
are the main body of students likely to be able to offer?

This is not a question that has been objectively investigated, to our
knowledge, in the sixty years since a 'second examination' in literature was
set up. However, it is fair to point out that all A-level teachers have
sufficient experience of the broad contrasts between written course work
and mock examination essays to offer some provisional judgements. Many
that we have met during the project would agree with the following students,
working for an A level which included a course work folder as part of the
assessment.

Having just taken the English mock 'A' Level my first reaction is that I am very
grateful to be taking the Leicester Syllabus and to have the opportunity of
submitting a course work folder, mainly because I feel that the essays I write

under exam conditions are not — and never could be — my best. Comparing them to those I write for my folder they really seem absurdly scanty, generally just skimming the surface of the ideas which I have and not because I do not know the particular book or play, nor due to any lack of ideas on my part but simply because 45 minutes seems a ridiculously short time in which to tackle, for example, a question as wide — and interesting — as that of order and chaos in *The Tempest* . . .
When writing a course essay you have longer to plan and you can also formulate and clarify your ideas. The books on the syllabus are available for reference and you are therefore able to choose the best quotes to illustrate your opinions. You have more time for the preparation and actual writing of the essay and can write more because of the absence of pressure. More ideas, themes and illustrations can be found and the essay is more comprehensive and thorough.

By contrast, the three-hour paper seems extremely restricting. It is difficult to choose the points which best illustrate the themes you are discussing and because of the time-limit, the length of the essay is shortened. The planning of the essay is difficult because there is virtually no time to formulate ideas before beginning. The essay titles seem to be very general judging from past papers and mock examinations, and this is an additional difficulty — for instance there was a title involving imprisonment in *Little Dorrit* and the theme of utilitarianism versus imagination and spontaneous emotions etc. in *Hard Times*. Both of these titles seemed to encompass the whole book and it is therefore extremely hard to pick the most relevant and significant parts to write about . . .

These students were clear enough about differences in preparation, in formulation, and even in aims between written course work and orthodox examination essays. Equally significant are their comments on the generality of many essay topics in exams. In designing a single question, suited to a wide range of students without a text available, examiners are under severe restrictions. If chance factors are to be avoided, it is unwise to ask all students to base their essay on a specific scene in *King Lear*, for instance; a general question relating to the play as a whole appears preferable. On the other hand, it seems difficult to deny that forty-five or sixty minutes is an absurdly scanty time in which to offer evidence of one's appreciation of some aspect of such a major work. How do students cope — and especially, what pressures does this put on their use of language?

Again, we can find no extensive study of this commonplace practice. It is difficult even to find a small sample selected by someone without an axe to grind. The collection of a representative sample will be an important part of our forthcoming investigation. For the moment, the best we can do is to look closely at one or two instances commented on not unappreciatively by Frances Stevens in her book *English and Examinations* (Hutchinson, 1970).

We begin with an average student and his two opening paragraphs.

In *King Lear* the influence of evil on all the characters is very apparent, the whole play is full of evil which destroys both the good and evil characters: because there is so much evil in the play, much of it is set at night-time and during bad weather.

There are two groups of people in *King Lear,* the good and the evil, and both recognise that man's nature is essentially evil but the good, Edgar, Cordelia, Kent, Albany, try to overcome this evil, whereas Edmund, Cornwall, Regan and Goneril are quite content to live a life of evil and to use it to gain their own ends. The two different attitudes may be seen in the contrasting philosophies of Edgar and Edmund, Edgar believes that man can rise above evil and live a good moral life; Edmund bases his philosophy on self-interest and rejects the conventional morality, he is one for his own gain no matter whom he hurts in doing so.

There is, naturally enough, some evidence of floundering — a failure to articulate the force of darkness and storm, for instance. But this can be discounted. More important is the characterisation of the two groups:

those who try to overcome this evil
        believe that man can rise above evil and live a good moral life
those who are quite content to live a life of evil
        use it to gain their own ends (no matter whom it hurts)
        base [their] philosophy on self-interest and reject the conventional
        morality.

The difficulty here is that the language seems to offer no evidence of even the last remembered traces of an encounter with the play. If one were asked, on the evidence so far, what text the student had been reading, *Lamb's Tales* might be suggested, or perhaps a comic strip version of the story. It seems as though something general had to be said, and without the living contact with the experience, the language began to spin its cool web round the writer, 'this evil', 'gain ends', 'moral life' forming a kind of refrain.

Of course, it is important to recall that a similar abstractedness marked the first stage of the course work essay we looked at earlier. The earlier student had the opportunity to work from the text itself, and even that took time to rekindle. What happens to this particular examination candidate as he turns to specifics? The comments on Edmund are a fair example.

The 'evil' group do not try to live up to any standards. Edmund uses other people's weaknesses to his advantage, he uses Gloucester's credulity to turn him against Edgar.
    'A credulous father. A brother noble'
He considers which sister will be most use to him before he can decide which to marry, he says
    'Which shall I take
    Both? One? Neither?'
Goneril must kill Albany herself, for Edmund will not take the risk.
    'Let her who would be rid of him
    Devise his speedy taking off'
He uses his illegitimacy as an excuse for his evil deeds but he himself does not actually believe this. He only shows a better side to his nature when he is dying, saying,

'I pant for life, some good I mean to do'
and he explains that he has ordered Cordelia to be hanged, making it look as
though 'she fordid herself'.

There are obvious reasons for the hasty compression. But in terms of
language use what are the results? Possibly they are most marked when the
student actually refers to the text, commenting or paraphrasing. What do
these moments suggest he is making of the experience-in-language, as he
writes?

'A credulous father. A brother noble'
— he uses Gloucester's credulity to turn him against Edgar
'Which shall I take
Both? One? Neither?'
— he considers which sister will be most use to him before he can decide
which to marry
'Let her who would be rid of him
Devise his speedy taking off'
— Goneril must kill Albany herself, for Edmund will not take the risk
'I pant for life, some good I mean to do'
— he only shows a better side to his nature when he is dying.

There is no time, it seems, to engage again with the felt experience of such
lines. The verbs 'uses', 'considers', 'shows' all in some way evade the
particularity of the sources for action that the play expresses — the devil-
ment, pleasure, immense self-possession, frightening coldness, reckless
drive. . . . There *is* enough to discover about 'evil' in those lines alone, but
not it seems with this task, on this occasion.

We started with an average student and his or her difficulties seem
obvious enough. Does a student who is rather above average experience the
same difficulty? Here are the opening paragraphs by one such student,
answering the same question.

It has been said that King Lear is seeking to answer the question 'What is essential
human nature?' and in answering this question he uncovers many truths about
the nature of evil. The play is greatly concerned with evil, for evil is the cause of
much of the suffering. All the characters are either largely good, or largely bad,
and amongst the wicked group we have Edmund, Goneril, Regan, Cornwall,
Oswald and even, to a certain extent, Lear himself. By studying these characters,
and their part in the plot, and their effect on the tragedy, we can see something of
the nature of evil.

From the evil characters comes the evidence that evil is self-seeking, completely
self-engrossed and therefore unscrupulous, and self-destructive. Edmund, in his
first soliloquy, gives his philosophy. He says,
'Thou nature art my goodness; to thy law
My services are bound.'
He feels that, because he is a son of nature, then he is entitled to live by the law of

Nature, that is the survival of the fittest by any means possible. He flaunts his
illegitimacy as a reason for his wickedness but he does not really believe that this is
so. He is, in a sense, honest. He recognises his wickedness and admits that even
'the maidenliest star' governing his birth would have made no difference to his
character. He is seeking self-aggrandisement and is completely unaware of pity for
those he uses to gain it. He wrongs his brother
       'on whose foolish honesty
       My practices ride easy,'
and betrays his own father, being the cause of all his suffering. Having thus
obtained all his father's lands and title he next plots to raise himself even higher.

Is this more promising than the previous piece? The start is little different:
the same broad generalisations are on offer. Then the 'wicked group' are
listed, including 'to a certain extent, Lear himself' — such is the effect of the
categories. However, this student goes on to suggest a different strategy: 'By
studying these characters . . . we can see something of the nature of evil.'
This sounds more hopeful. But the urge to generalise takes over again. 'The
evidence' offered by these characters *en bloc* shows that evil is:

> self-seeking . . . unscrupulous . . .
> self-engrossed . . . self-destructive.

Is it necessary to read Lear to reach this conclusion? We doubt it: for the
student is intelligent enough to remember, as he considers Edmund's first
soliloquy, that 'He is, in a sense, honest' too. 'He flaunts his illegitimacy as a
reason for his wickedness . . .'. This takes us a step nearer the audacious,
ruthless candour of a unique individual, and even suggests for a moment
('flaunts') the fascination that is mixed with our horror as we regard him.
But the rest of the extract deals with Edmund largely in the same limited
form of paraphrase:

'. . . he is seeking self-aggrandisement . . .'
'. . . completely unaware of pity . . .'
'. . . wrongs his brother . . .'
'. . . betrays his own father . . .'

At this point some readers may already be recalling the notes on 'The
Poison Tree'. There too 'evil' is observed, but with a difference. First, the
notes offer a fuller account of particular, awkward, uncertain and increasingly complex responses during the encounter: 'lively, strangely attractive,
insidious . . . terribly chilling, frighteningly revealing'. (The words might do
for Edmund too?) Secondly, they remain to the end fully open to character
in action — to 'the state of mind he is left with at the close'. Curiously
enough, in making generalised comments on a play, the two examination
candidates lose contact with the drama as action, and record nothing of
what they felt moment by moment in response to Edmund's audacity,

ruthless drive and black humour, or to his final words. Evil, an abstract category, seems to have taken their eyes off the very particulars from which they might have learnt, if — with Shakespeare and Blake — they had dared to realise the human complexity in Edmund, the poison tree and themselves.

How significant are these examples? For the moment they are merely samples of a danger inherent in the generalised examination question. How representative they are it is impossible to say, since so far as we know no study of the danger has been attempted. That it exists and could possibly be widespread seems difficult to deny.

Actually neither of the two students above suffered in terms of qualification: the first was awarded an E, the second a C grade. All that suffers in a sense, then, is teaching and learning to read literature.

The acceptability of such evidence of reading suggests the unanalysed, 'orthodox' expectations that may have grown up during the sixty years of the 'second examination'. A critical survey is badly needed of the language used to articulate the interpretations, response and reflective understanding that good 'reading' involves.

Many teachers have agreed over those sixty years that if one wants to know what students have gained from reading literature at 16–19, a much wider range of evidence will have to be considered. We conclude this discussion, then, with two specific instances that, it seemed to teachers in recent seminars, challenged conventional views about the testimony students can offer of what reading literature has meant.

Transpositions
I looked deep into a mirror today
I was alarmed to see
someone was standing there,
brushing his clean hair free.

Times I feel his hand upon my shoulder,
an older frightened man looks round to see
in whitened room that makes the sun seem colder
there's no-one there, nothing but air, and me.

I am afraid of him and who he seems
who knows what he might say, or who might see
he gains control of me sometimes in dreams
and does things I might do, if I were he.
He frightens me, maybe I worry him,
I saw him stare from the mirror today
with a thin, grim look of alarm on his face,
and I in his place, a vision in air,
was regarding him, brushing his hair.

                                                                Peter

Teachers commenting on this piece by a 17-year-old have felt it offered strong evidence for several of their aims being fulfilled. They feel an implicit comment on self and others, a sense of discovering, ambiguously and uncertainly, a potential in oneself that one had not been aware of, an older man in us and in contact with us, alarmed at what he sees in our acknowledged self, and frightening in his turn. This is to paraphrase and generalise, of course, on what is presented fleetingly and yet concretely in the writing. Perhaps the most important moment for the writer is the transposition from 'I was alarmed', 'I am afraid . . . he gains control' to 'maybe I worry him'.

It seems a serious piece of imaginative work, then, to many teachers. But equally, they feel, it is a testimony to the quality of his reading. It is difficult to conceive of this student not enjoying Frost, for example. The piece is his own work, but he has learnt a great deal, in rhythm especially, from poets he has read. Indeed, as one teacher said, this is a student who, we can confidently feel, knows what literature means.

We could add many questions that arise: for instance, given his strong feeling for form, is Peter conscious of the contrasting line lengths he has used, and deliberate in moving out of a rhyming pattern — or not? However, the main questions are not about Peter, but about the quality of imaginative insight and of sensitivity to language that one hopes for from a literature course. Although it makes no direct reference to reading, is this piece of writing not evidence of a certain stage in the realisation of the hopes and aims expressed earlier?

If it is, then people who query the inclusion of 'creative writing' in examination syllabuses, and comment on the difficulty of assessing it, are addressing the wrong question. A piece like Peter's, we would argue, has a natural place in a folder of writing, some of which will be directly inspired by reading texts, but all of which has to be judged in terms of imaginative sympathy and awareness, and of sensitivity and precision in the use of language. It is understandable that with examinations exclusively confined to three-hour papers, and all the constraints that go with them, such evidence could neither be required nor expected. As course work evidence becomes accepted — as it now is in many A-level subjects — the kinds of qualities to be recognised need themselves to be reassessed.

Thus, within the imaginative work that arises in reading a text and in reflecting on it, there are many different processes that writing can foster and develop. Public examinations naturally tend to call for writing that is addressed at best to a wider public audience, and at worst only to a marker. The style of address is not far from that of lectures or books of criticism. For the common reader, however, this is largely inappropriate; a more natural setting for comments on texts one cares deeply about has always been in letters to intimate friends or a personal journal. The difference in sense of audience strongly affects what can be said. Consider the following piece of writing, offered voluntarily by a young student after a discussion of Auden's 'Musée des Beaux Arts'.

Icarus

Bringing day to earth
With elation he rose,
Soaring high,
Wonder took his heart;
Love shone on his wings
Reflected from his father's gaze,
As he hung below
Suspended on the wind,
The gentle movement below,
Heaven above, with light for all.

Fears and warnings disappeared in fantasy
And his father's call was a gull crying in vain
As haloed he rose on his way to everlasting life.
He would get higher than he thought.
Sadly his plumage fell from him,
Followed by an eternal dive,
Beautiful to behold, but
Love turned to grief
And the feathers were drowned.

Driving the flaming chariot
Let loose amongst the stars
Bringing day to earth
For the first time was his son;
With his name, son of Phoebus,
And his glory came his down fall.
He lost control in the fiery chariot
And ice caps melted,
Hills were burnt with human flesh
Till at last he fell.

A star came from the sky becoming a comet
His long fiery hair its tail while his father watched,
The lithe beauty plunging.
The shimmering beauty below put up green arms to catch him
Extinguishing his life and light.

To people who watch, not much they remember,
But life must go on
And the ploughman returns to his plough.
And the ship sails on.

                                        Susan

Again, we can read this in several ways. Perhaps in part it is a 'Yes, but' to Auden, a passionate affirmation that tragedy *does* happen, some do grieve and 'Hills were burnt with human flesh', even though '. . . life must go on/And the ploughman returns to his plough'. In part, it may be read as the counterpoise, an expression of the knowledge Auden himself was restraining as he checked the pain of suffering with the wry recognition:

> That even the dreadful martyrdom must run its course
> Anyhow in a corner, some untidy spot
> Where the dogs go on with their doggy life and the torturer's horse
> Scratches its innocent behind on a tree.

So the young writer is inspired to contemplate aspiration and suffering in her own way as well as his.

But on closer reading, the writer may be doing more than this. The more one looks, the more one sees that starting points in Auden were transformed in a special kind of way:

> **A** the white legs disappearing into the green water
> becomes **S** the shimmering beauty put up green arms to catch him.

> **A** the ploughman may
>   Have heard the splash . . .
>   But for him it was not an important failure;
> becomes **S** But life must go on
>   And the ploughman returns to his plough.

> **A** the forsaken cry
> becomes **S** And his father's call was a gull crying in vain.

There is room for tenderness in her writing, and less toughness. Indeed, returning to Auden one realises that, in the course of the poem, the attitude to human suffering actually shifts. At first, it is acknowledged to take place 'while someone else is eating', 'anyhow in a corner', while 'the torturer's horse / Scratches its innocent behind on a tree'. The tone seems laconic but still vulnerable. In the second section — the 'for instance' — there is a change. 'Everything turns away / Quite leisurely from the disaster.' The writer underlines again and again a new attitude: he is trying to face, not the human position of tragedy, but an appalled sense that humans will not give it a position.

From this perspective, Susan's piece is an implicit withdrawal from this change — this failure? — in the man she has encountered. Instead she makes constructive use of what she feels is best in him and his vision. Her transformations are an implicit criticism, we could reasonably say.

Many teachers we have worked with would like to see such imaginative work recognised alongside more explicit responses to the text or presentation. They are concerned, that is, about the narrowness that has grown up in orthodox essays and the failure to testify to the full range of imaginative contemplation and reflection that a genuine encounter may give rise to. Within many examination questions they sense a failure to recognise the power and shock that literature has as students become involved in the writer's vision and reflect on that experience. There is certainly a place for scanning a complex text to ensure that the paraphrasable sense has been faithfully interpreted, but only in the interests of a reading that carries the imaginative experience 'alive into the heart'.

It is these doubts about the actual standards being recognised in public examinations and the potential standards that may be being ignored that led our team to propose on the teacher's behalf an investigation of the evidence of qualities in reading literature that is currently available in examination essays and written course work. We shall be reporting on the findings of a national panel, drawn from universities and schools.

The prime difficulty about any such investigation is that, if teachers were right in thinking that the feedback from examination questions severely constricted what was produced in the course, evidence of a wider potential range of writing would be scarce, especially beyond the first year. A kind of vicious spiral would have been set up, whereby writing within the course would be progressively modelled on that required in the set papers, with all their acknowledged constraints.

However, it was for this reason that during their first year the groups of teachers we drew together to consider their common aims in proposing alternatives in A-level literature asked for three interlocking kinds of change:

(a) a set book examination in which the texts were available, and questions were specifically designed to promote use of the text in the examination;
(b) provision for a selection of course work to be examined, and for encouragement to broaden the range of writing in it;
(c) an extension to the number and range of texts studied, by basing a proportion of the course work on additional texts proposed by the individual department and agreed by the board, and by including an extended essay based on a subject and texts proposed by the individual student in consultation with teachers.

The year 1976 was a difficult one for any board to mount an additional syllabus; however, in the event one board — the AEB — did take up the proposal our team circulated on behalf of the teachers, and submitted a scheme to the English A-Level Committee for approval. The aims and objectives of the proposal included:

to extend the range of English studies in the sixth form and, whilst retaining the traditional critical essay on a set text, to give the opportunity for more varied work;

to widen the reading of A-level students beyond a limited number of set texts;

to enable the student to pursue in greater depth a particular interest in literature, whilst ensuring that he also reads major writers' work;

to give the student an opportunity to work under conditions which scholars would regard as essential, i.e. with access to texts and reference works and without a time-limit of forty-five minutes or an hour for a unit of work;

to provide an opportunity for the teacher to participate in the assessment of students' work and to have experience of assessment procedures;

to obtain and assess a wider and more varied sample of the student's work in English;

to maintain comparability with other A-level syllabuses by allocating the majority of marks to an externally set and marked examination but at the same time to provide an opportunity for individual choice in a substantial part of the syllabus.

Although in effect the experiment was limited to schools and colleges served by one board, by summer 1977 the AEB succeeded in setting up four regional consortia of departments, each consortium working closely with a moderator appointed by the board. By agreement with the board and the LEA English advisers, in three of these consortia the project team have helped to organise development workshops in which many of the issues reported earlier have been discussed.

This is the first major experiment in A-level literature to include a large and varied enough sample of English departments to give the results some national validity. Currently it is just completing its first year, and if the changes envisaged are as radical as the teachers believe, one must assume that at least three years will be needed to carry them through and exploit the new opportunities to the full. The implications for further curriculum and examination development are discussed in section 3.6. For the present, we will concentrate on the overall differences such an examination syllabus may make to the teacher's realisable aims.

By introducing open books, one brings the two set papers much closer to practical criticism — giving those words their full weight. 'This is an examination in close reading', one teacher asserted early on, and the idea came as a surprise even to schools already familiar with the Cambridge Board's intelligent and delicate use of the open book at O level. One paper will include unseen passages and poems drawn from a set anthology; the other will be based on a further four major texts, one of them a Shakespeare play.

The eight selected pieces of course work will cover at least six further texts chosen by the department. This allows teachers to develop a very flexible reading programme. Thus in the second term at Crown Woods School, for instance, students began reading one of the five set books, *The Return of the Native*. During the term three related 'course work texts' were introduced: *The Woodlanders, Selected Poems* and *Selected Tales*. A booklet produced by the department contained further suggested reading from Hardy; reading of 'other writers on rural themes', such as Flora Thompson and Ronald Blythe; extracts from contemporary notes, letters and diaries; and 'suggested assignments' — among other things.

This is an example of the way wider reading can grow out of interests aroused by a major text, the key point being that if students feel any of this work to be specially rewarding there will be opportunity later to submit pieces of their writing as evidence of quality of reading, and even to help them develop an extended essay, or 'dissertation', on some chosen aspect.

In these early days there is naturally great enthusiam; teachers see such a syllabus as a means of 'bringing the best out of our students in a way that can be academic, but also stands a greater chance of being intellectually, emotionally, and experientially satisfying'. On the teacher's side, choice from a very wide range is often stimulating 'a genuine learning-partnership between teacher and pupil, in such a way that the "leading out" of the potentialities of a student (and, I suspect, of his tutor) is more likely'.

Consortium meetings offer 'the security of constant discussion and evaluation with other teachers'. Teachers comment on the 'wealth of ideas' this offers: in one early session 'we heard of and experienced a poem that told us more about Lear's psyche than most "lit. crit." writing; exploratory notes that raised important questions about Ted Hughes's "Relic"; journals that recorded all a pupil read, as a basis for individual teaching by the tutor; descriptions of the dramatisation of a text, that looked closely into how stagecraft and actors' approaches illuminated a text; how various tutorial sytems were being used to cope with learning and administration within the course; how we all applied differing . . . approaches to the study-skill problems that the A level caused to emerge; and, from an Open University film, the reasons for discussion at the student's level . . .'. At later sessions, there has been animated discussion of selected students' writing and the kinds of advice that can be offered on work in progress.

Any new syllabus ought to stimulate fresh thinking. The significant fact in this case is the interest aroused in helping students to articulate what they have learnt from a text. Thus, a consortium discussed small group talk, with or without the teacher, and one of the departments, trying to define its aims, suggested: 'students should be encouraged to speculate, to wonder, to think aloud and formulate their own questions (as in writing); to prepare their own readings for the rest of the group and to talk about it afterwards; to ask about and challenge one another's opinions; to tape discussions, replay them and reflect on them; to record in the most suitable, convenient way ideas and opinions they may want to use in another form later on'. Talk is seen as a provisional, exploratory medium for moving together into the experience of a poem like 'The Poison Tree', for instance.

Similarly, in looking at students' early writing there has been a steady emphasis in various consortia on the need 'to explore each poem in some detail', and, even though a student 'seemed to want to grapple with the larger theme or generalisation', to avoid him being 'thwarted by what we felt was an inappropriate task at this stage of the course'. One meeting roughed out some broad stages in a student's response (without 'proposing a hierarchy'), suggesting 'that these different kinds of response . . . were all part of a cycle of changing perceptions and stances'.

Participating departments remain individual in their approach, but there is a strong sense of sharing ideas, and of enlisting other members of the consortium, including the moderator, in sifting the results of experimental approaches, and as 'a prompter of finer standards'.

The results of the AEB experiment will deserve very careful study. We have seen that there are a multiplicity of aims in teaching at this level. For many students the humanities experience of the course is the predominant value; for a smaller group the specialised preparation for an honours course, with the scholarly knowledge and analysis it demands, may carry an important, secondary weighting. It will be vital to assess how the experiment affects both groups of students and to analyse with care which aims have been effectively enabled — and even encouraged — in the course work sample, and which in the three-hour papers. In the case of Shakespeare there will be writing available from both contexts: any differences in quality and scope will be particularly worth scrutiny.

The open book questions will enable teachers and the boards to reconsider the most effective uses of a three-hour common paper. The potential range and variety of open book questions has not been explored before at A level, and in this case, the close contact between the group of participating departments and the moderator offers a special opportunity for suggestions and proposals to be made (and tried out) in a collaborative way, as is already happening.

As the course develops, there will be continuing discussion, too, of the range of writing that may offer valuable evidence of the fulfilment of the aims of teaching literature. For many English teachers this is a question of central importance today. In seminars with local and national groups of teachers we have discovered the difficulty of setting adequate questions in a mass examination, and the multiplicity of traps into which the examiner recurrently falls. In discussion with students and teachers working for other, long-standing 'alternative' A levels with a course work element, we have found how restricting the three-hour paper can feel to those who know they can present other evidence of the value of reading literature. In the words of a student: 'I think the exam form of testing does not take into account the real difference in arts subjects' requirements compared to those of more factual subjects.'

The AEB experiment for the first time alters the form of questioning in the common papers, and allows for the text to be used; thus the consortia are free from many of the constraints on students' writing that were foreseen as long ago as 1918, when the system was set up. In addition, they actually do have that direct contact with the examiner that the English Association called for so long ago. We believe that the results of this enterprising work by small groups of teachers deserves the steady support and attention of a very much wider range of colleagues, if only because they enable us to ask again what evidence we would want to see of the value of education in one of the central human arts.

2.5   The Potential of Communication Studies

> . . . a lack of language is a lack of the means of communication and of thought itself.
>
> We have drawn a distinction between two aspects . . . the power of communication in English, and the appreciation of literature as an art . . .
>
> . . . the examination system should be applied as widely as possible to the power of 'communication' in English . . .   (Newbolt Report, 1921)

The first A-level syllabus in communication studies became available in 1976, and, for two-year students, the first examination has just been held as this report is written. Perhaps only two or three of the teachers concerned studied communication as part of their higher education. Indeed, many readers may be unfamiliar with the underlying ideas, and especially with the directions these have taken in recent years. To make matters worse, some of those who know least are already airing their prejudices in the press.

In these circumstances, it has been the aim of the project, in the critical formative years for the new subject, to support teachers who were exploring and clarifying its possibilities. Our main objective in this section, therefore, is to exemplify and analyse a range of work that this new A level has encouraged teachers and students to attempt. Our project booklets will supply much further material and help to correct any overemphasis that arises from the constraints of space in this report. Finally, we will invite the reader to stand back from the current examination syllabus and the work it has inspired to date, to consider the longer-term potential of this subject and its relation to English at A level.

We shall begin in this case by taking a sample of more than a hundred students in their first year of the course, and asking what they hoped for and wanted from it. Their perceptions at this stage offer another guide to the aims in process of realisation.

'I wanted to do something new.' 'It is a challenge.' Not every student will be prepared at 16+ to opt for what may look like a totally new subject. For those who do, that sense of breaking new ground (and knowing your teachers are doing so too) may itself be a stimulus. In communication studies the territory is not altogether unfamiliar, but the idea of studying it systematically is an extension beyond any previous course. 'I thought it would open up as wide and varied a field of opportunities as possible.' 'Many A level subjects are specialising in one particular area . . . I chose this course because of its broadness.' 'It seemed a very wide subject, which I could later on choose one aspect of perhaps, because I'm not sure exactly what I want to do.'

We have already noted the major recommendation that English courses at A level, while allowing for early specialism in some cases, should also be providing for a delay in specialist choice. If communication studies combines a broad offering with the possibility of developing specialist interests later in the course, this is a major contribution to fulfilling such recommendations. The question is, how will teachers develop a course that meets the desire 'to broaden my knowledge' while at the same time ensuring that 'a student can concentrate on the sections that interest him most'? In some ways this seems to call for new forms of group work or individual assignments.

There were other indications that students would differ both in what they might well contribute to the course and what they might be relating communication studies to in the rest of their work in college or school. 'It was an obvious choice with English literature and film studies', wrote one student, and looking at out chart on p. 44 one can see why. Indeed in our sample, English literature is the A level most likely to be taken in association with communication studies. But there are other and different possible associations. 'Chosen to help further my knowledge of the background to art work, i.e. how we are affected by visuals.' 'Seemed to offer a practical supplementary study to my other subjects, sociology and political studies.' 'A useful subject to combine with my languages, French and German.' In addition, though they are not represented in our sample, we have been working with one college where the majority of students are taking science A levels.

Each of these students has a valid point. Within communication studies there are elements concerned with the use of language, visuals and notational symbols as media for thinking, expressing feelings and attitudes, and communicating. Thus there are connections to be made with literature, art, modern languages and scientific thought. And since speaking, writing and

THE TEACHERS' CENTRE
WORCESTER STREET
MIDDLESBROUGH
CLEVELAND TS1 4NT

communicating inevitably occur in a social context, there are equally links to be made with the social sciences. Embryonically, then, communication studies is an area where the interests of many different subjects overlap. If individual students or groups are to explore these potential links, once again the course is going to demand a structure that is not characteristic of more specialist A levels.

In a few colleges this integration of communication with the rest of the students' course was simpler, but different again: we know of two colleges that have already included the communication studies A level as an integral part of their OND courses, and another that has directly linked it with a vocational course in residential child care. Thus the syllabus is seen to have potential relevance both to other academic subjects and to a range of vocational courses. If so, it may have a very important contribution to make to our thinking about courses for the majority at 17+ and 18+.

Up to this point the focus has been on the potential range and connections of the course. What of communication studies itself? it may be asked; what was its intrinsic value, in these students' eyes? There is little doubt of their answer. 'It seems it will be useful to help communicate with people and understand society.' The demand for practical experience and an increased mastery of communication recurs throughout the sample: it indicates the gap in A-level provision that the new syllabus was designed to fill. But the desire for greater social understanding is also emphasised surprisingly often. Many students seem to have chosen the subject because of an 'interest in people'. 'It will help me get a better understanding of people and life.' 'The idea of communicating with people (large audiences or small) appeals to me.' 'Communication is all about us and therefore the under-standing of it will be beneficial to each of us in our role in society.' 'The "human communication" section [in a first-term course] was very appeal-ing.' 'I'm personally very interested in the way people communicate, often without even realising they are doing so.' This humanistic concern is borne out by the vocations many of the students were considering: in social work, child care, speech therapy, nursing, journalism, personnel work ... and as a minister of religion.

At the same time there was a feeling that studying communication 'gives a greater understanding of the way society works'. 'One is made aware of the way people and organisations communicate'; it 'deals with the role of media in our lives'. 'A study of the media I confront every day' may enable a student 'to see how one is influenced by the media and one's whole life is governed subconsciously by them'. Thus in studying a cross-section of communication one may develop 'a general and basic understanding of society around me'.

There seem to be three connected strands in what students are hoping for: an increase in expertise and skill; a deepening of their personal understanding of people as they make contact with them; and a sharper awareness of society through an analysis of the patterns of communication it adopts and the way these are used.

It is not necessary to elaborate on the connections with English at 16+. And perhaps this is the place to note that among the hundred students were some who wrote that communication studies was 'as near as is possible to get to an English language A level'; 'a very interesting course — it's like taking an English language A level'. They opted for it because 'I enjoyed English at school', 'I wanted to do English language at A level but no course was available', or 'I wished to study English to a higher level, though English literature did not appeal'. 'There was a choice', wrote another student, 'of either A-level English literature or communication studies . . . I chose the latter because (a) I had not taken O-level English literature and (b) of the two subjects, communication seemed more relevant to my career in nursing.' Among those who *were* doing English literature along with other A-level subjects (and an A/O in drama) was a girl who thought 'I may decide to teach English, therefore the communication studies qualification would prove very useful'. This group of comments seems to point its own morals.

To sum up, then: among the first hundred or so were students attracted to communication studies by its breadth, choices and challenge; by its relevance to other academic subjects, past and present, and to a broad range of careers; and by the desire for a better mastery of communication and a deeper understanding of people and of society at large. It will already be obvious that, for the teachers designing the course, these aspirations in themselves offered a massive challenge.

Considering that almost all teachers were necessarily new to the subject, what was expected of them was a major curriculum development project in its own right. As the nearest available support team, we still feel the limitations in the direct help that was offered and regret that, like others involved, we did not make clearer publicly the sheer magnitude of the task teachers were taking on — willingly and with enthusiasm. These students' hopes, we must recall, are in part a reflection of the teachers' initial attitudes as they set about translating the syllabus into a two-year course.

Like most pioneers they had to be direct and simple in their early plans, and to begin with we shall try to emulate them. Among the five aims of the syllabus, two seemed to propose the central activities:

> to undertake practical work in communication in order to improve the student's own ability and to gain an understanding of the nature and usefulness of the resources available;
> to investigate the use and appropriateness of the various means of communication in such fields of human activity as family life, immediate social groups, commerce, industry, politics, education, entertainment and the arts.

This combination of practical work and analytic investigation is re-emphasised throughout the 'Expanded Notes for Guidance' and in two of the major components of the examination: a course work project (written, taped or audiovisual) and a 'case study' paper, requiring the analysis and selective use of a set of communications on a given issue. We shall illustrate and discuss both these central aspects of the course at this point before turning to the remaining parts of the syllabus. Both illustrations are drawn from the first two terms of the course and were presented by the students at the third London conference, organised by the project team in 1978.

Detailed briefing for the project we shall be describing was given in the first term of the course at Melton Mowbray College. The class were asked to divide into groups and, following a carefully designed assignment sheet, to produce their presentation by the end of term (six weeks). They were expected to consult Joyce Eyre, who set up the assignment, at specified points in their planning and production, and a second teacher, Derek Jackson, was available throughout to help with the technical side.

We discussed with two of the class, Rick and Dave, how they made a start. 'We split from the Church group . . . I knew quite a few mentally handicapped people — I'd dealt with them before — and it was really my idea, wasn't it?' 'Yes, we went to three . . . places; Silverdale, where mentally handicapped adults live; the day centre; and . . . The Mount, which is for mentally handicapped children.' The first two 'greeted us with open arms and I then wrote to County Hall, asking for permission, and that's where the wheels stopped . . . It wasn't a matter of not getting permission, it was getting through all their departments — it was a formality really. During that time we sent out a letter to all the parents asking for their permission . . . you see they've got guardians.'

In such cases there is as much to learn practically about communication in the planning as in the process of production and the final presentation. 'I was phoning them up, asking for a certain department. I'd be put through to another department . . . they were having an office changeover . . . And then the letter was lost, so we wrote another letter — it was a good three weeks.' Meanwhile the two students had decided to try to make a videotape of mentally handicapped adults 'to show that they do work and they are part of society'.

'First we went down there planning, when we got permission. Then — it was on a Wednesday morning — we started off . . . and took the cameras down.' ('I set them up,' said Mr Jackson, 'then I left them and let them get on with it.') 'We'd planned it, but you can only plan so much; you have a general sketch that can be altered . . . I wanted to concentrate on the hands because it was work . . . There are shots of faces as we scan around. I go to Phil's face when he's working . . . to bring out . . . the concentration.'

They got about fifteen minutes of film on camera and used about 50 per cent. There is a detailed editing script, noting the sequence of images and cuing in the narration and music. 'To produce the sound track you have to go over it time and time again. We had difficulties with the music: in one place it finished fourteen seconds too early, so we found a part where Richard is talking where the sound's low, stopped the record, and took it back . . .'

The sound track starts: 'This short film is about mentally handicapped adults. Its aim is to show that these people have a place in society and are not people who should be ignored, put out of sight and be the burden of a social stigma.

'Here the mentally handicapped adults from all the surrounding area come five days a week to participate in normal working activities. Their jobs are varied.

'Here they are putting airball refills into sachets: many local firms send jobs like these down to the centre. They are capable of many tasks from metal-work and wood-work to gardening and cookery. . . .'

We see people doing normal jobs, welding railings, glueing and sanding down chairs, and shampooing and setting hair. The film is about the dignity which work can give to people.

The effect is achieved by concentrating on the slow and deliberate care with which all the tasks are done. The first shot is of hands slowly and carefully filling and shaking a plastic sachet: indeed in almost every instance the boys focus our attention on the activity before moving to more general shots.

The commentary is kept to a minimum. We see one girl shampooing another's hair, gently rinsing out the lathered soap. Later we have the delighted grin when the job is finished and she goes under the hair dryer. The only comment is: 'Many of the women who obviously take great pride in their appearance use the hair salon at the centre. Here they wash, set and even perm each other's hair. Each week they have time allotted to them for these domestic activities. They decorate the area as they like.'

The boys took great pains, however, to choose songs as a background which provides comment. At the beginning the Beatle's song 'I get by with a little help from my friends' makes its point before if fades into the simple 'Here they are putting airball refills into sachets'.

The film is never patronising; as Dave said, 'The idea of the programme is not to get sympathy'. Some of the most effective shots were those of the men and women washing up and then putting the cups and saucers away. It is such an ordinary domestic activity that it emphasises the security which homely routine provides for us all.

The film has now been shown to a range of audiences: members of the class, teachers and fellow-students at the London conference, the handicapped people at the centre and their parents, and the local police. So the two students have had the opportunity to compare the positive response of audiences with very different interests, to make changes suggested by viewers and to add extra tape.

This, then, is an early example of the practical work the new syllabus has encouraged and will reward. From the same class alone, we could equally well have chosen groups working on slide and tape presentations or longer written projects. The topics and audiences might have been very different: 'The Play's the Thing?' — a guide to encourage theatre-going among young people; a cartoon film for TV showing; 'Music and the Child', a tape and slide presentation; a tape 'walk-about' for the city of Exeter, with supporting brochure; a guide to the working of The Samaritans; 'Drug Abuse', a broadcast for schools and other institutions; communicating with the blind; a prospectus of sixth-form studies at high school for the coming year; a study guide for A-level psychology; the uses of video equipment in teaching, for example.

What aims can be realised in such work? Students can learn to develop an initial brief, in consultation with their teachers. They can take on an independent, adult role in planning and organising their projects, especially in those that depend on meeting and negotiating with people outside — as some will, though not all. They can learn to use teachers as consultants, people with greater experience in certain technical and general fields, who can give initial guidance but still leave the major responsibilities to the student. They can take on new responsibilities to the potential audiences for whom they are producing. They can develop a better understanding of the medium they select, learning about its capabilities through their awareness of mistakes as well as successes. They can learn to discuss and evaluate their own work.

These are some, but by no means all, of the gains to be made as students learn to become practitioners in communication. From the perspective of such work in communication, we believe there are important lessons for the potential of English at 16–19, and the value of a close relationship between the two subjects.

As it happens, the project we have selected does encourage the students 'to observe people and things more closely', 'to appreciate the complexities of life' and 'to widen their understanding of the human state' — aims that were articulated in the previous section. Such aims may be an important part of the contribution English teachers can make to communication studies. But equally, have not English teachers something to learn now from the adult roles that can be offered students as they write and produce presentations for a variety of real audiences?

How is such work to be assessed? One of the major past constraints on English course work at 16–19 has been the failure to take account of anything more than a sixty-minute essay written in examination conditions.

The AEB examination syllabus provides for each student to submit to an external moderator either an individual project or a group project to which he or she has made a clearly identifiable contribution (recorded in a personal project file). Each project is accompanied by a short assessment of the objectives achieved and the problems encountered. Finally in an oral examination the student is given the opportunity to discuss the aims of the project, and to clarify and expand points that arise from the finished work: this is an internal examination externally moderated.

These three elements, the project itself, the written evaluation and the oral examination on it, offer a range of evidence as to what a student has gained from such work. They assess not simply practical mastery but the underlying understanding of the 'purpose of the project', the audience 'for whom it was intended', the 'resources used', the form of presentation, the 'control of . . . material and techniques', and the uses the presentation can be put to (to quote the 'Notes for Guidance'). It is practical *understanding*, not simply one instance of practice, that is being assessed: this is a distinction of far-ranging importance, in English as well as in communication studies.

Summarising the approaches it hopes to foster, the board believes that 'no student can succeed in the course without a sound grasp of . . . presentation and interpretation' in verbal, graphical and other media. We have followed it here in starting with productive work; however, as students later look back at what they have produced, they are already moving into the complementary study of 'interpretation'. Indeed, there is an inevitable interplay between 'productive' and 'receptive' studies: Dave and Rick pointed out to us how their VTR editing had been affected by parallel studies of advertising in television and magazines, and the recognition that 'music . . . was the easiest way to the emotions'.

Our second detailed illustration of the potential of the course is drawn, therefore, from many practical investigations of communication reported in the 1977–8 conferences. In this case, the whole class were involved in the analysis, as we shall see.

The first-year course at Redbridge College had already included some studies of perception — colour, perspective and composition — leading to a simple assignment in which each student selected an advertisement and commented on its effectiveness, bearing in mind the article advertised, the audience aimed at, the colours used and the composition. The next step was to apply the simple principles on a larger scale by taking a critical look at several local exhibitions. The first opportunity came in the spring term when Ilford Town Council mounted an exhibition to test public response to their redevelopment plans.

Before the visit, Donald Pohl, the lecturer in charge, asked the class to consider, as they studied it, the purpose of the exhibition, the audience aimed at, the variety of methods of communication in use, and having done so to assess the methods employed, first for their suitability to the purpose and audience, and secondly for their likely effect in this case. 'The questions acted as a very good guide', a student commented; 'we probably wouldn't have noticed what we did if it hadn't been for the questions.'

Each student made notes and in the follow-up session 'we worked out our ideas through discussion and used the blackboard to plot our thoughts'. At one point, using statistical methods already studied, the students took a vote, to rank the methods used in terms of potential and actual success achieved. A report was then written and sent to Ilford Council with an accompanying letter, asking for comments. That was the basis for the following report presented by students to the London conference.

Report on the Visit to the Ilford Redevelopment Exhibition made by Members of the Redbridge Communications Group on 10 March 1978

The exhibition was arranged in order to communicate information to the residents of Ilford. The aim was to highlight problems in Ilford and to publicise redevelopment plans. Should members of the public have had any objections after seeing the exhibition they could voice these objections and express their opinions at a follow-up mass meeting.

In order to meet these aims the exhibition had to be directed towards members of the public generally, but particularly those with an interest (be it resident or commercial) in Ilford. It was therefore important that the plans be communicated in a simple non-technical way and various methods of communication were employed to ensure that this was effectively accomplished.

Ten methods were identified and the students were satisfied that no major method of communication had been overlooked by the exhibition organisers. In addition to this, when these methods of communication were ranked by students for suitability and effect, a high correlation between these two aspects emerged. This suggested that the students felt that the potential of each method was well exploited. The communication methods were ranked in the following order of importance.

Suitability	Method	Effect
1	Plans	2
2	Models	1
3	Photographs	3
3	Maps	4
5	Written information	6
6	Human contact (Council rep. to answer questions)	7
7	Posters	5
8	Layout	8
9	Questionnaire	9
10	Colour	10

(A)   The information was graphically conveyed by the first four items on the list. This ensured that the proposed development could in fact be perceived visually, which made the information readily meaningful.

(B)   The visual methods were supplemented by means of written information (labelling, documents, printed handouts). While these make less of an impact on the 'man in the street' they do provide detail and interpretation which purely visual material cannot communicate.

(C)   Where both graphic representation and written information failed, a council representative was on hand to answer individual queries.

While the students therefore approved of the general plan of the exhibition, they did have some points of criticism as to details.

(i) The model they thought, though effective, could have made freer use of colour. It was predominantly white and thus lacked impact.

(ii) The display maps were mounted in such a way that details at the tops of the maps were too high up to be seen. While some students felt that these maps were useful in clarifying the issues at stake, others found them too technical and confusing. One student went so far as to suspect that the confusion evoked was deliberate in order to avoid objections from the public.

(iii) While the use of photographs was generally applauded, two students pointed out the limitations of the photographs for this type of exhibition. They could obviously only disclose present conditions and could not, in any way, reflect the proposed redevelopment.

Human contact in any exhibition such as this is vital and the council is to be applauded for fulfilling this need, despite the obvious cost it must have added to mounting the exhibition. Some students felt, however, that the official was too anonymous and an identifying badge would have been useful. While it was appreciated by some that the official should not be intrusive, others felt that he could have asserted himself more to overcome the shyness of the public and their reluctance to admit their confusion.

Among the questions answered by the council representative were the following. The official was able to explain that although the exhibition was limited in space, it had initially been on display in the Kenneth More Theatre where it had been seen not only by those who specifically came to see it, but also by the theatre patrons. *Then* the layout had been assisted by greater floor space. The representative also assured us that, although the space was limited in the new Town Hall venue, those who attended never caused major congestion, as the people arrived in a steady stream throughout the day, not all at once.

Less satisfactory was the answer that was received by one of the group. The student concerned felt that while the exhibition emphasised the advantages of the proposed redevelopment scheme, it played down the disadvantages. While it was acknowledged that 420 houses would have to be demolished to cater for the needs of a ring road, the exhibitors suggested, by implication, that all such properties were run down and neglected. The exhibition photographs of properties to be demolished showed unoccupied buildings boarded up. There was nothing to indicate that many of these buildings were casualties of earlier redevelopment schemes that had failed to materialise. Properties had deteriorated after they had been acquired by the Council under the compulsory purchase scheme. The new scheme involves these houses, but also further homes that are at present occupied and well maintained by their owners. The sugestion that Ilford would benefit from the loss of these unsightly buildings was thus inaccurate.

The student reports, 'When these points were raised with the Council representative . . . he was evasive and said that there was little point in emphasising the disadvantages of the scheme when it had so much to offer. He did admit though that there was no conscious effort to make it clear that these (well maintained) homes would be lost and that the people living in them would have to be rehoused on a new Council estate. He did not think that these facts had been deliberately suppressed but that they were simply unimportant.'

One final criticism was voiced in the form of a question 'Who is going to pay for all this? Does it mean an increase in rates?' No one who saw the exhibition could answer that question.

The council's reply was 'most gratifying', and the group are now hoping in a modest way to work with the council in future developments of the scheme. Two students currently have this in mind for their 'project', and other exhibitions are being analysed by smaller groups, with the additional aim of collecting the responses of a cross-section of people visiting them.

This is an early illustration, then, of an analytical investigation in one 'field of human activity' mentioned by the syllabus. We might equally have chosen studies of communication in smaller social groups.

What aims might be realised in such an investigation? Students can begin to consider more critically the very wide range of 'ideas, information and attitudes' presented ostensibly in the interests of the public — whether local or national. In doing so, they are learning in this instance to use a framework of ideas introduced by the teacher — purpose, audience, method or medium, suitability and effect. (Later, the 'model' of communication these ideas imply will itself come up for scrutiny, as we shall see.) They are also learning to apply simpler studies of the effects of colour, composition and perspective to a much more complex display. Within such a display, they are beginning to weigh up the contribution of different methods of communication.

With these aims it is not difficult for the teacher to give direct help. But there are others that depend on student initiatives. The students too are learning to ask questions — one of the most important being a question about the *interests* the exhibition is serving. Is it slanted towards acceptance of a scheme, or does it consider alternatives? 'You're supposed to give an opinion both ways, aren't you?' said a student in a later discussion. 'Well, he was employed by the council.' 'A spokesman is likely to favour ideas from the council . . . they don't like to draw attention to the fact that houses are going to be destroyed.' 'I expect they've already decided — it's just a public relations exercise.' 'No, the public *do* get a greater say nowadays.' 'How does this work you've done fit into the course?' the teacher asked them. 'It's about how an institution can communicate with the public.' This seems to be a very important discovery.

There are deeper aims to consider, then. In sending the report these students are learning to see themselves as active rather than passive members of a local community. They are learning to take the public interest seriously, and confidently to expect others to do so. This is a contribution to their 'understanding of the way society works', and they are learning as serious-minded participants, not as readers of textbooks.

How is work of this kind to be assessed? Once again, in English the past approach to examining the interpretation of informative and persuasive documents has been limited to 'comprehension' questions, focusing almost exclusively on words and phrases. The AEB examination provides for a three-hour 'case study' paper. The student is offered a choice of three case studies, each drawn from an 'area of life in which communication problems arise', and is able to study the documents for up to two days before the examination proper. During the three hours, students are asked to undertake a critical analysis of the material, to state the results in a suitable form and, adopting a given role, to draw selectively on the material for a piece of written or graphical work designed for a further audience. The Redbridge students are learning to do the real thing. The basic idea of the paper is to simulate conditions in real life, so that students who have undertaken a variety of such practical investigations will be able to tackle the assignment with confidence.

This, then, is the second major element of the current syllabus. Both the case study and the project are concerned with 'practical understanding' — allowing the full weight to each word. Students will discover that some of their course work projects will lead them to 'find and use sources of information', make analytical and critical notes, 'classify material' or 'prepare abstracts': indeed these are among the stated objectives for such work. As they carry out such preliminary tasks, however, they are already developing the kinds of competence called for in case study investigations. Equally, some investigations may lead them, as we have seen, to write what amounts to a minor project, adapted in 'style, method of presentation and content' to the intended recipient, as the syllabus says. It is only at an abstract level that the 'productive' and 'interpretative' sides of practical communication can be kept apart.

This coherent core of practical work has been taken first. Nevertheless, the AEB syllabus envisages more than that. Alongside and — it stresses — integrated with such practical work, it calls for a deeper understanding of the process (communication) and also of the cultural and institutional systems producing it (communications). We shall attempt to clarify what this implies.

We have just been considering four means of communication: an exhibition, a guide to it able to answer questions, the letter to Ilford Council and the video-recording. At different times, as they produce work for an audience, students will be faced with a choice of means, and when they investigate other people's work, as we have seen they may want deliberately to weigh up which means of communication has most to contribute. This implies a closer study of the different effects oral, written, graphical and other forms of communication are best suited to achieve. In the case of the Redbridge students, they took a vote on it: further analysis would help students to justify or modify their vote.

The means we use and need will vary with the context. Individuals think things out 'through inner dialogue', perhaps using jottings, diagrams, notes. Small groups talk things over face to face, using facial expressions, eye contact, gestures and stance to signal to each other, as well as complex vocal means. 'Industry, commerce, government and other institutions organise their lines of communication and their publicity and information services.'

Thus, standing back, we can see how a study of 'means' might alert students to the use of different modes of communication (verbal, visual, others) in different social contexts (individual, informal or formal group, bigger social institutions). The syllabus calls for a variety of means to be studied closely in different contexts.

The means of communication is only one factor — though a vital one. To gain a fuller understanding of the process, students have to consider what other factors to take into account. The means may be well chosen for the task but 'the needs, capabilities and weaknesses' of the audience may be ignored. Or, alternatively, the producers may either be very unclear about their purpose, or open to criticism about it because of the way they are abusing their powers. A rough 'model' of the factors to bear in mind can help to focus attention and prompt analysis, as the Redbridge student commented. 'Starting with a simple formula such as Lasswell's *Who says what in which channel to whom and with what effect?*' students will gradually learn to take account of more complex factors in the proccess of communication.

In doing so they should be introduced to psychological evidence of 'aids and barriers to communication' and encouraged to look with critical care at 'the uses and abuses of communication techniques in education, indoctrination, advertising, propaganda and brainwashing'.

The study of the key factors (besides means) and of more complex models of the process of communication is headed 'theories of communication' in the syllabus. 'Means' and 'theories' form one half of the analytic work; the other is concerned with 'cultural and institutional systems'.

We have seen earlier that large social institutions have their own way of organising communications — and sometimes their own means. The key examples, of course, are those which produce communications for a mass audience. The press, radio and television include professionals with a sharp awareness of ways of using these three different means of communication. For this reason alone they would have to be studied. But the emphasis in the syllabus is rather different — less on means than on intentions. Under the heading 'mass communications', it calls for an analysis of the purposes for which the media are used — and specifically of 'their contribution to social, political, educational and cultural development'. The organisations producing the media are seen as active agents, in some degree able to 'generate, influence [and] interpret social change', whether this is 'in the home, at work . . . in politics, education or the arts'. Thus the main form of study is evaluative — and it is extremely broad.

The remaining section is historical. 'Technical and industrial advances' are recurrently affecting printing, cameras, receivers and indeed the whole television output in the near future. The syllabus proposes an historical study of the way such advances 'have interacted with social and political change to produce the media and methods of communication we know today'.

Thus there are four 'sections' of analytic studies to be integrated with the practical work:

> Means of Communication and
> Theories of Communication;
> Mass Communications and
> Development of Communications.

Currently teachers are not equally happy with all four, and for obvious reasons. The first two sections are intrinsically concerned with the process of communication; thus, as we have seen, they are bound to arise in all work that fosters practical *understanding*. The media are rather different. They offer particularly rich examples of, say, a news story being adapted to the medium of print, radio and television. Their practice, for better and for worse, is bound to influence all other productive work, including students'. And their use and abuse of their power is a particularly important part of 'the way society works', a key instance for students to discuss and analyse.

The problem lies not in their inclusion, but in the form of study the syllabus appears to demand — 'their contribution to social . . . development' seems too large a task to take on. Similarly with their historical development; it is a fascinating study over the past 200 years especially, but to combine an understanding of changes in the media over that period with overall (international?) social and political change would be asking a lot, even of people already well-grounded in history. In a nutshell, many teachers are afraid that this section will have no effect on practical understanding, and will encourage shallow, second-hand opinion rather than deepen the students' analysis of major issues.

The form of assessment makes this difficult to avoid: students write four essays, one on each section, in a three-hour paper. Obviously, a great deal will depend on the kinds of question that can be developed, and the way these help students to demonstrate the value of their practical experience as they try to sum up some of the lessons they have learnt. Readers might like to consider for themselves the following questions from the 1978 paper.

Means: What means of communication are available to management intent on promoting safety at work?

In your answer, consider the relative effectiveness of your examples.

As a communication specialist, what advice would you give to a politician on the structure and style of an election speech:
(a) at a general public meeting to be reported in the press;
(b) at a factory gate meeting during the lunch hour.

Theories: The 'noise' factor is evident in many models of the communication process and most indicate that because of 'noise' the reception of the message is diminished.

Interpret the concept of 'noise' and apply your interpretation to five examples of communication situations.

David Gates, of the group 'Bread', wrote the song 'If' which begins: 'If a picture paints a thousand words, then why can't I paint you? The words would never show the you I've come to know.'

How far does this quotation make sense? Why does the song-writer feel that the words can never show 'the you I've come to know'?

Mass: Discuss the merits and demerits and also the impact of
                   the popular press.

                   Discuss the ways in which the social and economic expec-
                   tations of people have been influenced by the media.

Development: Take any one of the systems and innovations that led to
                   the great increase in communication in this country in the
                   nineteenth century and describe its particular contribu-
                   tion.

                   Modern technology has made entertainment abundantly
                   available. Illustrate the effect of that abundance on *one*
                   social institution.

These questions and the whole examination were thoroughly discussed
at a follow-up meeting organised by the board, to which all departments
were invited. The examiners reported fully on the answers to each question.
Thus they noted, for instance, 'the enthusiastic approach' of most of the
candidates who attempted the question prompted by 'If' and felt it had
been valuable to include something 'partly phrased in a more modern
idiom'. Most answers had concentrated on the contrast between verbal and
non-verbal communication, with 'two excellent examples comparing song-
writer, poet and painter' and 'the emotive aspects of communicating in the
chosen medium'. Some candidates, they were also pleased to see, had
realised that the quotation included a *non sequitur*.

The examiners themselves proposed a number of changes in form or
wording of questions, and there were constructive suggestions both from
individual departments and from a London working party representing
nine colleges and schools. Scripts and projects were available at the meeting.

At this point, we must recall that the AEB syllabus is the first attempt to
define the subject at A level. This is a major undertaking in itself. Within
any growing subject there are conflicting tendencies and, over the period of
a generation, manifest shifts of emphasis. 'Noise' is a reminder of the
dominant influence of communication engineers in the 1950s; 'eye movement', in another question, of the influence of social psychologists in the
1970s. Those who produce a syllabus, then, have the difficult task of striking
a balance between jostling pressures to send the new subject off in several
different directions. That balance comes from trying to achieve a longer-
term view of the value of studying communication at 16–19.

We can best understand the underlying issues by comparing the 1976
AEB syllabus with the syllabus produced only a year later by some of the
same people, in the N & F commissioned group convened by Dr John

Gardner. What are the significant differences? We would suggest four.

First, the 1977 N & F syllabus is designed from the start as 'an integrated theoretical and practical study'. As a result the understanding of major processes in communication arises from studying both 'society and . . . the student's work and experience'. For example, 'in the course of carrying out projects — in planning, discussing, formulating preliminary ideas, criticising drafts, or interviewing members of the audience — students will become aware of other contexts for communication, including inner dialogue, one-to-one tutorials and small working groups . . . (for instance). Thus, in the course of their own productive work, as well as in studies of the work of other communicators, they will learn to look closely at the participants in any communication, and especially at their social relationships.' Possibilities of this kind of integration were not explicit in the 1976 syllabus; they are first touched on in the 'Extended Notes' published later that year. Similarly, the 1976 syllabus did not explicitly foresee 'theoretical understanding . . . derived from and applied to practical communication', as the N & F syllabus does. Theory was still received information: by contrast the 1977 syllabus expects students to theorise — to 'devise and use models related to their own experience and appropriate to particular tasks' as well as studying models already developed.

The second difference probably arises from the greater coherence of the 1977 syllabus: it replaces the four discrete sections — means, theory, mass communications and development — by 'five major aspects of communication'. The first three are concerned with 'processes and modes of communication, and their social contexts'; the final two with relating theory to practice and the 'critical analysis and appreciation of selected communications (including students' work)'. In effect a historical treatment is discarded, and 'the communications industry' is regarded as one specific social context for work in communication.

We have seen that the 1976 syllabus was strongly aware of the historical context for communication. Thus there was an explicit interest in the effect of the media on 'social change', and in the interaction between 'social and political change' on the one hand and 'technical and industrial advances' on the other. The ambition was to paint a very broad canvas, and the difficulty was to relate this to 'practical understanding'. By contrast, the 1977 scheme puts the emphasis on the 'social context' for a given act of communication. As we have seen in the Redbridge investigation, this allows students to 'raise ethical and political issues' directly, with respect to a specific exhibition, and then to generalise from that example (as the students began to) about the political decision that faces a council, whether to consult the community they serve about possible social change or to inform and persuade it. The historical context is so broad that students have to focus on 'patterns of development' at a rather high level of abstraction — as we can see from the questions. The social context, on the other hand, can be considered as each 'selected communication' is evaluated. This is a third major difference, we feel, between the 1976 and 1977 versions.

Finally, the 1977 syllabus is more explicitly aware of different functions of communication. To begin with, it appreciates that 'a communicator will often . . . express his own personality, emotions or mood. At times, indeed, the main force of what he produces may be expressive rather than informative.' Emotion and feeling were not specifically referred to in the 1976 syllabus. The model of communication tended to be that of the fifties, when information and persuasion were the dominant research interests. Thus, the suggested projects too were implicitly informative and instructional, though a broader range is certainly allowed for in practice. Similarly, though there was reference in places to literature and the arts, there was no explicit statement, as there is in 1977, that the 'imaginative' function should be studied alongside the 'informative, persuasive and regulative'. In this respect the 1977 syllabus is broader in what it acknowledges and prescribes.

We have suggested four significant contrasts between the two syllabuses produced to date. There may well be others. However, although we should admit that in the view of many teachers these changes are probably for the better, perhaps the more important point is the underlying questions they raise about the new subject.

(1) How coherent and unified should the course be at 16–19?
(2) Should the media be treated in some ways separately?
(3) Should the context for communication be studied in terms of broad historical patterns at this stage, or more empirically in terms of the social roles of the participants in specific examples?
(4) Should the communication of feeling as well as thought be studied?
(5) Should the imaginative function be included alongside the informative or persuasive?

Whatever our own opinions, each of these questions seems worth careful consideration as the new subject develops through its formative stage.

Having said that, we should equally remember that 80 to 90 per cent of the current syllabus has already been welcomed by a wide range of students and teachers, because of the challenge and scope it offers. Currently there is no other syllabus at A level that gives the same opportunities for students to develop 'a sound grasp of . . . speech and writing . . . listening and reading' — quite apart from graphical and other media. The setting up of a broad communication studies course has stimulated some English departments to join in, and many more to reconsider the gap in existing provision at 18+. This merits a further section.

Before turning to it, however, we should consider the significance of this new subject in the overall curriculum. For the coming generation of students it offers a striking shift towards broader social (and vocational) uses of language and other modes of communication. It introduces the study of mixed media, and especially the visual and verbal, into a curriculum hitherto dominated by specialist approaches. In doing so, it manifestly encourages students to undertake a more independent, adult role in the society they live in, and critically to evaluate the characteristic role and products of the dominant media.

This seems a task worth undertaking. What will be crucial for its future, however, is the quality and range of in-service support that is offered to teachers who see its value to the students coming into the sixth form or college.

2.6   Continuing English to A Level

> During their Sixth Form years they will need to use language to express more difficult ideas and to develop more extended and complex arguments than they have met before. . . .
>
> A pass in 'English Language' at Ordinary level at the age of 16 does not guarantee effective communication at the level of an 18-year-old.   (Crowther Report, 1959)

In the last section, we have seen a surprising anomaly develop: in order to gain credit for an advanced mastery of spoken and written English, and careful investigations of many of its uses, students must now opt for an A level in communication studies. As it stands, this is a polarised choice. Without a broad English qualification at A level, the 18+ curriculum has a significant gap in one of its central areas, we would argue. It is unthinkable that this should continue as the number entering A level continues to rise.

As a project team, we have already discussed this issue at a preliminary delegate conference, with fifty LEAs represented. The teachers and advisers who came believed strongly that the students already exist who would benefit from and desire a broader English course. However, the point has not yet been reached at which a specific syllabus has been designed: that is a matter for teachers in dialogue with the boards. What we shall aim to do here, threfore, is to set before the profession some of the main questions that will have to be answered, if such syllabuses are to be given a secure foundation. These include:

(1) how broad should an English course to 18+ be?
(2) how flexible a course should the examination allow for?
(3) what fundamental aims and objectives should be examined?
(4) what conceptual study of language should be expected? (See next section.)

There is an obvious interlock between the potential answers. In discussing each question, we shall draw on existing experience and on syllabuses under discussion, including the following: the AEB English (language and literature) A level, with a core of literature and an additional language paper; the N & F English syllabus commissioned for discussion from the NATE 16+ Committee; and the discussions in Schools Council of the English A Level Committee's recent working party on language. In addition we shall refer to work arising from both the literature and communication studies A levels.

How Broad?

Despite sharp differences in emphasis and aims, there is a surprising amount of common ground between these existing syllabuses and proposals. Thus all include:

(a) both practical mastery of English and the critical investigation of its use;

(b) some work in spoken as well as written English;

(c) implicitly or explicitly, the exploration of 'informative, persuasive, personal and imaginative, and evaluative' uses of language;

(d) studies based on books, periodical literature, the press, television and speech in various contexts.

The fact that so much is agreed seems to point to a well-established view of English — and effectively, we would say, one that derives directly from many teachers' experience up to 16+. From the sixties on, the main movement in English teaching 11–16 has been to broaden the subject and integrate its parts. This movement has already been carried a stage forward to 17+ by the departments exploiting the opportunities of CEE.

At 18+, the major immediate difference, it seems, lies not so much in the components as in the degree of integration expected: the AEB syllabus appears to accept the division of the subject customary at O level, while the NATE group explicitly comment that 'the fact that English specialists have developed a habit of dividing this area of study and naming its divisions "language" and "literature" is regrettable, and our familiarity with this usage disguises its illogicality'.

To avoid unnecessary argument it is worth bearing in mind that, in its broader, traditional usage, 'literature' includes informative and persuasive works as well as imaginative — essays, tracts, sermons, speeches, biographies and autobiographies, journals, letters . . . even 'table talk'. If we think of students working both productively and receptively across such a range of 'literature', it is difficult to see where the division from 'language' is to be made. Alternatively, if the word is used in its narrower sense to refer to fictional works in drama, prose and poetry, then the tradition of Milton, Defoe, Coleridge, Dickens or Lawrence suggests that the two sides can in fact be intimately related. The common interest, surely, lies in the sensitivity and understanding with which language is used, whatever its purpose and audience.

However, there may be a more fundamental difference hidden behind the literature/language dispute, and perhaps obscured by it. At times language takes us into the heart of human conflict and passion, but on other occasions it is used in a workaday fashion to transact the matter-of-fact business of one's life — social, vocational or academic. It is the balance (and relation) of these two poles that may have to be established.

Again, the current syllabus and proposals all make reference to such matter-of-fact uses of language in the course of study and practical work:

> 'to simplify for the purpose of giving general information in notices, minutes and . . . news reports';
> to recognise 'salient ideas' and 'extract the essential message';
> to 'incorporate selected material' in a report, memorandum or article.

Language uses such as these would benefit from further scrutiny, we believe, for two reasons. The first is that they may be more generally valuable than they have appeared — because of an extremely restricted tradition in 'language' examinations. Understanding the structure of ideas in an argument or discussion; being alert to the strengths and weaknesses in the logical presentation of a case; analysing the viewpoint and attitudes adopted and allowing for bias; appreciating the exact force, or the ambiguity, of key expressions; synthesising divergent points of view and demonstrating the pattern of agreement and disagreement; assembling the points to be taken into account in coming to a decision . . . objectives such as these are fundamental not simply to specific workaday tasks but to living in a society struggling to be more democratic.

The second thing to be scrutinised is the context in which such objectives are demanded. Traditional examining lifted them out of context and turned them into purposeless exercises; recent teaching and examining have begun to restore the real (or realistic) context that makes them essential. This point was brought home to our project team in a series of workshops with vocational and sixth form teachers, reported in our booklet *Active Comprehension*.

In terms of breadth, there is one further element that a comparison of syllabuses brings to one's notice: oral, written and possibly dramatic presentations for a specific audience. Again, it might be easy to dismiss this as a rather minor aspect of oral or written work. Our team's experience with communication studies has taught us otherwise. When students present work to a real audience they have to match up to adult standards, and take on adult roles. They learn to take a practitioner's interest in technique, whether in the pace and style of delivering a talk, or in the preparation and editing of a magazine. The appreciative comment and criticism they encounter is an essential stimulus to greater control of material and technique.

Perhaps this is the place where aspects of English not much mentioned in 18+ syllabuses, but current in many comments from employers, need to be taken into account: audibility, coherence, directness and poise; care in spelling and punctuation, clarity in organisation; and, on the negative side, the avoidance of redundancy, irrelevance, ambiguity and inaccuracy. It is a context in which critical care to such detail can be seen to pay.

How Flexible?

We have seen from communication studies the potential links that individual students can make with a variety of other subjects, courses and career intentions. In a broad English course a teacher may be able to foster similar links and allow individual students to develop special interests at certain points. However, the overall flexibility of the course is bound to be affected by the syllabus design and the method of assessment.

Currently two approaches to the examination syllabus are being tried. The first model lays down core units plus a range of options: this is typical of A-level literature syllabuses and was suggested in the brief that the NATE N & F group were given. Each of the options, it turns out, is capable of being related to the core, but is separately examinable. This allows for a fairly tight definition of what the individual student has to cover.

The alternative model is that used in the language element of AEB English (623), in communication studies — and, in fact, in O-level language. A broad syllabus is outlined and teachers are left with the responsibility for ensuring it is adequately covered. For the final assessment a rather narrower sample is taken, sometimes (notably in communication studies) with room allowed for individual interests, whether social, vocational or academic. Overall the definition of what an individual student has to cover in the course is less tight. In terms of the syllabus this seems to be the more flexible approach.

However, it is possible for the examination to remove most of the gain in breadth. English language syllabuses leave the door open for a very wide range of reading, but the examination usually closes it again by offering no choice in the passage set. At A level the communication studies approach, whereby a candidate selects from three 'case studies', rewards students who have broader interests, by giving them a choice, and in any case allows for divergent interests among students as a whole.

Similarly, the treatment of the passage in traditional 'comprehension' questions is (a) stereotyped and (b) divorced from any conceivable experience of actually using what one reads. Thus, students who during the course do learn to read *and use* a variety of informative, persuasive or instructional documents gain no recognition for the breadth of their work, and little direct help in tackling the kind of question rewarded in the examination.

Although in the case of writing there appears to be an element of choice in language examinations, the actual effect is little different. Students may learn in the course to undertake some major written assignments, to write for various purposes and 'to address a variety of readers'. The constraints accepted in the traditional essay paper prevent this kind of competence from being examined.

Thus the examination of students' competence in writing is based on a single essay, and their competence in reading on a single passage. It may seem flexible, and even liberating to demand so small a sample, but in practice no such effect is guaranteed: rather the contrary. This is a short-coming teachers have pointed to in the current AEB English papers. There seem to be two lessons.

First, the constraints of a three-hour paper (or an oral examination) need to be recognised and taken into account. The English tasks selected need to be suited to the restricted setting, the time-limit and the impersonal relation of mass examiner to candidate. On the face of it, the context seems best suited to language work that is businesslike, practical and analytic in style. If the taste of real experience is to be introduced, rather than neglected, some kind of simulation or work in a given role needs to be considered. English examiners have perhaps most to learn here from work in the OND in public administration and from case study assignments in general.

On the other hand, the admitted limitations of this kind of sample can be balanced by selective assignments undertaken during the course. The NATE group follow reformed O levels and CEE in suggesting a folder of writing with perhaps fifteen pieces covering four major language functions. This is the tighter method. The communication studies N & F group, revising the A-level practice in this case, proposed one major project (4000 words in length or ten minutes' listening time) and two minor. This allows for some range of work to be specified, but is more flexible.

What Fundamental Aims and Objectives?

Probably none of the current proposals would claim to have treated this question in the depth it deserves. However, taken collectively, they do indicate a range that needs to be borne in mind. Even if an A-level syllabus finally has to select part rather than the whole, some plurality is inevitable, we believe. Our provisional chart in section 2.3 demonstrates this clearly enough. Equally, 'what gives an English course coherence is the recognition of the interrelationships between its varying elements' (NATE N & F). Perhaps our most important function in this section, then, is to eschew faction and make clear the potential range of interests that need to be borne in mind and drawn into relation with each other. In conclusion we shall try to illustrate with writing by 16 to 17-year-olds the kinds of work that may be recognised and rewarded within English.

Following the chart on p. 44, we shall start on the left-hand side with literature and the imaginative uses of language. We have already discussed teachers' hopes that in this work students will reach a deeper understanding of themselves and others, and of the complexities of life. In a broader English course, the NATE syllabus suggests a two-way process, in which 'the student, through his reading and consequent growing awareness of the nature and quality of creativity, will have the opportunity to become aware of his own potential in personal and imaginative writing. He should be encouraged to experiment in a variety of forms, and to use the process of "practical criticism" on his own work, as well as on the texts presented to him.' For some students, we suggest, but not all, this practitioner's interest in imaginative literature may become a major element in the course. We have already illustrated some students' work, but we will add at the end of section 2.7 some further examples from personal writing. In our view the fundamental contribution of such work remains the sensitivity and perceptiveness with which students can enter into other people's experience and visions of life, and the self-knowledge they gain from doing so.

Moving to the second column, we see that along with literature in the broader sense there will be studies of reports, articles, programmes in the media and live speech. What are the potential aims of such work? The AEB syllabus encourages students to write on 'current events and movements' and to study 'a range of books' and other material 'giving information and expressing views on aspects of modern life'. The central interest, we take it, is to study the language used as a range of people inform and persuade each other on important contemporary issues, and thus for students to gain deeper understanding of contemporary life — and possibly a critical perspective on some of 'the ways society works'.

In the departments we have worked with, these studies — currently confined to the first year of the sixth form — are taking two forms. At the national level (the macrocosm) they may lead to an intensive study of the reporting of a major event; of documentary radio, television or text; or of a major social campaign, for instance. At the local level (the microcosm) students may be involved in library research or in visits and 'attachment' to a variety of local groups, firms and organisations — sometimes simply to study them at work, sometimes to get a better understanding of local problems. Work of the first kind tends to be critical and evaluative in the main; but the local work based on first-hand observation and personal research offers students themselves an important role in presenting their findings to the class and other interested groups. We shall try to illustrate later the variety of personal and social interests this allows students to pursue in some depth, and thus the potential importance of this element in an English course.

Perhaps it is worth recalling at this point that there is an inevitable overlap between the informative, persuasive, personal and imaginative aspects of language. Thinking of the two fields we have looked at so far, a combined interest in imaginative life and social man is part of the tradition of English letters, and is evinced today in writers as various as Achebe, Baldwin, Naipaul or Solzhenitsyn. The difficult task, in which some departments today are playing the role of pioneers, is to find out how 16 to 19-year-olds can make a positive and mature contribution of their own in the study of contemporary culture and society. In particular, as English breaks out of the constraints of the examination essay and the limited tasks it suggests, teachers want to find out the kinds of informative and persuasive presentations students themselves can produce, and the variety of forms (written or oral) they can tackle with advantage. There is a new territory to be charted and, again, we must remind readers that among the things a book cannot represent are the presentations (arising from attachments, study visits or the analysis of media material) which are given in the form of talks with slides or with taped interviews incorporated.

Visits, attachments and presentations, we have come to realise, are contributing to the objectives of English courses in two ways. The first arises from *what* is studied and presented — the subject, the understanding it calls for and the care needed to interpret it adequately. But the second stems from the *way* it is studied. This leads us to a third group of aims.

All of the English syllabuses we have noted explicitly refer to what are often called 'basic' or 'study' skills — from taking notes and summarising an argument to incorporating selected material in a report. There are parallel 'oral' skills to be considered too, as the NATE syllabus notes, in such contexts as 'interviews, committee work and role play'. As visits and investigations are planned by groups in the class, or as the material they have noted, recorded or summarised is being jointly organised for presentation, we have observed these more workaday objectives being achieved in English lessons.

Again, this is difficult to illustrate in a book, though we shall look more closely at new approaches to basic skills in section 2.7. For the moment the main point to be made is that 'basic' and 'study' skills do need to be taken into account in designing A-level English, and that work is at last going on to exploit their practical value within English, rather than leave them as abstract 'exercises'.

We come, then, to the third column, to language and the student's awareness of its uses. To be honest, this seems to be left very non-explicit in the available syllabuses, but we feel we should at least raise the question of whether some explicit objectives should not be considered as a contributing element to a broader English course.

Thus, for example, there is reference in both the AEB and the NATE syllabus to the critical understanding of 'logical argument'. For our own generation this was offered in a very practical way by people like Susan Stebbing and Robert Thouless, university teachers with a philosophical training but well able to address the common reader. Their careful and unpedantic treatment of logical problems in the discussion of current issues seems to be worth developing for a new generation. If so, the objectives would need to be clarified.

Similarly, as a second example, both syllabuses wish to encourage students 'to criticise, appraise and assess speeches, letters, reports, advertisements and newspaper comments', and to 'become aware of the influences bearing on them' from such material. This suggests some study of the emotive uses of language, and especially of implicit attitudes, feelings and implications. The foundations for this work were laid, we believe, by Richards and Empson, and popularised by other writers. Again we wonder whether some explicit understanding of the emotive side of language would be worth including in the objectives.

Thirdly, all three syllabuses are concerned with 'effective presentation', the NATE group explicitly referring to the need to adapt 'style, tone and register to take account of [the] audience'. Here are four concepts already that might bear closer scrutiny in class: style, tone, register and audience. Scholars such as Randolf Quirk and Andrew Wilkinson have shown how the common listener and reader can be interested in such things, and the new kinds of understanding they may gain.

These three examples are enough to suggest how A-level students could benefit from an analytic study of language and the way it is used. We have tried in this section to consider general rather than specialist possibilities, which will be discussed in the section that follows. However, from these three examples alone it does seem that an element of explicit language study could play a valuable part in the course for some students — if not for all?

To sum up: there is already surprising agreement about the elements to be included in a broader English syllabus, and with care these can be flexibly organised to leave room for differences of emphasis. Since 1965 there have been valuable experiments in the examining of English, and a more critical conception has developed of what is required to make the method of assessment searching and valid: fortunately these findings also encourage greater flexibility in the course. Finally, some schools and colleges are learning to relate the different elements in such a way that what were hitherto barren exercises become a necessary part of the students' methods of work, especially in their longer projects and investigations.

Some students would already gladly choose such an A level. By the 1980s there may be many more. Thus, provision on these lines is one of the most urgent immediate tasks for English teachers and the boards.

To conclude this section, we should like to illustrate the range of language that might be recognised by this new qualification. Clearly at present one can do no more than indicate future possibilities. Some of these have already been suggested in section 2.4 when we discussed the varieties of writing inspired by literature. What additional kinds might be worth considering? There is room for some, but by no means all, here. What we have tried to represent, with the help of teachers, are some of the character-istic qualities that might be encouraged. Most of these extracts from longer pieces were written by 17-year-olds: however, we hope they will suggest a competence in English that is worth developing on to 18+, both for broader social and personal ends and for its relevance to academic and vocational life.

Personal and Reflective

At 16 or 18 any discussion of a shared experience may spark off the desire to write about a past experience of your own, or to reflect on the experience you are living through. Sometimes, students write autobiographical pieces — too long to include here, in the main; sometimes, their personal reflections on things of importance in their lives. Here are two.

> All through life you reckon the bit you're up to at the time is the most important, when you are at your best, you're most mature. Well, that's what I think now. It's natural really, you remember the present most vividly, what you have done recently best matches your aspirations.
>
> Perhaps it really is experience that counts, and the further one progresses in life, the more experience one has, which sharpens one's awareness of what really is important. More probably only the past can be placed in perspective and the present should not be judged, it is just that up until now things have got progressively more important. But you get more mature in your reactions to them.
>
> No longer the mad panic before exams, but the realisation that things don't seem to turn out in general as badly as you feared that they would. Everything seems to sail past in an air of refinement and unruffled smoothness, things that just two years ago would have sent me into throes of agonising panic, and even a year ago thrown me to the utmost despair, now bring about a raising of eyebrows and a shrug of the shoulders.
>
> But the reason isn't just maturity or experience, it is also a sense of apathy and resignment creeping on as you realise just how long you have been at school. Sure it's necessary but by the time A levels are reached it becomes a huge effort to raise oneself to a peak. Yet behind it all is a nagging, not fear, fear is too strong a word for it, anxiety perhaps, that maybe at some stage of your life you will make a wrong decision. For example, A-level subjects. A mundane sort of example, but I was undecided upon whether to do maths, physics and chemistry or maths, history and economics. Yet my decision will have altered my entire life, and it was a decision that had to be made without experience, and anybody will tell you it is

impossible to make valid decisions without the 'light' of experience.

That last bit of essay sounds as if it is something I've been wanting to get off my chest, well it is.   Anon.

. . . At four, one accepts that school is a necessary part of one's existence and to me it seemed no different from playing at home or out of doors with my friends. Learning to read, write and calculate are vague, hazy memories that seemed insignificant events in my life compared with the importance of being able to roll your plasticine so thin you could curl it round on itself a couple of dozen times. Throughout the infants I don't think I realised that it was for the writing and arithmetic that I went to school and that there would be more and more. School blended with the rest of my life and didn't seem a separate part until I was into the juniors. I was perhaps eight years old when I saw that I had only come a short distance on the conveyor belt of learning and that there would be no clearly defined point at which I would be told to get off, as surely as I had been put on. However, I didn't worry about that question. At primary school if I was happy with the present, I forgot about the future.

As far as academic achievement went, though more emphasis was placed on marks, grades and positions than in secondary schools, it bothered me far less, possibly because I had some idea that everybody had a fixed rate of earning marks which determined who got the As, who the Cs etc. and there was nothing you could do to help the people who, shortly before taking their eleven-plus, were having difficulty with their three times table. I also had definite ideas on intelligence and what it was. At eleven, most matters seem black and white, and easier to resolve than people make out. It's only later that varied shades of grey appear. But isn't this one of educations aims, and/or effects? To introduce grey areas in the answers to questions which previously seemed to have only one or two alternative replies. For instance, to me, then, intelligence was the difference between those who could finish an exercise in ten minutes and those who couldn't attempt it after twenty. In other words, the quickest learners were the most intelligent.

In a class of forty-six, like my last one at primary school, the slow developers didn't stand a chance, and were mown down by the ridiculous exam which packed a third of us off to grammar schools and the rest to secondary modern schools. Now, I often ask myself what intelligence is. I find it far harder to link it with achievement. Do I gain intelligence (thinking of it as in measurable units) simply by learning? That means those with the best memories are the wisest. But what happens when dealing with unknowns in an unknown situation? Memory is of little use then. . . .

[In secondary education] by half way through the fourth year a lot of my attitudes had changed, and things no longer seemed so simple regarding my future. The main question was 'Where will it all end?' Acute depression set in for a couple of months and all I could see, looking ahead pessimistically, was an obstacle course of work, exams, marks and grades, hopefully university, more study, more exams then a job. Following on from that, I was asking myself, 'And that's all there is?' and 'What's it all for?' and finally just 'Why?' However, on that occasion, several weeks respite from work during which I put most of my energies into my social life, revitalised me. I realised that since I *had* to stay at school till I was sixteen, I might as well work. I promised myself I'd consider such questions as 'What's the point of education?' after O levels . . .   Alison

Documentary

Young adults begin to search for an understanding of a range of people beyond their own peer group, sometimes in an older generation, sometimes just a few years on into the experience of marriage, work and the challenges of adult life. Documentary film, radio and television can be a valuable stimulus. So too can writing biographically. This extract from a student's biography of his grandfather suggests the quality of imagination, knowledge and empathy that may be called for.

> . . . Stephen like all good Christian English men was highly patriotic and when the war broke out in 1914 he wanted to join the army. At first his father stopped him but at the end of 1915 he signed on with the Hampshire regiment. He was sent away for brief training then in 1916 he heard he was to be sent abroad on Empire protection. Fearing leaving his sweetheart, he married her in the Spring of 1916. After they had had one week of married life, the regiment moved.
>
> They left in an old cargo steamer at Southampton, destination unknown. After mixing with people of all classes in his childhood he got on well in the army. They crossed the Mediterranean to the Suez Canal, stopping at Port Said and Suez.
>
> For someone who had rarely gone outside their home town this must have been a wonderful if not frightening experience. Soon he missed his wife and the familiarity of the life he left. No more quiet market days leaning on the railings watching the animals, or letting loose your pigeons, or Sunday tea parties, choir or games. From Suez they moved to the jewel of the empire, India, and to Bombay. Here he wrote emotional letters home during a long stay.
>
> After the home-sickness left he enjoyed the new experiences. Still today these army days are some of the most vivid in his mind. Mostly he enjoyed the new company, the leisure of the Raj, the Saturday night dances. The Hampshire regiment then moved to remote north India and Rawalpindi.
>
> In 1917 the war was just starting to go the Allies' way in Europe, when in Russia a revolution started. The Hampshire regiment was ordered back to Bombay where they boarded another ship and made for Vladivostok, East Asian Russia. They travelled through storms in the South China and East China sea, only stopping at Hong Kong. Finally they crossed the Sea of Japan and put in at Vladivostok.
>
> The aim was for the British to give support to the Anti-Communist White Russian Army and defeat the Communists.
>
> When they arrived the men were restless, not understanding the plans and not being interested in the foreign civil war. Conditions at Vladivostok were bad. Stephen organised a camp outside the town. They then had to amuse themselves while their leader argued over a train and the general plan. The men were later joined by the Londoners regiment. During this time fights started due to the oppressive heat and lack of things to do.

Finally, a train was found which was to get them to Irkutsk in Siberia. The train was old, and the men in the regiment were piled into cattle trucks while the officers were in good trucks. Stephen's duty was to see that all went well with the driver of the train, a Russian who had with him on the engine his whole family.

This young market town man must have felt bewildered as they crossed Manchuria and Mongolia into Siberia. Yet what sights he saw as the train crossed the mountains over 6,000 feet above sea level. This was very different from India, and at the stops in China, for example, Harbin, they were treated with suspicion from the Chinese. After many months he got to know the Russian train driver who knew a type of English. In Siberia they crossed the deep blue Lake Baikal finally getting to Irkutsk. Siberia with its beauty yet hostility really proved too much for him, he was now so cut off from his family, his young wife and friends at Basingstoke . . .									Simon

The Address to Specific Audiences

Some speech and writing needs to be specifically shaped in the interests of a particular audience. This is not an easy task: to tackle it confidently students have to feel they have something worth saying and an adult role. Our first extract shows a student's attempt to design a booklet for parents; it is a 'simulation' from which she hopes to learn more. The second is an article by a comprehensive school student, published by the *TES*.

Parents often suspect there is something wrong with their child, yet they avoid having their suspicions confirmed because they are frightened of facing the truth. Once the doctor has told them, then they have nothing to cling to for hope. Many parents put off going to the doctor for as long as they can, but there comes a point where they can no longer deceive themselves. Yet when the doctor says 'Yes, your child is physically/mentally handicapped', it comes as a terrible shock. Some parents refuse to accept the verdict, yet in their heart of hearts they know it is true. Some parents may never recover from the shock while others are dazed for a few months. However it may affect you — remember your child is still there — a child who depends on you totally and relies on you to provide the best you possibly can for him. You owe that to your child!

No good ever comes of hiding your child behind closed doors because you do not want people to talk. By being secretive, you do encourage rumours to fly around and add substance to gossip. It is not your fault you have a handicapped child, so you should not be ashamed of him. After all, it is not fair on your child, to keep him locked up. So make an effort to go out with your child as you would with any other child. Of course, people will gossip but remember gossip only attracts attention when something is a novelty.

Guilt is another bridge to be crossed. It is easy to go back through the family trees searching for the cause of your child's affliction and then start blaming each other. What good will it do? None, for your child's condition will not improve, just because you find out which side of the family it came from. Yet it can break up your marriage and that is no basis for any child, handicapped or otherwise, to start life on.

Although it is so very hard to stand by, watching your child painstakingly eating or dressing you must resist the urge to help him, if you know that he can do it himself. He will not be grateful for your help, especially when he is older for every child likes to be independent, but he also likes to know that he has the security of a loving family behind him when he is having problems. Do not reject your child, but do not over-protect him either — a happy medium is desired.

The more handicapped your child is, the less he realizes how different he is from ·other children and the more chance there is of people saying tactlessly 'Put him away', or 'Forget him'. This attitude makes you determined to keep your child — no parent will give up a child willingly, no matter how much trouble he is. The more helpless he is, the more one's heart bleeds for him . . .   Anna

As a pupil studying O-level English literature last year, I had expected the examining board to have a more subjective type of evaluation, so that the five essays, to be compiled in the allotted two and a half hours, would receive credit for creative ability and proof of deep understanding of the text.

That is, that the examination would provide an opportunity for the examinee to demonstrate his own personal interpretations of the material.

It was disappointing to discover that this was apparently not the case. I had been taught by an extremely capable man — highly regarded by all members of the school. He constructed his lessons in such a way that full participation, enjoyment and clear understanding were attained by all. It was expected that I would do well in this examination, but in the event I failed.

The result was such that the head, an English specialist, recommended that the paper be re-marked. This was not only in the hope of an improved grade, but so that any comments included might prevent similar occurrences in the future and provide useful feedback for the staff. The examining board's reply proved to be totally unhelpful in this regard.

After an interval of two months I recommenced literature classes with a different teacher, attending for only one hour each week. This course was orthodox and uninspiring, but subsequently I received an 'A' grade, after the re-sit in November.

The first method had been interesting, discursive and probing, so that individual views were developed. The second was the conventional itinerary of teacher-directed responses, and the regurgitation of rote-learned model answers. This approach was infallible to the extent that a colleague of mine passed the examination merely by attending lessons, finding it unnecessary to read and decipher the listed text.

It is my opinion that the examining board should reconsider its approach, so that allied courses can be less limiting and restrictive and more capable of, and intent on, developing not only knowledge, but desirable attitudes towards this important aspect of our culture.   Murray

Informative and Evaluative

There is a long tradition of sixth form study of the media and, through the media, of information and opinion on contemporary issues. In part, the best that is spoken and written there is a stimulus to young writers. Perhaps the two students below are beginning to see *themselves* as journalists! Equally they learn to look selectively and critically at the way language is used. These two extracts come from articles sent in to *Feedback*, a magazine produced by communication studies students and currently edited at God-alming Sixth Form College.

What Is an Alternative Paper?
In the 1960s the restless youth-culture was very much concerned with finding a different way of life from the nine-to-five-mortgage-repayments-existence that their parents seemed content to lead. That was the age of the Polaris Missile and the Nuclear-Fallout Shelter when it seemed that the two major powers were hell-bent on pressing that button and burning us all from the face of the planet.

The young people dared to consider that maybe there was something the whole establishment was doing wrong. From out of this disquiet, this search for an alternative existence, was born the Alternative Press.

Pioneered by early papers like *IT* and *OZ*, the list of Alternative Papers now numbers some 68 publications run on a regular basis and a further 28 occasional publications in Great Britain, ranging from *The West London Street Press* to *The Aberdeen People's Press*.

The journalists of the Alternative Press see the need to report to local people news events which will affect them parochially, without letting it first filter through the censorship of the politicians, the companymen and all the other restrictions that are put upon the commercial papers in their struggle to make money. Facts cannot be distorted, diluted or drowned in the need to show the shareholders a profit, because the Alternative Press doesn't have that restriction.

What is RAP?
RAP first came to print in 1971 and was originally printed in Moss Side, an underpriviledged area of Greater Manchester, but there was some fear that Moss Side Press hadn't got a future, so its editors, David Bartlett and John Walker, raised the money to buy their own press and now produce the paper in the basement of David Bartlett's Rochdale home.

The paper is very much in contact with the local community: the back cover has the invitation 'Come and meet the *RAP* people, on Thursday evenings in the Carters Rest', and as well as being a community platform it provides cheap printing facilities for local action groups like The Women's Group, The Socialist Workers' Party and The Samaritans, who all have regular slots in the paper. With a circulation of approaching 7000, *RAP* is now coming very close to breaking even with sales revenue at 6p per copy. I asked David Bartlett about that other source of revenue, advertising . . .   Ged

The mass media do show clearly through their products that they have a definite view of what their audiences are like. When a programme or magazine is put together, it is aimed at a specific audience. It therefore reflects the image that the message originators have of their target audience. The product will contain what the media policy controllers think that the audience wants to see, read, or hear. The message will reflect, overtly and covertly, the lifestyles, norms and roles the audience are thought to have. That these products are presented in certain conventionalised formats shows that the media produces expectations of its product in the minds of the audience, which it then fulfils. Also, having created these expectations, they do not deviate from them, as it might not prove popular. Such programmes as *Coronation Street* and *Crossroads* are supposed to be taken by the audience as directly relating to their lifestyles. These programmes reinforce, and in some cases modify, the world view of the target audience. They also create stereotypes of other people's lifestyles. Do the characters in Emmerdale Farm truly represent typical rural Yorkshire folk? Are the Archers ordinary everyday country folk?

The mass media present our view of the world and its events. Often one hears people passing judgements on issues and situations that they have never been involved in, concerning places they have never been to. Our only knowledge, for the most part, is that gained through the media. Therefore, the media have great power over what we think. The *way* that issues are presented affects our view of them, as much as the content of the actual message. The media also choose what they think are the important issues. One could suggest that what is considered to be important has as much to do with the management structure of the media and with sensationalist appeals to a mass audience, as it has to do with actual newsworthiness.

A few months ago, an estimated eighty thousand people went to London on what was probably the biggest demonstration since the war. It gained little press or television coverage. Whether one thinks that the march was important or not is immaterial. The majority of the press did not think that it was anywhere near as important as the disintegrating marriage of Princess Margaret. There is a belief that news reporting is basically impartial and balanced, especially in television or radio. This can be questioned. A supposedly balanced coverage frames our conception of the issue as much as an 'opinionated' one . . .   Simon

Understanding One's Use of language

Many older students can learn to gain more control of language by analysing closely its actual use. Sometimes this will raise the need for specialised concepts; sometimes — as in the following extracts — for a refinement of common sense. From many possible uses, we have chosen two students' comments on their own writing in the sixth form.

. . . I enjoy English more as a subject, but I find writing for history somewhat easier. English essays demand an organisation of ideas which is also necessary in history, but the difference is that ideas in English often have to do with verbalising feelings, while history essays deal with what you think. English demands a rigorous examination of your own reaction to a novel or poem, while in history the difficulty is not so much the formulation of ideas as the marshalling of facts, and the clarification of notions which you had all along. It is because English has more to do with the non-cerebral part of your mind that it is more difficult to write about and more satisfying at the same time. History essays may be slightly easier (though often the marshalling of facts is just drudgery), but they are less satisfying: indeed, the age-old story of human failure is often downright depressing. Nevertheless, although an individual part of an English essay may be satisfying, the longer length of time spent on it means that one is more aware of its failings and shortcomings, and yet powerless to correct them (due to tiredness, or boredom, or something else). A history essay can conform more closely to a perfect and almost attainable plan set by teacher; it may be infinitely inferior compared to an English essay as far as personal expression goes, but it can be almost perfect. Thus history essays are generally more satisfying because they can earn A+, whereas in some ways English essays are more satisfying because they express something one has been wanting to say for some time, and the sense of achievement is greater because the transference of ideas from the inexplicit (or implicit) to the explicit, intellectual, and cerebral part of the mind is such a difficult and time consuming process. Of course, it is possible to write essays on both subjects which leave the writer dissatisfied . . .   Robert

I find about all my writing, whatever form it takes, it is never *exactly* what I meant to write. This is partly, perhaps, my inadequate handling of language but also the inherent nature of language. What a particular word means to me might be totally different from its associations in another's mind. Abstracts obviously will have widely divergent associations, but even mundane concrete objects have different contexts, however minute, for each individual — a broom has a fairly standard design, but it is stored in a wide variety of places, used on a wide variety of surfaces and through time and familiarity a broom can assume an individuality according to the scratches of the varnish, the sweat marks, etc.

Therefore, I find truly subjective writing extremely frustrating, for when I start a sentence in which I am trying to express something very important to me, the words on the page assume a new life, semi-independent of their life in my head. Having written something down, it no longer is true. This is why I don't keep a diary, which is supposed to be the most personal form of writing. When I did start one, I found myself becoming self-concious and posturing. Diary-writing is merely an attempt at externalising one's emotions in order to define and, perhaps, resolve them. However, it can produce excessive self-preoccupation and stifle any inclinations to communicate 'deeply' with people. I, personally, prefer to externalise my emotions by discussing them with my close friends, because often they have been present at the focus of the experience and thus they are not just sounding-boards but diffraction gratings which filter my emotions, and metaphorically straighten them out . . .

I think everyone prefers to express themselves in the medium at which they are most proficient. I write very little for pleasure, (1) because I do a hell of a lot during my A-level course and (2) writing is not my natural medium — I express myself better verbally, because I am talking at someone's face not just a piece of paper. By talking one gets a much quicker response than by writing and thus much quicker interflow of ideas. Writing is a very lonely business and must by nature be somewhat formal — both facets which discourage me from practising it.

Footnote
This has *not* been a hint that I haven't enjoyed the Study Group. If I had not been forced to write I might never have found out how bad I was at expressing myself in writing.   Andy

2.7   Language Studies to 18+

The first A-level syllabus to encourage the analytic study of language became available in 1978, as this report was being written. It was offered by the London Board as an optional paper within the existing English literature syllabus. This follows over a decade of argument about the aims and definition of such studies and their potential role in English and other subjects. It will probably not be claimed that London has found the final solution to those debates, but at least it has set up a test bed on which teachers, students and examiners can experiment with very varied course work and refine the methods of assessing it.

A specialist interest in language and its analysis may currently take several different forms; unfortunately these are not too well integrated in practice, though there is some overlap between them. The oldest is the study of the language of earlier English texts, an analysis of changes in grammar and vocabulary that owed a good deal to classical studies. The second is the more systematic treatment of spoken and written language that developed in 'general linguistics'. The third arose from the study of individual language development and has come to include the social context for its use. For 18+ students it is the second and third that have recently stimulated most interest, because their potential application might be quite far-reaching. However, the difficulty has been to define what an *applied* study of the mother-tongue would entail, either in higher education or at 16–19. This has not been made any easier by the fact that the aspirations and theoretical sweep of linguistics and associated studies have been through an international boom since the early sixties.

Of course, teachers and students of 16–19 are already aware *to some degree* of the way language is working as they use it, or investigate its specific use. There seem to be three questions to consider, therefore:

(1) How explicit an awareness should be aimed for in 'language studies'?
(2) How systematic should a student's ideas be?
(3) Should the student be involved in systematising — or simply be informed about existing systems?

The answers depend in part on what teachers hope the students will gain from these studies. In discussing alternatives we shall draw on two recent sources: the London syllabus and specimen paper, and some 16–19 study units prepared by a group of Cheshire schools and colleges, co-ordinated by their (then) English adviser, Geoffrey Thornton.

To illustrate what English teachers may have in mind, let us take some of the lesson units tried out by the Cheshire group. Thus, in the later part of a sequence on 'Who do you think you are talking to?' come the following suggestions:

The class should consider short extracts from a variety of styles of writing and see if they can judge what audience the writer had in mind, i.e. age, sex, intelligence, level of knowledge, interest, etc. Some suitable sources of material are: instructions from a workshop manual; a handicraft book for children; history textbooks on the same topic for junior and secondary ages; teenage magazines, etc. It can be fruitful to compare the definitions of the same word in a children's and adult dictionary or the same recipe in cookery books for clearly different audiences e.g. children, novice cooks, expert cooks. These are some of the questions that can be used to compare the extracts:

(a) Is the audience directly addressed? (e.g. 'Take care not to cut yourself!')
(b) Is any technical vocabulary used and, if so, is it explained?
(c) Is any of the vocabulary clearly aimed at a particular age group?
(d) Are the sentences simple or complex?
(e) How much knowledge is assumed?

The initial focus is analytic, then, and we note that the students are invited to move freely between an open question — what audience did the writer have in mind? — and a set of closed questions that might turn up useful evidence. The student is alerted to some specific linguistic features (complexity of vocabulary and sentence structure) and other features not specifically linguistic (the knowledge implicitly assumed). But the basic aim seems to be to make the students more aware of the fact that writers do have an inner sense of audience, and adapt their language accordingly, in many subtle ways. It is not difficult to see how this could be applied on occasions when the students themselves address an 'audience', or when they study how effectively others have done so.

Thus, in language studies of this kind the focus may be on the writer or reader, as well as the linguistic medium. The student has to bear in mind the whole communicative act and not just the verbal element of it. The basic interest is as much psychological or social as linguistic. Such a conception of language studies was not entirely unforeseen in the early years of this century, for example by Sweet and de Saussure. However, today both would probably be used as the basis for an alternative form of study. How would it differ?

On the alternative approach the same pieces of text could be used, but the primary task would be to analyse their typical features. Thus the student would be taught, let us say, to take 'history textbooks for junior and secondary ages' and to describe in an objective way some of their constituent parts, using linguistic terms. (The London syllabus in fact contains a list that would prove useful — lexical and grammatical items, sentence types and functions, clause and phrase structure . . .) Given a sufficiently large sample from history textbooks and newspapers, say, one might then be able to point to generic differences in their linguistic features.

In the first approach the analysis may be built in part on the reader's intuitions and experience; in the second it will properly be systematic. Thus there are two poles towards which (following our ideal types) 'analysis' may be directed. In the one direction the student learns to look closely at the language in abstraction from its communicative context, to classify with increasing precision the various elements it is composed of, and on that basis to describe typical features of language drawn from certain contexts and contrast them with the features of language from other contexts. The study is descriptive and systematic.

In the other direction, the student learns to look closely at a particular utterance or text in relation to its context, including the speaker and his or her listeners. Part of the evidence is covered by linguistic concepts, part moves beyond them as we have seen already. And there is an important difference in the questions that arise: although initially descriptive, they will tend finally to be evaluative.

The inclusion of evaluation is a crucial point. Let us take the treatment of persuasive language. As it happens, London's specimen paper contains a question asking the students to 'discuss some of the distinctive features of the language used in TWO of the following examples of advertising copy and comment on their effect'. It seems as if the analysis of distinctive linguistic features is intended to be entirely descriptive — we are not sure.

By comparison the Cheshire unit on 'propaganda' is explicitly evaluative. Thus about halfway through the sequence of lessons, the following suggestions are made:

> Give examples of other kinds of persuasion: a football report in a local newspaper, where the journalist must be obviously partisan; an article on trade unions in newspapers such as the *Daily Express* or the *Daily Telegraph*.
>
> By this time the group should be beginning to realise how often the clever half-truth can be used to influence the reader's/audience's view, or how broad generalisations, when not subjected to closer scrutiny, can form our opinions. The art of much propaganda is to convince us that we thought the whole thing out ourselves.

The objective of the unit is to help students appreciate 'the pressures, influences and deceptions to which they may be subjected without realising their full implications'. The feature which calls for comment is generalisation — and particularly, we would say, unqualified generalisation. In itself this feature may be quite innocuous, and indeed the broader verbal context may eliminate false implications. It is only in specific contexts ('trade unionists say', 'employers say' — some? many? most? all?) that one may well suspect the writer's intentions.

This example brings out a number of points. First, linguistic features are descriptive categories which apply equally well to sense and nonsense, false and fair implication, truth and deceit. Thus in judging how language is (ab)used on a given occasion, one must always be drawing on other criteria. Secondly, the context for a given expression will need to be taken into account. Thirdly, although all language is fascinating to the inquiring mind, there is probably a case (as Acton said of history) for studying problems: the difficulties, for instance, in trying to persuade the reader without taking unfair advantage, and conversely, the need to be critically aware of the grounds on which one has been convinced.

Admittedly there are acts of analysis that may be helpful in themselves. Thus a Cheshire unit on 'structure' contains the following suggestions:

> Students should be asked to bring to the class copies of paragraphs from various types of written English e.g. newspaper, detective novel, hobbies magazine, textbook, etc. In groups or pairs they should attempt to work out the organising principle of each paragraph. Asking some of the following questions might help:
> (a) What is the paragraph about?
> (b) How does it differ from the preceding and following paragraphs?
> (c) Do the sentences in the paragraph have to be arranged in that particular order or could they be rearranged?
> (d) If the order is more or less fixed, what is the relationship between the ideas in adjacent sentences e.g. chronological, spatial, inductive, contrastive, comparative, etc?
> (e) Are there any words or phrases which indicate the relationship between ideas e.g. 'therefore', 'but', 'on the other hand', 'similarly', 'likewise', 'however', 'in addition', etc.?

Actually, in the course of such an investigation students would probably learn a good deal. If a difficult abstract paragraph were chosen, for example, the underlining of words and phrases indicating the structure could lead to a diagram of their overall pattern — and thus to a stronger grasp of the meaning. Similarly, as the unit later points out, these cohesion features might reveal where a paragraph or utterance was not too well organised, and thus explain why it was difficult for the reader or listener to follow.

Equally, there are issues in using language about which people are bound to go on arguing — and may do so more sensibly if they have studied some simple facts. Thus the London specimen paper contains a delightful invitation to 'write a letter to the President of the Queen's English Society explaining why you agree or disagree' with its aims 'to dissuade public speakers from committing the following blatant, but common, literary offences:

(1) Ungrammatical use of "I" or "We" . . .
(2) Wrong use of words, more specifically of "anticipate" . . .
(3) Wrong pronunciation . . .
(4) Ungrammatical double comparatives . . .
(5) Vogue words . . .
(6) To try to eliminate "try and" . . .'

With notions of 'correctness', as with a number of other warmly held views about spoken and written language, a cool study of past and present uses of English can be a great stabiliser.

However, though a number of different interests may need to be accommodated, obviously some overall coherence is essential. In the London syllabus, this is possibly provided in the list of linguistic concepts which students should be able to use: they are largely concerned with language variety in spoken and written English, and with the elementary features of prosody. vocabulary and grammar that display that variation. The focus is very much on language and the categories are entirely linguistic.

The Cheshire units are introduced on an alternative method. Language is set in two main contexts of use: first in thinking, and the inner speech which is 'the starting point for our conversations'; secondly in social relationships, in vocational or academic work, and in particular in literature. A diagram indicates the interplay between 'personal expression' and the 'imposed conventional patterns' which 'we feel constrained to use' in formal or public roles. This leads into the main sections on:

Language and thought
Language and social relationships
Writing, and responding to literature
Language and vocational or academic work

To sum up: currently there are two polar directions that may be taken by language study at 16–19. In practice, of course, a working partnership between the two is possible, and even desirable. Thus, at times the evaluation of language in a social context is bound to demand some attention to objectively described linguistic features. This is the broader approach. The converse relation does not hold: it is possible to undertake elaborate systematic analyses without raising evaluative questions. As it happens London's pilot venture calls among other things for the study of 'educational, occupational, social and contextual factors affecting the forms and uses of the language' and explicitly rejects the idea of systematic analysis. It will be very interesting to observe the balance that is struck as the actual courses get under way.

There is one remaining contrast, which readers may already have noticed. Many of the Cheshire units set up a process of investigation by groups of students, and thus encourage speculation, hypothesis, empirical study, cross-questioning and critical review. These processes seem worth encouraging at 16–19, particularly when there are many cross-currents internationally in language studies and few received opinions. On the other hand, the questions in the London paper do tend to leave less room for active investigation, we feel. Perhaps this is a consequence of the demand for a 'specimen' before one has run the course. But it may well be that questions of a rather different design will be needed if an investigatory approach is to be encouraged.

2.8   Choice and Scope from 16+: the FE Contribution

We deliberately began our analysis at 18+ and invited the reader to reconsider the kinds of excellence to be recognised there, bearing in mind some of the fundamental aims and objectives of English teachers. We question whether A level should be exclusively concerned with specialised academic achievement, especially when, even now, the majority of the 66,000 students who enter for English are not destined for higher education. And in future, there will be even more reason to allow some of them the choice of an English syllabus with a broader view of social and personal uses of language, and thus with scope to develop interests of vocational as well as academic value.

We began at 18+ because the majority who currently stay on beyond 16 want a two-year course, and, whether they are in FE college or in the sixth form, a very large proportion of those who stay for two years finally take A levels. We have been discussing the courses, therefore, for the largest single group of full-time students at 16–19. However, within a decade this may well have changed. As the proportion staying on beyond 16 rises above 50 per cent of the age group, an increasingly large section will want targets other than A level. Currently, they have four main options:

(1) an entirely vocational qualification, generally with communication/ English as an important element;

(2) a combination of vocational and academic qualifications;

(3) a re-sit of the 16+ academic examinations in language, literature or English

(4) a qualification in English specifically designed for 17+ students (CEE or A/O)

Although separate figures for English are not available, we do know that overall in 1975 the largest groups were the third and the second (probably in that order), and the smallest was the fourth. This was not a matter of choice, for either students or institutions. At the time of writing this report, the CEE pilot work encouraged since 1971 remains nationally unrecognised, and uncertain as to its future. Indeed, it would be fair to say that the whole issue of 17+ qualifications is still unclear and, with 100,000 students involved, a national policy is already overdue.

It is in the first and the fourth options that active developments have taken place during the period of the project, 1975–8. On the vocational side, first TEC and then BEC have demanded a national revision of syllabuses, and this has already affected the communication element in some scores of courses preparing for specific vocations. Meanwhile, although hampered by lack of recognition, several regional groups of schools have been taking the opportunity offered by CEE to design a new stage in English beyond 16+. The project has been linked with both these main lines of development. In our view both have made important contributions to the choice and scope of courses, and a new synthesis may now be possible.

We must remember that while some students may leave the fifth form with a strong commitment to prepare for a specific vocation, many others will be uncertain or undecided about their future, or interested only in a very broadly defined area of work as yet. Others again may be wondering if they have the confidence to tackle a fully academic course to 18, and wishing they could keep some options open. As we review the new approaches in FE and schools, we need to keep all four of these groups in mind.

What, then, is characteristic of the FE contribution at its best? Primarily, we feel, its practicality and the business-like approach to the course. We begin by illustrating what this implies, using instances drawn from departments linked with the project and from the series of FE workshops organised jointly with Bolton and Garnett colleges during 1976–7.

In the eyes of FE teachers, 16+ students (and young workers in day-release classes) are users of language facing increasingly heavy demands — in college, in work and in adult life outside. One of the basic pressures is to use language to get things done. Thus in handouts, instruction manuals, schedules, forms, notices, technical reports, letters, public information pamphlets and advertisements, 16 to 19-year-olds face a barrage of information, advice and arguments to use or act on and there will be an equal bombardment, of course, in oral form. How can they cope? What can the teacher do to help? Many of the assignments and workshop materials we have seen take these demands to heart, and offer individuals or groups the chance to work on those that are directly relevant to them. But some go a step further.

To take one example: an advisory leaflet, *Free Prescriptions,* turns out on inspection to be very complex reading. However, there is a way in which it can be simplified, because of its underlying structure: it can be converted into a set of YES/NO questions, each one leading to specific advice on actions. Thus students can be helped to produce an algorithm on the lines shown opposite.

Reading a leaflet may seem a rather trivial lesson on communication, though admittedly useful. But suppose the teacher and class are concerned, not simply with *that* specific leaflet alone, but with a generalisable way of analysing and organising ideas — in this case, with the use of an algorithm. In a sense, this offers a fundamental understanding about the way some ideas are structured. (In effect, the boxes on the left indicate subgroups of the population, carving it up first in terms of age, and then, between 16 and 60/65, in terms of specific criteria.) This experience has many other applications, which teachers can elicit in further discussion.

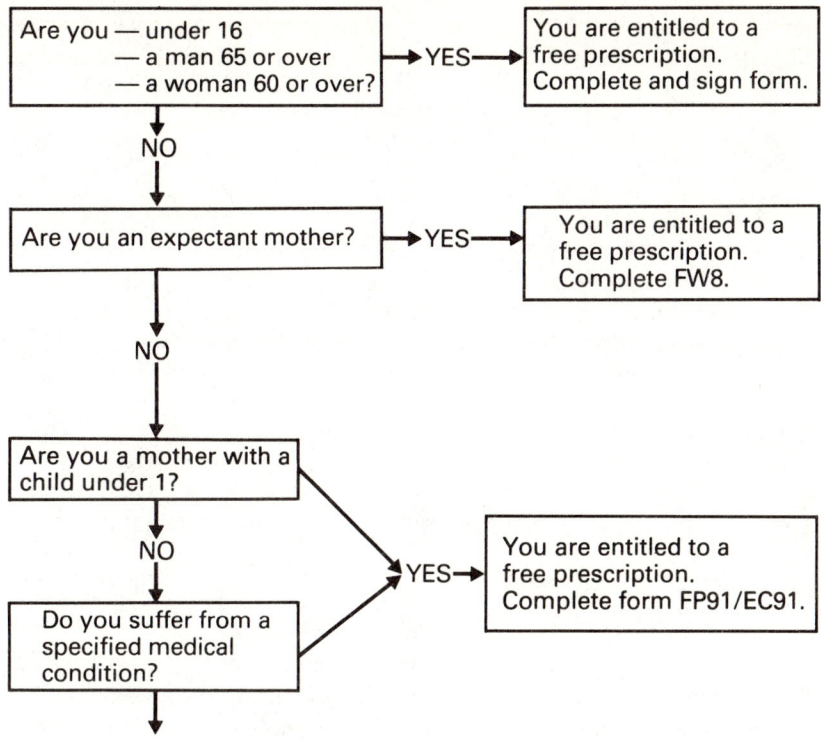

Thus what starts as a practical lesson on the content of a given leaflet becomes a much more basic lesson on a method of analysing and representing certain kinds of instructions and choices. It is very important to the teachers we have been meeting that the lesson should offer students success in a practical, mundane task they feel relevant; but, for some, it is equally important that the actual method of achieving success should be useful in many other contexts. We shall return to this interlock later.

The leaflets and written material in our initial list are one kind of language demand that can easily be foreseen, but there are others, sometimes related to the attachment work in a specific vocational course. In these circumstances, the teacher begins to see the students as clients, facing demands with which they need assistance; one way of helping such clients is to review the language they are learning to use, or about to need.

Thus, in one of our workshops a teacher brought in a tape of discussion with a group from a nursery nurses' course. Where had they thought it was important to communicate well?

— when you're writing for a job . . . they're going to judge you on your written letter

— if you go for an interview . . . [to] answer them rather than just saying yes and no . . . [to] express your feelings . . . bringing out your personality

— then there's the book side next, the reading; it widens your vocabulary so that's going to affect your oral outlook and your reading

— you have to be able to speak to the children in the nursery as well . . . expressing what they'll have to learn

— if a parent comes to see you . . . and you see her child is not dressed suitably . . . you've got to be able to tell that parent very tactfully . . . You don't want to hurt the mother's feelings . . . you've got to get round the mother so that she will understand and not feel embarrassed by it, and she won't embarrass you

— personal relations . . . orally as much as on paper

— I was shy at one time; as the English teacher brought me into debates I became forward . . . it's good to argue your point of view

— but you've got to be able to listen, haven't you? . . . that as well as talk and understand . . .

In a short tape these girls brought out a very important group of ideas for the communication teacher to underline. For instance, talking involves confidence, an ability at times to argue your point of view, express your feelings and incidentally bring out your personality. That is an important objective. But equally important is the ability to take account of the audience, to consider their feelings, to explain tactfully (in the parent's case) or in an interesting manner (in the child's). Writing may also invite a personal relationship — as we shall see in a moment.

With encouragement from the teacher this class are well on the way to framing some of their own objectives for the course. Their attachment work gives them direct criteria for judging the value of what they are learning in communication, but it is already clear that the objectives they now foresee are going to be relevant on many other social occasions. How can they learn to tackle these broader objectives, with the teacher's help?

There is a range of possibilities, the teachers would reply, ranging from real encounters with people to simulations, games and role play. The appropriate form depends on the objective. Suppose you are expected at work — or in college — to master a lot of written information quickly on a new topic: one method is to draw up a set of questions you can answer from it. Thus, let the whole class provide questions based on the information, study the data-sheet, and take turns in a 'Mastermind' contest to see how well it has been absorbed. Finally generalise on the method.

Letters can take us a step nearer realism. With the nursery nurses, for example, begin by asking what ideas they have of the different kinds of letter they will be asked to write, hoping to elicit at least three main types: letters to your 'masters', to parents and to specialists. Illustrate with a file of letters, slightly fictionalising on a real nursery. Take two examples for groups to read, discussing 'How would you feel if you received this letter?' — as a nurse, as a parent, or as a local authority staff member. Move to class analysis of the tone and sense of audience for single letters, some badly judged in tone. Define with the class a demanding situation for a letter, asking groups to prepare and exchange drafts. Study one together perhaps on the OHP, to consider whether all the challenges had been met. Finally, try to list questions that might be used as an aid in drafting:

What attitude are we taking and trying to convey?

How should we organise our points? Etc.

These ideas come from two teachers planning in a workshop. But it is important to have a practical outcome for such preparatory work. Thus, it is a great pleasure, one teacher commented, to have students actually say 'You'd better sit us down and teach us how to write a letter', simply because they have the real need to produce a good one. Not all demands will be external, though. A first-year group of catering students, for instance, planned a radio broadcast, spending in all six weeks in preparing and finally producing a series of tapes. There was discussion and planning of items to include; writing, criticism, and in some cases précis of sections of script; and the formal presentation on the tape. The first bulletin, which started with the week's news in the catering section (including gossip) and the description of a trip to a catering exhibition, was in heavy demand during tutorial time. This is a task which brings simulation a step closer to reality — and thus to the demands and satisfactions of actual success.

Sometimes, however, the work will take students out of college and we have reported fully in our booklets how a first-year group of mining technician students became involved in a serious study of the Vale of Belvoir issue, a social question of direct relevance to their industry. The point of such projects, in the teacher's view, is the demand they inevitably set up for reading and research, field study, organisation of visits and interviews, the interviewing itself (whether face to face or by phone), the selection of material and the preparation of reports — a very wide range of practical comunication tasks with a clear sense of purpose.

What has particularly impressed us in projects of this kind — whether in FE or schools — has been the care taken when briefing the students both to offer them an independent, adult role and to alert them to the need to check and consult at specific stages in their work. In this way communication objectives are often explicitly brought to the students' attention as they work on their assignment. Here, for instance, is part of the initial briefing for a second-year diploma group of photography students.

> *Aim.* The aim of this assignment is to provide you with a practical task through which specific skills of communication may be developed. You will be involved in communicating information through: the spoken word, the written word, photographs and graphics.
>
> *Brief.* Your task is to choose a particular aspect of the city environment, to carry out research upon it, and to produce a report of your findings in the form of a display for an exhibition or conference, or an illustrated article for publication in a magazine. Your work should be geared to public information. Photography should be an integral part of the task.
>
> *Deadline.* You will be given a deadline to which you must work. This encourages disciplined work and is typical of commercial practice.
>
> *Subject. Set out below are some topics from which you might choose.*

. . . .

Discuss your choice of topic with your tutor.

Approach

(1) *Planning.* Decide exactly what topic you wish to tackle and outline your *aims* in following it through. You should write out details of the *method* of working you intend to employ. You should also list possible sources of information. Plan your work and discuss it with your tutor before beginning the research.

(2) *Gathering Information.* Consider all possible sources of information and select those which promise to be most useful. The library tutorial classes should have equipped you to find your way around most libraries. Letters should be handed in to your tutor; after checking they will be typed and posted on your behalf.

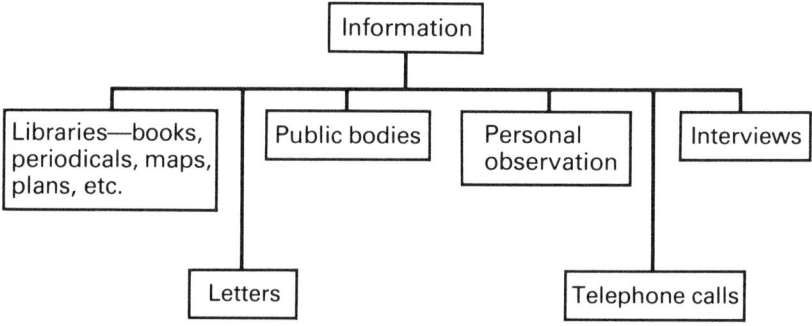

(3) *Recording Information.* The methods below are obvious. Choose the most appropriate approach for your own situation.

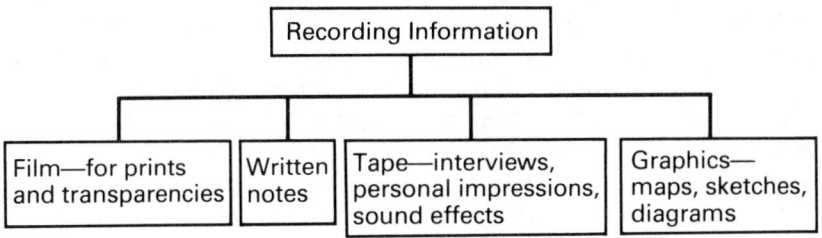

(4) *Evaluation of Information.* An important task in any assignment is to decide how relevant and how useful the information you have collected actually is. Obviously you should keep in mind the *aims* of your assignment. Remind yourself of the terms of your *brief.* The important thing is to reject irrelevant information and to organise what you have retained into a logical sequence.

(5) *Presentation of Information.* Your main concern here is *communication* of what you have found out. Whatever form of presentation you choose, the report should be informative and easy to follow. Two modes of report back are involved: a presentation and a short talk.

To sum up so far, then, we have learnt from colleagues in FE workshops the value of:

(a) tackling mundane practical tasks that arise as natural demands on the young adult and offer the reward of functional success;

(b) using methods (such as the algorithm) that offer a generalisable approach to similar difficulties in communication and thinking;

(c) eliciting from students, especially those with attachment experience, the range of communication demands they realise they will face, and basing explicit learning objectives on such discussions;

(d) designing a range of games, role play and simulations as a preparation for real encounters and the communication demands they make;

(e) offering the students independent roles, with a carefully prepared brief that emphasises the things to be learnt and checked at each stage of a longer project.

This is what we meant by business-like practicality. It involves the teacher or, better, the communication workshop team, in considerable preparation of materials together with very careful, explicit discussion of their objectives at each stage, but it can also leave them free in the classroom to act in a consultant role, eliciting problems, monitoring progress, responding to requests for advice, criticism and guidance.

This is a very important contribution, we believe, to all courses with a communication element, and thus to English teaching. There is evidence of the same trend, to be fair, in a number of sixth forms, and especially those which throw weight on practical enterprises in CEE English or in general studies — community work, attachments and environmental projects, for instance. But there are also sixth form teachers who seem apprehensive about something that feels alien in the approach. In part, they are right: cut-and-dried efficiency cannot apply to all uses of English, as we shall see, and there is a weakness in the discussion of communication in the fifties and sixties which reveals a certain blindness to major functions of language. In part, however, we suspect an element of romantic literary revolt against rationalism. For both reasons we feel the need to place the vocational interest in communication positively and clearly within a wider range of language use. This is the task of the next section.

2.9   Where Schools and FE Meet

Some, but not all, of the communication objectives arising in FE work have a family likeness. Completing forms, acting on advisory leaflets, following an instructional manual, mastering impersonal information and responding to questions on it, explaining procedures to parents — these and many other kinds of language activity in everyday life lead to successful outcomes, or failure. And if we turn to the objectives underlying the course units we have been referring to, these show in considerable detail the points where success or failure in a bigger task may occur: thus, the young miners investigating the Belvoir issues were explicitly aiming:

— to identify the information sources relevant to the problem, or their section of it;
— to distinguish the people or instructions most likely to respond to requests for information;
— to select the appropriate procedure for communicating with these sources;
— to make precise and courteous requests for information, both in writing and speech . . .

These were the first four objectives drawn up for one section of their overall course at South-East Derbyshire College, and applied, in fact, to other, minor assignments before the longer project. We are not suggesting that there will necessarily be total success or failure in any of these objectives, but there might be. This is because all these and similar uses of language involve 'getting things done'. For this reason we have come to call them 'action-oriented'.

Action-oriented language was something pupils learnt to follow rather than use in the past. In fact, it is the weakest part of the traditional course in English language, mainly because the pupil *did* so little — except follow the specialised instructions of teacher or textbook. At work, however, and especially in jobs that call for further study, using language to get things done is a natural and even perhaps the central task; similarly in active social life (including academic life in college) there are many points where success or failure in this form of communication will count for a good deal.

We have found that sixth forms and colleges that offer students independent, adult roles, naturally tend to set up the demand for success in 'action-oriented' language. Frequently, like the Melton Mowbray lads, students find they have to persevere in 'finding the appropriate procedure' to obtain information, permissions or an opportunity for an interview. Their early efforts are sometimes very naive, from lack of experience or background. This suggests the benefit they derive when the school or college takes explicit responsibility for seeing they can cope with such quite elementary and essential uses of language and communication.

When that happens, some departments make an interesting discovery. As recently as 1975 teachers tended to think in terms of learning to use *language*. But in our earliest seminar on FE objectives the point was well made by John Pearce, an assessor for ONC/D, that in much communication students are also learning to cope with new social roles. The difficulty of the nursery nursing students, for instance, lay partly (as they saw) in learning to be confident in tactfully guiding people much older, or much younger, than themselves. They might have the linguistic resources, but the role itself might feel new and strange.

In their particular job, independent responsibility might be very important on occasion. For others, like the miners, group responsibility might be equally important. Thus collaborative roles need to be considered also. We have found this reflected in FE objectives, which may now include both:

— to plan individual work in response to the requirements of the task, and the resources, including time, available;
— to practise in their work techniques for the organisation of thinking, particularly those which promote
   (a) flexible, exploratory thought and
   (b) rigorous self-criticism;

and

— to contribute to the planning and organisation of collective work;
— to demonstrate ability to work as a member of a group, including the tackling of difficulties which may arise from variations in working methods, personality, etc.;
— to practise in their work techniques for the organisation of thinking, particularly those which
   (a) facilitate creativity,
   (b) diminish blocking and other retarding behaviour, and
   (c) use criticism positively.

Planning, organising and reaching sensible decisions, whether jointly or individually, are an important part of learning to get things done, reflecting that combination of social and linguistic know-how we have referred to. The possibility of incorporating them into educational aims seems worth serious consideration, in school as well as in college.

Once again we have found FE teachers interested to draw students' attention explicitly to the communication processes involved. Thus in a London workshop, a teacher reported how in each group working on a joint task she had asked one student to listen to the discussion and record on a specially designed sheet whenever members of the group (a) initiated a new idea, (b) agreed and took it up and (c) disagreed. By numbering each utterance it was possible to see and discuss the pattern of interaction, and to consider the relative weighting of each member's contribution. One group of three found they had agreed a good deal and contributed almost equally, but perhaps needed to be more critical. A larger group found they had let one member adopt a 'teacher' role, so that there were fewer members initiating ideas till the later part of the discussion. These were second-year students in business studies, and the task and comments were quite sophisticated. However, first-year apprentices can also learn to spot 'blocking and other retarding behaviour', and to use such perceptions constructively.

We have been impressed, therefore, by the way FE teachers have brought action-oriented language and the accompanying social roles into their explicit objectives for courses at many different levels of complexity. This is by no means all that they are doing, but it is a very distinctive and important contribution to the design of new courses from 16+ on. In part at least their attention to this aspect of communication has been focused and strengthened by the widespread demand in vocational boards for syllabuses based on 'objectives'. Before moving on we should look closely at the positive and negative results of this demand — which has important consequences for communication and English.

In principle the idea of objectives focuses attention on the students, and the tasks they are able to carry out with success as a result of the course. Equally valuably, it has encouraged FE teachers and some employers to look with critical attention at the actual tasks that have to be carried out in a particular job — and often to realise more about the kinds of communication going on. These are obvious, long-term benefits.

However, because some jobs require only standard tasks and the criteria for success or failure may be very simple, the notion developed of defining the work in terms of highly specific and measurable objectives. This was taken up by TEC and put forward as a demand for all submitted courses. It is not difficult to demonstrate that, unfortunately, language samples rarely come in standardised packs. Even the most elementary objective requiring students 'to fill in forms correctly', say, would be unmeasurable in practice since the linguistic and intellectual complexity of forms varies, and success in one case cannot guarantee success in another. In the attempt to fit TEC's Cinderella slipper on to the Ugly Sisters of ordinary language and communication, some odd things happened.

Nevertheless, filtered through common sense, syllabuses in the form of lists of objectives did appear and, as may be seen from the quotations we have been using, the demand to think fairly concretely about the kinds of competence involved was very beneficial whenever teachers based their objectives on a careful analysis of actual communication. This was not something that happened overnight. Indeed, some objectives still owe more to the study of earlier textbooks than to actual uses of language at work. Even when actual uses were taken into account, there was a good deal to learn; more sophisticated models of communication were only gradually brought to bear. Thus earlier sets of objectives, such as those in the City and Guilds Foundation Certificates, for example, begin to look broad and undefined in the light of later experience:

— Accept, understand and relay oral messages.
— Use the telephone with confidence . . .
— Participate in discussion groups or business meetings to formulate decisions.

These three objectives are intended to cover oral communication in community care work. They certainly offer rough indications of areas of competence that should not be overlooked. But more recent work has shown the need to take a harder look at the processes to be learnt. Thus the first objective may be interpreted simply as memorisation and transmission of a sentence; or as selective recall of the relevant parts of a longer message; or as the preparation of detailed notes on the basis of a phone call in which the student may have had to query and establish certain key points, for the benefit of a third party. Similarly, the 'confidence' with which students use the telephone will depend on who is addressed and for what purposes — on the social roles and the uses of language that are called for. In these and other ways, it has been realised that early attempts at defining objectives were concerned with surface behaviour rather than the analysis of the process of communication students actually had to learn.

The demand that teachers should be as specific as possible in their objectives has had the effect, therefore, of producing much clearer analyses of communication processes. It has also produced extremely long syllabuses, with scores of objectives listed in sequence, each introduced by a verb in the infinitive. For those without experience of producing them — including most English teachers — they make intimidating reading. That is a pity. As experienced teachers of English ourselves we would make two points. First, the use of lists and infinitive phrases is an excessive formalism; actually the same points can be made in well-composed paragraphs — and with better communicative effect for most readers. Secondly, if English teachers start from specific course units and then consider the objectives that apply, as we have tried to do here, they will soon find whether these infinitive phrases throw new light on what a student has to learn, at work, in college and in social life.

THE TEACHERS' CENTRE
WORCESTER STREET
MIDDLESBROUGH
CLEVELAND TS1 4NT

However, they will not find that all the major functions of language are included, or treated equally effectively. 'FE has a better picture of what they're preparing [vocational] students for than schools . . . they're used to planning always with an end in mind — Where do I get them to because of external demands?' This comment by Diane Brace, currently chairman of the ALE, makes a key point. Syllabuses defined in terms of specific demands met by part-time students will inevitably tend to take action-oriented language as their prime target. We have tried to show that some FE teachers are not only doing that particularly well in practice, but also have analysed their objectives in depth, and thus have an important contribution to make to almost all courses from 16 to 19. Equally, some of them fully realise that 'the situations we place students in are . . . on the functional side: you've had an accident on your bike — what particular things do you have to cope with (what forms, who do you have to contact, and so on)? They are different in the degree of *specificity*. There seems to be a slightly different emphasis in schools on generalised appreciation as opposed to specific functional success.'

This puts it in a nutshell. There are two poles, as it were, in communication and thinking. Towards the one end students are thinking of 'functional success' in coping with specific, everyday experiences of getting things done. We have called this action-orientated communication. But there is the other pole, concerned, as we have seen earlier in the report, with appreciation and understanding of other people and oneself, and with notions of how society around one actually works. Language towards this pole is a medium for developing awareness, interpreting the life we encounter and reflecting on it. For brevity we have dubbed it 'notion-oriented'. It leads to objectives of a different kind, much less specific and directly practical.

Many of the teachers we have been working with believe that these two poles need to be kept in contact. Some schools, for instance, have been reviewing the fairly tough demands made by academic texts and assignments at A level. 'It is being recognised — it's a bit of a scandal — that there is a whole stratum of communication skills which our most able sixth form pupils can't necessarily cope with; partly study skills (how to research, sort out and organise notes, and solve problems they may face) and partly the more mundane skills of communicating with people at different levels — giving or receiving instructions, for instance — all those things you may never cope with in your traditional A-level course, though the general (course in the sixth may be making positive efforts to help.' Conversely, as FE colleges review the actual uses of communication and thinking in the young worker's life as a whole, they begin to argue about the need for understanding and awareness as well as skills. 'At the moment . . . we're talking about problems like insuring a motor-bike, getting a job, claiming money from social security; very specific, concrete and in a sense limited communication tasks. Now is there a way in which the same model can be used to deal with rather more complex subjects, unemployment, for example? Does this model operate? — is it possible to deal with something as abstract as that?' 'I think many of the assumptions about what is vocational, well-meaning though they are, are very limited and limiting,' commented Dr Frank Foden, an OND/C assessor. 'The vocational area is encapsulated in a much larger area of language use, and that has to be our concern.'

The need for a broader view of language use is particularly clear where the job itself calls, in its very nature, for personal and social understanding, 'community care' or 'public service'. But it is hard to decide where to draw the line beyond which it could be said that social understanding is irrelevant to the young worker! Within technical education, for example, with its tradition of general studies, there is an important debate at present about the recognition and weight to be given to objectives that go beyond action-oriented communication.

Certainly, in 1978, FE teachers are bound to recognise some very different 'demands': we have learnt this particularly from the West Yorkshire Communication group. There are local areas where, whatever their skills in a given vocation, some young people will not find work at 16, or even at 17 — and will have to face what that means in their personal lives. Many anxiously trying for jobs month after month also need help and encouragement to make a positive assessment of themselves, and to look more objectively at themselves as others see them. Both of these groups are showing in extreme form that work affects who you feel you are, where you think you are going in life and what life in your society has to offer. Equally these young adults today are a bitter reminder that, with or without work, you somehow have to achieve a personal grip on life, and it may not be easy.

How can a school or college provide positive opportunities for the kinds of awareness and understanding that make people confident and independent in work and adult life? We believe there are already positive answers, and that, fully implemented, these would make education 16–19 a new stage for the majority of the age group.

2.10   A Bridge from School to Community and Work

While vocational courses have been swept up in a wave of reforms, centrally promulgated, the 'academic' options for most one-year students remain much as they were a generation ago: they cater for GCE O level. In 1977 the NFER published a survey of the results. In their sample of 365 one-year students studying for O-level GCE in schools and colleges, a fifth passed in two subjects, a fifth in one, and two-fifths failed to gain a single pass. As they report, 'The wisdom of employing O level as the examination staple for so many one-year students is thus open to serious challenge'. Indeed, if the figures are borne out nationally, it is a disincentive to staying on at all.

Nevertheless, it is plain that the number of students staying on at least a year for additional 'academic' qualifications has steadily increased, and will continue to increase if the right courses are made available. So far as English language is concerned, we have already reported the authoritative criticisms made of traditional O-level examining, and indicated the limited effective range of the syllabuses. Since 1971 the way has been open for pilot schemes to produce an alternative qualification, the CEE. The irony is that while renewal on the vocational side has been vigorously pressed for by TEC and BEC, together with the RSA and other examining bodies, the main academic reform remains without national recognition. Thus in a critical area, where change is manifestly needed, teachers have had to work against the grain, as uncertainty about the recognition of this work grew. Some schools have reverted to O level; some have thrown their energies into the City and Guilds Foundation courses, a development of importance in its own right. Nevertheless, some have continued, despite the uncertainty, to strengthen and develop CEE work, because of its obvious benefits to their students.

In observing this work in schools, and discussing with the teachers their underlying aims, we have come to realise that a new stage is possible in one-year English courses beyond the fifth form. English can become an essential part of a bridge between life as a student in school, and life out in the community, in work. We believe courses designed on this principle are now worth serious consideration nationally. What is more, as a contribution to thinking about English and communication, they form the complementary half to the FE work we have just described.

The essential thing these students want is a chance to broaden their experience and reflect on it. English lessons confined to the classroom are not the answer. 'In the past we've constructed the lives of young students so that they are deprived of social access and the sorts of life business that would generate understanding and skill in communication.' But English can include learning from people direct as well as through books. When the students we are thinking of are offered that chance it can have remarkable effects: 'Most English lessons, you go there, either you do comprehension or you write an essay. I find it boring — I just don't like it. But when you go to a CEE group you have discussions, you have people coming and talking to you, you meet different people, you go to television studios and different places — you really learn a lot from it. And it alters your outlook on life . . .'

The speaker was a young immigrant in an inner urban school, and her folder of writing testified to the truth of her final statement. What kinds of course elements, then, are helping such students to alter their outlook on life?

Some help the student to move direct from reading to active inquiry. Thus, 'I was trying to think how I could throw them into something that was very different from CSE courses. It just so happened I laid my hands on a copy of Studs Terkel's *Working* . . .. I picked out three different interviews . . . we went through them, and talked about them. One of the things I was focusing on was the whole way in which he'd written up these interviews . . . I feel he's very good at getting people to speak for themselves and you really get the feel of each person as a separate individual.' So the class – on a C & G Foundation course — discussed the ways an interview can be written up, from the most boring to the most interesting, and considered the kinds of people whose work they would like to inquire about, to see what it meant in their lives. Questions were prepared and criticised, and armed with note-book or cassette recorder each student went off. Back in class they worked on a rough version in written form, with individual help and suggestions on structure. Here are some extracts from Junior's final version, which ran to over 1500 words in all.

Lois is a state registered nurse and now holds a nursing sister's post . . . Lois is twenty-seven-years old and is married. She is attractive and friendly. . . .

I wanted to know what she really did during working hours in detail. She does her rounds in the morning, reads out reports to nurses (male and female), gives nurses their duties for the day, watches students and pupils use equipment and machines, also makes sure that pupil and student nurses do the right things required. During the afternoons she sets tests (written and practical) for the students and pupils to do and gives them small lectures. After what she told me I said, 'A lot of the students must be frightened of you'. She said she makes them feel comfortable and she lets them feel free to ask questions. She tries not to be a bullish ward sister as she remembers that when she was doing her training she felt nervous at times and did stupid things. I asked if she ever lost her temper during working hours. She replied 'No'. The only time she lost her temper was when she was a student nurse and a patient threw dirty toilet paper at her. . . .

Sometimes we wonder what makes people choose their jobs. In Lois's case her mother always brought up the subject, as she did nursing. She felt odd when she started her training as she never fancied nursing but eventually she got the hang of it and when she got involved it was too late to opt out. . . . When she gets her holidays (six weeks) she misses the place and always looks forward to getting back on the ward.

That may depress some people, she says, but she has done that sort of work for quite a while and it would take her ages before she could adjust to another job, as she has done this since leaving school. She says many men and women can't stand the sight of hospitals but its different when you actually work in one. People who make these remarks usually go to hospitals to visit someone or have a medical but when you work in one it's just the same friendly atmosphere as a school, office or factory.

Her advice to young men and women is that nursing is a good profession and you don't have to stick to one place or hospital. Nurses are always wanted at hospitals all over the world, and once you're qualified you can earn good money in many other countries. Lois also emphasised that there are many other courses in the nursing field you can do, she says you can always get to the top if you work hard and further your education, as she is hoping to do. . . .

I enjoyed talking to Lois and as you can see she enjoys her job although it was not her choice but she made a go of it and reached somewhere. To end the interview she said she was scared of leaving school to start a life of her own but nursing is her profession now and it would be a waste of time to change it for something else. She can still remember that day, years ago now, when she went onto the hospital ward for the first time, after a six weeks introductory course in nursing school, when she pinned on her cap and the patients called her 'Nurse'.

Interviewing someone like this in depth gives the student the opportunity to learn from his or her experience and, at times, to show a 'generalised appreciation' of what a job means. Through anecdotes they can begin to see the moments of pressure in different kinds of work, and the control and assurance that is needed to carry a job through successfully. It is a first step to probing for a fuller sense of life beyond school, its problems and rewards.

The obvious complement to asking students to set up interviews of their own is to invite in people working in the local community (and beyond) to discuss their experience. The broader CEE course offers many opportunities for such visitors. Thus in some courses that we have observed a special effort has been made to bring in 'writers, journalists, television workers, photographers, Theatre in Education' and similar groups to discuss their aims and hopes, their work and the satisfaction they get from it. This direct contact with people producing elements of contemporary culture helps to bridge the gap the students often feel, especially in a working-class district. Students begin to realise that this, too, is a kind of vocation — that there are people behind the seemingly impersonal products. It is also a stimulus to many follow-up activities and suggestions, as we learnt in mid-course interviews with the students. 'We have been to quite a few theatres to see plays. We've interviewed actors and asked them questions. We tape it and then write a full report.' 'Hoxton Hall [Theatre] decided they wanted our school to come and see a play they were making, because they'd never done it before.' 'My depth study is about theatre work.' 'I think we should read more books in class together — *Of Mice and Men, A View from the Bridge, A Taste of Honey.* . . .' If the teachers were 'to get more poets to come in and talk to us, probably . . . [it would be] a much better way for us to understand what poetry is all about'.

A second kind of interest comes from social workers. In a CEE/A-level course we observed, the first half-term began with the theme of living in a multi-racial society. The course was built up from discussions of a series of local radio programmes, *Conflict and Contact*, and led to visits from 'five knowledgeable men . . . to discuss and put forward their individual points of view on the problems and solutions, if any, to some of the unrest which is now all too evident', to quote a student reporter. These included members of the Race Relations Board and the AFFOR Foundation (All Faiths for One Race), a Barbadian serving as an Anglican priest in Moseley and two police officers. Meeting a variety of people allowed the students to compare a range of different experiences and observations, to assess different attitudes, and eventually for some of them to make personal studies in depth.

Obviously such visits give initial access to a very wide range of social and vocational experience, in circumstances where the teacher is able to be of direct assistance in helping students to elicit what the speaker has to offer. Almost invariably, though, the teachers we have worked with see this as a first contact and hope to encourage volunteers to follow this up, as we have seen, by going out independently to observe, interview and study something about which they may feel deeply concerned. We notice that where CEE is assessed on a written folder these studies tend to become 'extended essays'; where there is provision for an oral examination, including a presentation followed by questions, they may take more varied forms.

Sometimes, such depth studies may be entirely personal. Thus Elizabeth, the student who felt the course had changed her outlook on life, chose to write an anonymous case study of the struggles of a girl who by the age of 21 had been left by her husband with two young children. The story made great demands on Elizabeth's capacity for imaginative understanding, not only of the girl's actions, but of the reactions of the parents, and the behaviour of the boyfriend she ran away with and eventually married. As we read it, it did indeed seem a task worth doing.

Others may arise from further visits or formal attachment: thus we have seen individual work, or work in pairs, taking students out to study theatre groups, local newspapers, community action groups, immigrant organisations, local authority services, nurseries and primary schools and a wide range of different kinds of social organisation. We have also noted the overlap between this approach and the kind of placement in industrial and commercial firms, or the social services, called for by the City and Guilds Foundation courses.

What is to be learnt in this way? Very often, teachers comment, it takes time for students, however interested, to learn to formulate the questions they want to study, the observations required, the secondary inquiries and library research that may be needed and the overall organisation they want to give the material they have finally gathered. As a result, however, these projects often become the highlight of the one-year course, the embodiment for the students of the advance in learning they have achieved. Carrying out the project sets up demands, that is, not simply for communication in different roles with people outside school, but for mastering certain basic processes in independent study.

For example, students opting for weekly placement in a local primary school were briefed among other things:

(a) to spend some time walking round the area, looking at the facilities, the variety and types of houses, possibly the mixing of different ethnic groups, etc., and to consider how the neighbourhood might influence the children they met;

(b) to keep a detailed diary, describing feelings and reactions, and recording incidents each week;

(c) to select one child to try to describe in depth from personal experience.

Thus the teachers have to help to focus attention, but at the same time to be open to individual interests and questions aroused by the actual experience. We are especially interested in the effect this has on them.

'I am enjoying my work with the CEE/A-level sixth enormously. . . . I find that I am really "learning with" rather than "telling". This is largely because the content of the course cuts across normal categories' . . . 'I particularly value the opportunity CEE gives to draw into the school issues and individuals that pupils identify with the outside world rather than with the somewhat glasshouse atmosphere of school.' 'I have had great pleasure in watching the growth of both self-confidence and social awareness. . . .'

We have emphasised up to this point what is new, but equally interesting is the way the elements of direct experience — visits and visitors, attachment and placement — are integrated with the established parts of English, already discussed earlier in these sections. To schematise the teacher's choice, we now see a pattern in which six elements may be closely related:

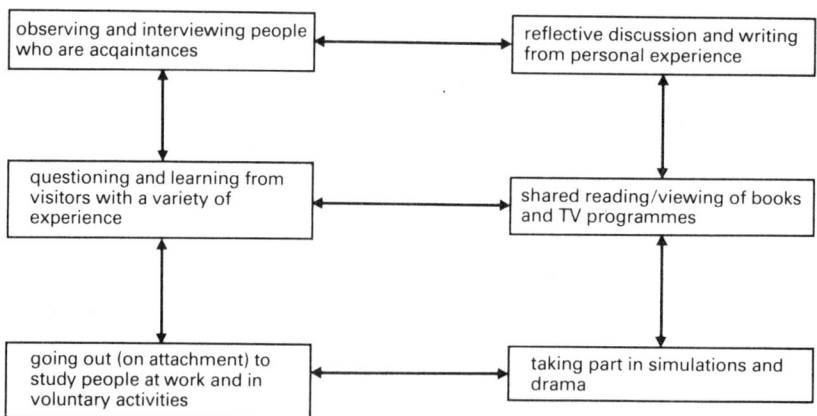

Thus we note that as well as discussing with people from the council's housing department students may watch *Cathy Come Home*, or play a Shelter simulation game that involves role play in problem housing situations.

'Documentary drama' helps students to encounter the experience through the eyes of an individual, to realise what it is to live through an experience. This is the role of 'literature'. By contrast even the most graphic interview is likely to tend towards generalisation and reflection. Both are valuable.

Drama, poetry and story have therefore an important place in the kinds of course we are considering. Sometimes they relate to direct possibilities or questions in the minds of young adults: leaving home, struggling for independence, setting up a home, deciding on the woman's role and the man's. . . . Sometimes the possibilities are much less direct, though they are significant enough to affect a whole generation, and its view of the world. Thus within the CEE folders we have recurrently found work that points to the importance of imaginative sympathy beyond the immediate, personal demands.

'Who you think you are' and 'where you think you're going in life' cannot be discovered in any deeper sense without an imaginative involvement in the lives of very varied people. At their best literature, film, television, songs and ballads can offer that possibility and strike an awakened response from many 17+ students. When that happens, their use of language may take on an answering quality. Thus in poems, autobiographies, character sketches, scenarios and a wide variety of forms we have seen the value for such students of the encounters already discussed in section 2.4, and the writing this stimulated has been fully illustrated in our booklets on one-year courses.

Overall, then, the one-year courses we have studied already show how English and communication can be broadened in the first year of the sixth form, so that social and vocational interests are allowed for and encouraged. A new strand of education, 'learning from people', is being interwoven with the more traditional strands of learning from literature, drama and television. This has important consequences. In undertaking independent 'depth studies' and similar assignments outside school these sixth-formers are actually facing some of the demands on 'action-oriented' language that have been studied so closely in FE. 'They recognise their own inefficiency in getting people to respond to them.' They have to learn to arrange their own visits, and to report and present their findings when they return.

The link with FE is of profound long-term importance. But so too is the potential link with two-year courses. It will not have escaped our readers that there are elements in the work we have been describing that would be equally proper and valuable in broader English/communication studies courses to 18+. In a sense this is not surprising if, as we believe, teachers have been making a major effort to define a new, central place for English and communication in education beyond 16.

To judge by the one-year courses we have been discussing, this will incorporate six basic criteria:

(a) Are students having to communicate and cope with a broader range of people, in adult roles?

(b) Are they learning to study and investigate independently?

(c) Are they learning to work, plan and organise as members of groups, with a contribution to make in presentations for the whole class?

(d) Are they facing and deepening their understanding of various practical decisions in their lives, present and future?

(e) Are they seriously considering the importance of certain experiences and general issues in their lives?

(f) Are they extending their imaginative sympathy, understanding and vision of life?

Criteria such as these call specific attention to what FE might refer to as 'communication', 'study' and 'coping with life' skills. They suggest a balance to be found between the uses of language for successful action, and its uses for reflection and contemplation. And they propose a direct interest in people in action, in the community and at work, as well as in documentary and poetic presentations of human experience. What is now needed is national support for the enterprise these teachers have shown.

2.11   The Criteria for One-Year Courses

It is time to stand back and take a more general look at the pattern of courses and qualifications needed at 16–19, using English and communication as our guide.

First, let us consider how many students may already be needing a general educational qualification below Advanced level. In 1975, according to DES statistics, they amounted to half the students entering sixth forms. Some would not be taking A-level courses; some would start them but leave before the examination; and some would enter the examination but gain only one A-level pass or none. Their estimated numbers were as follows:

First-Year Sixth, 1975
55,000+ not taking A-level courses
10,000+ taking A-level courses but leaving early
35,000+ likely to gain one pass at A level or none

These 100,000 students, then, plus a smaller parallel group in FE colleges, were relying for their main leaving qualifications on something below A level in standard.

We know from the NFER survey in the same year that there was a very wide range of attainment within this group. A proportion of those on a one-year course would not achieve an A–C grade at O level. On the other hand over 20,000 of the total group were likely to achieve A level in one subject. Nevertheless, for all these students — the largest single group staying for a year beyond the fifth form — only one nationally recognised target is currently on offer: GCE O level.

Common sense tells us there is something wrong. A qualification below A-level standard is manifestly needed; equally the standard set in its higher grades has to recognise achievement beyond O level. With so many students potentially involved it is time something was done.

The question of the levels of achievement to be recognised is the first hurdle. The second concerns the general aims of these students and the design of appropriate syllabuses. The vast majority of the 100,000+ students currently involved leave school or college for work. It would be unwise, therefore, to design the syllabuses as if they were inevitably destined for higher education. On the other hand, as the NFER survey showed, a surprising proportion of those opting for a one-year course *in certain institutions* (notably tertiary colleges) actually stayed for a two-year course. It would be unwise therefore to plan one-year syllabuses as educational cul-de-sacs, offering no way through to higher levels of qualification.

Again common sense suggests that on these grounds neither the A/O examinations nor the CEE pilot schemes are in *themselves* the final answer, though an answer is actually available if their positive features are combined. One normally assumes a university-oriented course, the other a terminal qualification without links to higher levels: these are their negative features.

On the positive side, CEE has produced broadly defined courses through to 17+ which it would not be difficult to link with an English or communication studies A level at 18+. On the evidence of the one communication studies A level currently available, many universities are beginning to recognise such a broad qualification and equally it is beginning to attract significant interest among the professions. Thus a combination of academic and vocational interests does seem possible. Given broader A levels of this type in different areas of the curriculum, an A/O style of qualification might then encourage exactly the kinds of courses that CEE has piloted. Thus, many English teachers would now like to see a broad syllabus in English at A level. So the 17+ student who did well at the intermediate level would then be able to stay on for a crack at the A level, and equally any students who found A level beyond them at 18+ would at least have a post-O-level qualification to try for.

What remains to be resolved? The main question that calls for national discussion and policy decision is the balance of interests in such syllabuses. In discussing the new developments in one-year courses we have shown how some teachers of English have extended the possibilities and challenges they offer their students. The 'personal development' model characteristic of the sixties has had a stronger 'social development' element grafted on to it. As a result, their students are learning to face adult demands and take on adult roles in their use of language within school and beyond. The inclusion of depth studies and 'attachment', for instance, allows wider interests to be harnessed: some students are encouraged in their search for a vocational commitment, some in their desire for social understanding and participation. From the student's point of view both are important extensions to the value of a course of general education.

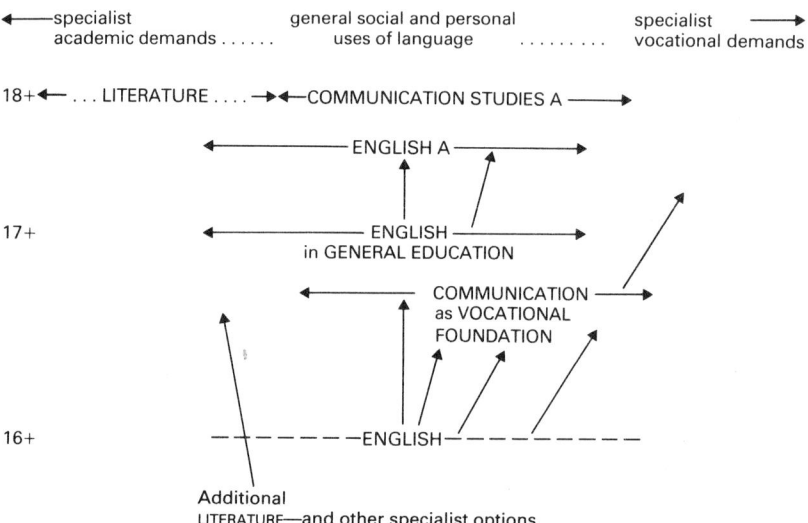

REVISED RANGE OF QUALIFICATIONS NEEDED

This seems to us a prototype for the immediate future. As the demand for general education continues to grow, this central group who opt to continue it beyond 16+ (currently rising above 100,000) will become increasingly important. Some will carry one subject through to A level; all will want to carry a range of subjects through, potentially beyond O level. For many, English and communication will be a key element of their course for one year or two.

There is an alternative choice, a minority one at present, but worth long-term consideration. The students who 'stay on' in general education do so because, to some degree, it offers them some confidence or reward. But there are others who, as we discovered in depth interviews, are finding equal or greater sources of confidence and reward in a foundation course with a vocational orientation. At present full-time provision of these courses is fairly patchy, particularly in schools, and thus the potential demand is difficult to estimate. However, it will be clear from the preceding sections that there is a wing of FE work in communication which is already taking 'social and life skills' into account as well as the broadly vocational.

Following the recent initiative by City and Guilds, such foundation courses are increasingly being set up by FE and schools, sometimes in collaboration. It is too early to take stock of the full potential or limitations of this particular approach. What can be said, however, is that an integrated course, with provision for attachment in a vocational area such as community care or business studies, offers some students a strong basis for a broad education beyond 16, and, if anything, communication should be playing a more central role than it does at present.

To sum up: the map of qualifications inherited from 1951 needs urgently to be remodelled in the interest of potential students in the 1980s. In the year beyond the fifth form, the largest single group for the next decade will be those who achieve not more than one A level and who now badly need a recognised general qualification with grades beyond O level. Some students would try for this at 17+, some at 18+.There are already signs that a second group may be developing, still looking for a non-specialist course beyond the fifth form, but preferring a vocational orientation from the start.

We could say that both these groups, in effect, require a 'foundation course' beyond the fifth form, the one oriented towards general education, the other towards vocational. However, it is not enough to think of them as 'one-year' students; in some 16–19 institutions a surprisingly high proportion opt to stay on for a second year.

If some of these students are to be encouraged to work to achieve A-level standards after two years, the 'post-O-level' syllabuses they follow need to be related to broader syllabuses at A level.

Further but slower growth can be expected in the second largest group at 16–19, those taking two or three A levels. Here, too, some students would benefit from the provision of broader syllabuses, while others would continue to need the specialist syllabus that fits end-on to a degree course.

Finally, the third and currently the smallest group of full-time students are those following specialist vocational courses. We look forward with interest to the development of the integrated courses recently proposed by the BEC, and for the lessons these may have for other groups.

A Footnote on N & F

In essence N & F is a proposal for a five-subject curriculum. This is a decision that should involve all teachers and many people beyond education, since it depends on a prediction of the kind of advanced education likely to be needed for living in the twenty-first century, to meet and fulfil personal, social and vocational purposes.

The facts are that at present the largest single group staying beyond the fifth form combine O and A levels for at least the first year of the sixth form or college, and are thus already likely to be taking five subjects or more. The main question, therefore, is whether those taking two or three A levels only, with the hope of HE ahead, should be expected to broaden their curriculum or not. It may be that on general grounds England and Wales would be unwise to persist much longer in the degree of specialism encouraged since 1951: this is really beyond our competence as a specialist project team.

What we can point to is the lack of an intermediate qualification between O and A level. Some students may already wish and be well advised to follow a broad five-subject curriculum. If they achieved five high grades at an intermediate level, for many purposes this might be equal in value to two or three passes at A level.

Thus if N & F is *not* agreed, we would emphasise the immediate need first to produce an intermediate level of qualification, between O and A, and then to ensure that higher grades in five of its main areas were recognised as a valuable entry qualification for broader HE courses.

PART THREE

The Need for Local and National Support

THREE LEVELS OF CO-ORDINATION

3.1 At the Local and Departmental Level

By a historical dislocation, rather than human design, education provision 16–19 has grown into a muddle; the struggle to give it a more rational shape had only begun in 1976 and was still very indecisive. The dislocation goes back to the days of grammar and 'modern' schools, on the one side, and colleges of commerce or 'techs', on the other. With the school-leaving age set at 15, many modern schools were unable to develop a fifth form for those pupils who wanted a crack at O level. For a variety of reasons, most of these pupils transferred to the local FE college rather than the grammar school. Thus during the 1950s, many colleges began to develop an 'academic' side, not only for part-timers but for full-time students. A range of subjects was gradually built up at both O and A level, sometimes interlocking with vocational courses, sometimes quite independent. Thus during the 1960s FE had begun to see itself as the 'second chance' for the academic student who missed the opportunity at 11+ or dropped out of grammar school later on.

In addition, while the range of subjects available in the smaller sixth form was often quite restricted, the expanding FE colleges began to offer an increasing number of subjects beyond the school norms; institutionally they were well placed to advertise and recruit to new courses, catering for needs as they arose and sometimes anticipating them. Thus, by the time comprehensive reorganisation was well under way, there were many local areas where an FE 'academic' wing had effectively become a sixth form college.

In many regions this happened without a clear design or overall policy. Few people in education realised what the full implications were. To take a small but significant example: even in 1976, the DES statisticians continued to publish figures for the annual achievements of 'school leavers' without noticing that since the early sixties, when the detailed leavers' survey started, many school 'leavers' had become FE 'stayers', and were totting up further academic achievements there.

What are the implications? First, there are two different institutions providing and competing for 16–19 students who want an academic course. Secondly, one institution, the FE college, can always offer academic or vocational courses, or both, while many of the schools cannot, or can offer only a narrow range on the vocational side. Wherever the sixth form is small and the FE college large, they are competing on unequal terms.

It is no part of our project remit to review the different solutions that are being adopted to cope with the results of this dislocation. However, in considering how a broader range of courses can be offered to students 16–19, teachers inevitably face problems at this early stage of expansion, especially if they think solely in terms of their own small sixth form, let us say. In our experience four methods are being tried by LEAs to resolve or eliminate the problems of achieving broad local provision while the numbers staying on to 17+ or 18+ are less than a majority.

    (a) The grouped sixth scheme, whereby in Tower Hamlets, for example, all sixth forms are organised on the same timetable, and for minority subjects students attend either at the school that has a specially strong demand or at a local sixth form 'centre'.

    (b) The linked course scheme, where one or more local schools combine with the FE college and each run agreed elements of a range of courses (usually but not necessarily vocational).

    (c) The sixth form college.

    (d) The tertiary college.

It seems that one or other of these schemes may be essential, especially in the transitional phase we are now entering. When the proportion staying on in a local area is rising from 25 to 50 per cent, the range of provision has to be broadened, and yet the size of the average teaching group remains relatively small. Each scheme allows the 16–19 institution(s), with LEA encouragement, to co-ordinate the overall range of courses on offer, so that they meet — and stimulate — students' initial aspirations, and allow for growth and change between 16 and 19.

In the first two types of scheme, a key question is going to be whether the schools are expected to retain an entirely academic role, or not. If our diagnosis is correct, education for the majority 16–19 is going to increase the demand for courses with both academic and vocational value. Thus, we believe, some students — probably a rapidly increasing number — will need the opportunity to defer specialisation in English and communication, and to relate their studies to broader social and work experience. Schools that have been cast in an exclusively academic role will be ill-equipped to cope with such courses.

We therefore foresee less specialised institutions at 16+, and, where it still persists, an end to the academic–vocational gap assumed a generation ago. This implies joint briefing for 16+ students on the overall local pattern of choice, with individual guidance at this and succeeding stages. It suggests a pattern of branching choices, with opportunity for changes of emphasis within a course, and for transfer between courses. It has important implications, which we shall look at later, for the pattern of qualifications nationally available at 17+ and 18+, and the way these are interrelated. And it is bound to put new demands on teachers.

At the national delegate conference in 1974 that effectively led to our project, the working parties who came together for the final session were asked for any general lessons they had learnt. The one that came through with most personal conviction was that teachers from schools and FE ought to meet locally to exchange experience. Our three years on the project have convinced us how crucial that advice may be in the future.

In the main, both in schools and in the larger FE colleges, teachers have gained experience in academic English or vocational communication — but not in both. When they come together, it is not difficult to perceive how this has affected their underlying assumptions. 'I suppose vocational FE has a better defined picture of what they're preparing students for than schools, which traditionally have sent students in any one class on to a very wide range of jobs, as well as further and higher education,' said one acute teacher in a recent schools and FE conference held by the project. Thus, in considering a broader course, 'it's very difficult when you're used to planning always with an end in mind — where can I get them to because of external demands? I'm like a police dog in the wrong surroundings.'

A teacher who is already so aware of the predilections and special skills built up by past experience has not far to go in imagining the possibilities of a new and broader kind of course. This will not always be the case. Among the teachers we have met some of the most confident and pioneering in their own sphere of academic or vocational education have been prone to stereotype work in the opposite sphere — both school English and vocational communication — in terms of its worst exponents and results.

It would be a pity if such suspicions (and often ignorance) prevented an exchange of the best experience on both sides. The most promising opportunity for positive exchange over the past three years has been in the conferences discussing the design of courses for the new A level in communication studies. No one had all the answers; almost all were eager to gather ideas and extend the range of opportunities they could personally see in the course. It was realised early on that the AEB and the examiners had no wish to impose a specific way of interpreting the syllabus, and that they explicitly foresaw an exploratory stage, with teachers designing a flexible range of courses, each of which would meet the broad requirements of the syllabus and the three forms of assessment. If these circumstances recur as further broad qualifications are set up in English and communication, and provision for similar regional development meetings is made, the exchange stands a chance of challenging and invigorating teachers from both sides.

We foresee a further kind of conflict within departments and between schools, as general courses are built up alongside the current specialist provision at A level. Initially, at least, an A level in English will be an underdog, without the protective support of literature specialists in higher education. Unless there is a well co-ordinated structure of 16–19 provision locally, some teachers in a small sixth form may well see it as a competitor for already scarce resources and staffing — a competitor moreover against the affectionately (zealously?) regarded study of literature. If, in addition, the teachers involved in the new course are actually listening to FE colleagues or actively designing courses with them, one can imagine the stereotyping that may go on — 'betraying academic values', 'selling out to utilitarian pressures', and so forth.

Against prejudice the only hope is evidence and experience. Many English departments — whether the 16+ courses they teach are specialist or not — are going back to fundamentals and considering the range of language their students actually encounter and may need to master, for social and personal purposes, for broad vocational purposes and for academic purposes. The humanity of literature alerts us to purposes that might easily be obscured or dismissed — on the shop floor, on television or in social life, for instance. So much the better. Does it not also open our ears to our fellow men and their experience, so that we learn from them too?

What applies to the schools may apply equally well to the 'academic' departments of FE colleges, where it is easy for the individual teacher immersed in O and A levels, say, to be relatively oblivious to new developments on the vocational side, and vice versa. To date it is rare indeed for the teachers responsible for language and communication work across the college to have a common policy, based on a careful sifting and application of the new understanding of language that has grown up over the generation. As communication or English elements are woven more tightly into the business or technical course, it actually becomes less likely that the teachers responsible will be supported and critically assisted by colleagues with a special interest in language — or that they will have the opportunity in turn to feed back into an overall communication policy the insights derived from working in an integrated course.

If professional understanding of language were static, and formed an essential part of English degrees and of preparation for teaching, this relative isolation of groups of 'English' or 'communication' specialists would be no problem. As it is, none of these conditions holds true.

It seems then that, in order to be positive and confident in facing the challenge we have described, teachers of English and communication need regular opportunities to meet within their own school or college, both to understand and to make a constructive contribution to a wider range of courses, on the one hand, and to a common policy for language, on the other. Such meetings offer the teachers for the new courses an essential support, and in the long term should allow students to choose among a pattern of courses with genuine relationships, so that transfer is facilitated rather than ruled out.

Except for the tertiary college, this common understanding of the local pattern of provision in English and communication depends on teachers from more than one institution. If the project's experience is anything to go on, the design of new courses with a broader appeal offers an excellent opportunity for teachers from schools and FE to meet and learn from each other, providing the conditions for setting up the new course are right.

To sum up: each LEA, then, will have two kinds of responsibility. The first concerns the overall co-ordination of academic, vocational and 'bridging' courses of all kinds, through the joint efforts of several local institutions or through a local tertiary college. Within that system, the second responsibility concerns the right provision for a co-ordinated pattern of courses to be developed in each major curriculum area, and in this instance in English and communication. Without regular internal meetings of the English and communication team, we foresee plenty of scope for misunderstanding, muddle and failure to give adequate support to colleagues who have the difficult but potentially rewarding task of pioneering new courses. Given such meetings we see new hope of a better fundamental basis being hammered out for language work across the school or college.

3.2 At the National Level

The framework on which all this depends is the national pattern of syllabuses recognised for qualification. The bodies responsible for this task are still surprisingly varied, and by no means perfectly co-ordinated. Once again, the system has grown, adapted to new functions and been dislocated by broader historical changes. There are strange anomalies and stumbling blocks in the way of any attempt to produce a national strategy.

This first became clear to our project team when we considered the contrasts among five major bodies engaged in curriculum and examination development in English and communication. The most centralised are BEC, TEC and the City and Guilds Institute. Since 1975 all three have been involved with other vocational examining bodies in a radical restructuring of syllabuses and assessment. Sometimes a national communication syllabus has been laid down; sometimes colleges (or schools) have been asked to design their own, following guidelines issued nationally. In all cases, however, the much more complex task of interpreting these new syllabuses into actual courses has been left to the college or school. None of the three major bodies has a curriculum development unit; indeed, a national R & D unit for FE was not set up until 1977 and currently has a staff about the same size as our project. Thus, for TEC, BEC and the City and Guilds, development work is in some respects very straightforward, in others very difficult indeed.

There is a sharp contrast on the schools side. There, the Schools Council offers a range of support teams like ours to encourage and assist teachers developing new courses. In addition, in a major subject like English, many LEAs have appointed their own advisers, so that a national team is able to support and seek assistance from a network of experienced people with local responsibility. (FE advisers with a special interest in communication are very much rarer.) On the other hand, the Council — unlike TEC and BEC — has no direct control or influence over syllabuses and systems of assessment. This is currently vested in two separate groups, the university boards since 1918, and the regional local authority (CSE) boards since 1964. Thus on the academic side, for FE as well as schools, there is relatively strong provision for course development when the need arises, but little provision for a co-ordinated strategy among the large number of examining bodies.

Both arrangements have their obvious limitations. On the academic side, for instance, it would be fair to say that since their savaging by the Lockwood Committee in 1964 there must be few boards that have not carried out experiments in 16+ English syllabuses and assessment methods. In one or two cases there have been remarkable achievements. On the other hand, the news of syllabus or examination development in any given board seems to percolate to the others rather slowly, if at all. Few of these experiments are publicly reported, and there has been no overall survey of their results. Thus, there was no basis for a critical review of provision in English, when the pilot '16+' syllabuses and examinations were drawn up in the early seventies. Yet in English alone, the experiments made over the decade had been a massive undertaking.

One of the values of a decentralised system ought surely to lie, not in the mere proliferation of syllabuses, but in the opportunity to compare the results — the typical quality and range of work achieved in English under one syllabus as compared with another — and the relative ability of various methods of assessment to sample these achievements fairly and accurately. This potential benefit seems to be scarcely considered at present. On the other hand, with a centralised system it is natural to ask — especially in the present state of our knowledge of vocational communication — how the national committees responsible for syllabus and examinations are to be kept up to the mark, and alternative models to be tried out.

In these and other ways, then, there are strange differences between the groups of bodies severally or jointly responsible for qualifications — the main instruments in current education 16–19. What most concerns us here, however, is the fact that in a given subject area, such as English and communication, overall co-ordination may be completely lacking. How could this affect the generation in education 1976–2001?

Given the prevailing British attitudes to practical experience and education, it is perhaps not surprising to see vocational and academic courses treated in entirely separate ways. However, by 1976 the numbers were already approaching a majority at 17+, and there were authoritative demands, as we have seen, for courses that allowed a proportion of these students to keep their options open. The logic of this argument seems to demand not only branching specialisms in English and communication, moving off towards a specific vocation or academic degree, but also a central set of choices which are less specialised. The question is: how are these less specialised courses to be defined? Who should be involved in their design and validation? Should it include representation from both specialist branches, or not?

There is an obvious danger in inviting specialists in English and communication — whether honours degree teachers or education officers from professional bodies and other organisations — to define something for which they have no particular competence. On the other hand, there may be an equal danger (or loss) in leaving them out. If the central choices are defined without reference to the specialist branches, neither will learn or contribute to the other, and the links across will not be established.

It is easy enough to foresee problems in general terms. Yet, in actual practice, things are currently very one-sided. Both at 17+ and 18+ (as can be seen from our diagram on p. 130) the new central options are being developed by the academic boards. Thus communication studies has emerged as a very broad option and as a subject at A level; it could well be followed by a broad A level in English. If this pattern continues, there are two potential dangers. First, the opportunity for broader vocational interests in such options may be overlooked or given less weight. And secondly, the link with vocational courses and qualifications may be weak.

So far as English and communication are concerned, it would be rather stupid to say the least if either of these things occurred. Developments in the understanding of language have been common ground between some of the most respected and active teachers on both sides, as we have seen. In its first form, A-level communication studies has been put forward by a group of teachers whose experience was in fact strongly vocational. Thus, business studies teachers who studied the syllabus in workshops organised by the project were delighted by the possible links they could make. However, there is no direct way in which this or any similar syllabus can influence — or be influenced by — BEC and TEC. Currently, there is every likelihood that their syllabuses will go their own way, without reference to the central choices. And for the best of reasons: vocational communication has begun to be studied closely, and courses that offer a genuine preparation for it can at last be conceived. This is an urgent priority. Ironically, however, the very analysis that reveals what is going on in vocational communication also indicates how closely this is related to language and social skills in wider use. Thus, as we have seen, the FE consensus tends to demand something fundamental enough to be called 'life skills', as well as the specifically 'vocational'.

It is not clear, at this historical stage, whether the vocational councils and boards will remain so preoccupied with defining vocational communication that they fail to realise the broader base they too might be helping to develop. If we are not mistaken in thinking they might indeed fail, there seems only one answer.

What is lacking? What has historically produced such an ill-assorted pattern as the following:

(a) 1964 Two groups of examining boards for academic studies at 16+, without any direct relation between the groups.

(b) 1965 An R & D agency for schools and the academic wings of FE but not for vocational studies.

(c) 1975–6 A TEC and BEC without a direct relation to the academic examining boards.

(d) 1977 A small R & D agency for vocational FE, not directly related to the academic course agency.

It seems we must conclude that piecemeal planning is the main problem, and the source is the DES. If this is true, it is only through the DES, at national level, that some coherence and longer-term vision can be achieved.

An agency is needed to review 16–19 curricular provision as a whole, looking at some of the major areas such as English and communication in depth. None of the present agencies can take on that remit. To be useful, it needs to be done in a critical and detached spirit: the system we have has grown imperfectly, in response to forces now transformed out of recognition. Some of those forces, especially in the 16+ examinations, have been known for decades to be educationally negative, 'warping' and destructive of good teaching. Others have suggested a far more positive relation between syllabus-building, assessing and education. Syllabus choice may be very refined within certain specialist areas, but quite inadequate in its overall coverage: a better pattern of choice needs to be nationally agreed and implemented. There are key decisions to be taken about the balance between specialist and general education, and about the relation between academic or vocational preparation, on the one hand, and social and personal education, on the other. They will continue to be taken piecemeal and equivocatingly unless there is some forum where general principles can be established, with the twenty-first century in mind as well as 1979.

These are major issues. In addition, there is the recurrent need to review and co-ordinate the work of existing agencies, the Schools Council, the Business and Technician Education Councils and the examining boards. Effectively, we cannot see how this can be achieved without more central intervention by the DES. It is within such a framework, commanding professional and national respect, that teachers will have the best opportunity of moving out of their reluctant, passive relationship with examining systems and curricular bodies.

A POLICY FOR CURRICULUM AND EXAMINATIONS
DEVELOPMENT

3.3 Examining a Student's Work in English

. . . examinations can be of great service in communicating experience,
suggesting fresh ideas and exposing stereotyped methods . . .

(Newbolt Report, 1921)

We are easily manacled by unrecognised assumptions. In the foregoing
discussion it has been assumed that, for the moment, 16 to 19-year-olds stay
voluntarily in full-time education primarily because they want qualifications. Writing in a worldwide economic depression, with unemployment
among school leavers up to 20 per cent in some localities, it is difficult to
assume anything else: the competition for jobs is so manifest. But thinking
ahead to economic and social conditions in 2001, whatever they may be, it is
difficult to rule out the possibility that by then personal and social education may outweigh qualifications at 16–19, as they probably do for a
minority today. If they do, public assessment with all its admitted crudities
will be on the wane, while the kind of self-assessment that includes a
confident openness and a respect for judgements from a range of other
people will be on the increase.

Actually, any system of assessment which does not encourage such
self-assessment seems to be missing one of the key elements in the education
of young adults anyway. In this section, then, we shall be asking whether
there are not positive contributions that development in examinations and
the curriculum can make, first to the student's education and secondly to
the teacher's.

Contribution to their education? No doubt there will be some readers to
whom this sounds a shade high-flown. In fact, self-assessment is already an
integral element of one A level our team has been working on: all students
have an oral on their communication studies 'project', and an explicit
purpose is to consider what they retrospectively think about their earlier
aims, methods and the product they ended up with. There are two sides to
this. First, they are encouraged to apply their (theoretical) ideas about
communication to their own practice; secondly, they are rewarded for
maturer perceptions about themselves as learners.

This example is a reminder that part of a growing mastery of English as
communication is the ability to take stock of a draft, or a piece of work in
progress, and to decide for oneself whether it is essentially on the right lines
or has to be radically revised. This 'self-examination' is something an
advanced student can benefit from being quite explicit about. It is a
sensible objective for any 18+ course in English and communication. The
fact that it is ignored in traditional examining is a comment on the relative

naivety of our thinking at the time when the public examination systems were being set up.

The public 'examination' of a student's work — to give the word its original weight — suggests a careful scrutiny, an unbiased effort to see what is there. Mass examinations in English tried to simplify the examiner's task (a) by eliminating face to face contact and dialogue; (b) by excluding all the student's actual work during the course; (c) by substituting in its place a small set of standard tasks carried out in unusually circumscribed conditions. The experiments in assessing English that have been carried out by almost all boards since 1965 have altered the 'examination' in one or more of these basic points. Not all the earlier generation were at fault: as we shall show, these experiments have incorporated several of the key suggestions made by the English Association in 1920 to avoid the negative effects of mass examining.

Equally important with these changes, in our view, has been the recent decision to try to indicate explicitly the learning objectives a given 'examination' is concerned to recognise and take account of. After Hartog's famous relevations in the 1930s about the marking of English essays, the main effort in the boards was to make marks in English rather less unreliable. The focus on marking (severity and leniency, range and distribution, agreement, pooled judgements, mark schemes, explicit criteria, etc.) left obscure *what* was being examined overall. Thus while most boards could offer very refined observations on the marking not simply of the English panel but of individual examiners, few could say more than a sentence or two about what examiners were looking for in the 'examination' as a whole.

This is a very serious weakness. Ironically, in terms of communication, the English examiners in most boards have been operating on a kind of restricted code, a relatively inexplicit understanding, developed among a small group of peers, on the basis of which they reached a consensus whether any given 'paper' was an adequate examination of a student's English. Provided the team were selected to represent English teaching of some quality, it might seem that no great harm was done. But this is to miss the point of a 'public' examination. Without explicit indications of the range and kinds of learning to be assessed, the examination is effectively private. Indeed, no examination of English on these lines can be ultimately accountable, since there are no explicit and agreed criteria set out by the board against which a specific paper or other method of assessment can be judged.

It has come as rather a shock that examiners too ought to be examined, and in order to permit this should set out explicitly the range of learning they are expecting to find evidence for (and in the case of set papers, to invite or elicit). However, internally the boards are familiar enough with the need to scrutinise marking, for instance, with great care. The other side of the coin, external accountability for what an assessment of English is expected to offer evidence about, is not an insuperable problem. Indeed, as we shall show, the methods adopted in guiding and moderating mode III and II syllabuses have already begun to suggest a solution — and to build up informed groups of teachers, with a greater understanding of the difficulties inherent in assessing English.

For there was a fourth simplification in the mass examination system: the majority of teachers were excluded from the process of 'examining' not merely their own students, but any students at all. If you look on the examination of English as an arcane exercise, after the manner of Worldly Wiseman, say, this seems a merciful release — and heaven pity the poor devils who have to suffer it, to pay off their mortgages. But, giving the word its full weight again, what teacher is in fact going to abstain from carefully examining the work of his or her students, or from encouraging them at 16–19 to make a steady and balanced examination of their own work? None, we believe.

Teachers do 'examine' and assess, day in, day out. But their exclusion from a public system of examining has very important effects. Unlike public examiners, they may never realise or have to face the severity, leniency or unreliability of their own judgements (and gradings). They may never have to argue and justify to a group of colleagues their detailed or overall evaluation of a piece of work. They may never learn to be fully explicit about the criteria underlying their judgements, and to consider critically the alternative weightings that might be given to different qualities in English.

A teacher without recurrent experience of this kind is poorly equipped professionally. He is also in a very weak position to criticise the mass examination. Thus a vicious circle is established. Naive teachers are incapable of criticising the methods of sophisticated examiners. External examining develops a mystique. Internal assessing is written off.

Nevertheless, the teacher may be uneasy, and with justification. Compared with the evidence available and waiting to be examined every month in a good classroom, the evidence collected in traditional papers is severely limited. It is the teachers' turn to feel the naivety of the examiner's task, compared with the sophistication of their own. Yet, as we have seen, teachers' preparation for this much more sophisticated demand may be negligible compared with the examiner's.

There were two familiar roads from that point. One was to capitulate to the external authority of the examination and the board, to accept the notion that, in English syllabus-making and assessment, they set the standards and the school or college did not. This was a covert message to be read in almost all the popular English textbooks of the fifties. The other was to assert that alternative, internal standards did exist but were not examin-

THE TEACHERS' CENTRE
WORCESTER STREET
MIDDLESBROUGH
CLEVELAND TS1 4NT

able, and at some point had to be abandoned in the face of external demands. Neither road seems to lead to a responsible profession.

It is for these reasons that, in looking at developments in curriculum and examination, we shall analyse their contribution to the teacher's education. We see this neither as a side-effect nor as an ancillary aim. Indeed, in the long run, it is the evidence available in the classroom and the teacher's steady examination of it that offers the challenge and the foundation to any external system of assessment. If English and communication teaching offers nothing more than what a three-hour paper can collect, the mass examination is proved adequate. If its objectives — covert or explicit — are no wider than those of the three-hour paper, the external demands are reasonable. But if neither condition holds true, the boards must ask — as many of them have begun to — what further evidence ought to be assembled, what further learning objectives should be explicitly taken into account.

In the period since 1965, evidence from the best classrooms has challenged many expectations and assumptions about what constituted an adequate sample of a student's work in English, and an adequate examination of it. On the surface, oral English, drama and media studies have raised questions about the range of traditional 'papers'. Communication has offered a new, alternative framework. And, more fundamentally, a deeper professional understanding of language has, as we have shown, challenged the very assumptions on which the mass examination of reading and writing was based.

During this period, then, the design of syllabuses and systems of assessment has become a matter for negotiation between teachers and the board, and for genuine exploratory discussion. A new foundation had to be built in response to the challenge from the schools and colleges. Thus, though the mass examination system has spread to many more students, alongside it have been growing alternative systems that may be needed in the longer term to replace it. These assume (a) steady contact and discussion between a group of teachers and representatives of the board; (b) agreed methods of sampling actual work from the course; (c) the board taking responsibility for educating school representatives in the examination of student's work, and for giving them an agreed role in assessment; (d) the selection of standard tasks which can appropriately be tackled in examination conditions, and the adaptation of these conditions to remove unproductive constraints.

In these four ways, the boards have been learning to adapt the mass examination system and to take account of the quality and range of work students are actually achieving, with the help of their English teachers. It can be objected that such teachers are probably in a minority at present. If that is indeed the case, we must all ask what incentive or assistance the majority have been offered — and need — to break out of the vicious circle described earlier in this section.

3.4   The Changing Role of the Boards

In many ways English examining 1951–63 was a relatively static system. Changes, if they occurred at all, took place within a paper, or more likely within a particular type of question. All language papers — even those set by vocational boards — had a strong family likeness; similarly with literature. Differences lay mainly in the imagination and inventiveness shown by the examiners in designing each of the familiar sections.

By comparison 1964–76 has seen not only radical changes in the boards themselves, but a much more dynamic role for them in education. The 1951 conception of the curriculum effectively adopted the simple distinction made in 1921, in the first national report on the teaching of English in England: there was 'the power of communication in English' on the one side, and 'the appreciation of literature as an art' on the other. In point of fact, this formulation was open to question from the start: on analysis, the explicit contrast offered is not between purposes for using language (*Literature* v. *A. N. Other*! but between productive and receptive uses of it (*Power of Communication* v. *Appreciation*). What is more, since 1921 and indeed since 1951 there have been massive changes in the practice of communication in schools, in the prevailing technological media and in teachers' theoretical understanding of the role of language (alongside other semiotic systems). Although the way these changes have been taken into account is often piecemeal and fragmentary, various examining boards have played and are playing an active part in the curriculum and examination development that is called for.

Examination boards actively pursuing curriculum development! To old-timers in teaching this must still smack of heresy. Certainly it reverses the anticipated relationship between the Schools Council and the boards. But in various boards, as we shall see, the facts are clear. Moreover, the claim is now explicitly made. In a discussion paper presented to a recent seminar held at the Schools Council, Mr C. Vickerman, Secretary for Examinations to the JMB, provided a schematic outline of an examining board's role that is well worth considering in detail.

First, Mr Vickerman considered four ways in which 'decisions taken by examining boards . . . must have had a direct influence on the curriculum'.

(1) 'They can influence the curriculum in relation to existing individual subjects e.g. their boundaries, their content, and the skills which are to be shown in handling content.' Positive examples include the decision of CSE boards to include oral as well as written English; a negative example, we presume, would be the decision to continue to exclude oral English from GCE O levels.

(2) 'They can introduce completely new subjects which extend the area
     of the curriculum . . .'
     In our case, obvious examples would be drama, media studies,
     communication studies and what we have called language studies.
(3) 'They can combine or integrate existing subjects . . .'
     Thus language and literature were integrated into 'English' by most
     CSE boards.
(4) 'They can redefine and rearrange aspects of the content of existing
     subjects to produce what become new subjects . . .'
     This would be the case if 'English' on the lines discussed in section 2.6
     were introduced at A level.

Thus, both by positive and negative decisions, the boards' power to create
and reshape the curriculum in terms of examination syllabuses is very
far-reaching. In discussing positive changes, Mr Vickerman put forward an
'active' view of public examination, which he rightly said 'has very far-
reaching implications . . . for the relationship between the examining board
and the schools which it serves'.

Mr Vickerman began with changes of boundaries, content and skills —
changes of type 1. 'The formulation of the examination syllabus starts with
the question *what are the aims of teachers of the subject?* It proceeds to *which of
these aims could or should be examined?* Or, in other words, *what should the
objectives of the examination be?*' On this analysis, then, the new or revised
syllabus is founded on what teachers see to be realisable aims. In our terms,
any changes are the board's response to the challenge of practice.

With changes of other types, and especially with new subjects, the board
responds to proposals put forward by 'interested educationalists' or 'from
individual schools or groups of schools'. If the demand becomes widespread, the board brings together 'the various groups who had put forward
their own proposals . . . (on which special examinations were provided
initially) to draw up an agreed syllabus and scheme of examining which
would be generally available'. On this analysis, the board is again responding to changes outside, but this time in the form of proposed examination
syllabuses, not practice — since in a new area, practice itself may be
fragmentary.

Concentrating for the time being on these two major ways in which
curriculum change occurs, Mr Vickerman asked how this had affected the
boards' role since the days when they traditionally thought that their job
was 'to provide an examination, not to dictate to teachers what they should
teach or how they should teach it'. As he indicated, boards may now be
providing a range of additional advice on new syllabuses, including 'notes
on appropriate practical work' and 'advice on teaching strategies'. Moreover, 'if syllabuses have introduced topics with which some teachers may be

unfamiliar, the [Joint Matriculation] Board has encouraged appropriate university departments . . . to organise in-service training courses'. Thus, as Mr Vickerman pointed out to the assembled Schools Council project teams, the boards are necessarily involved in curriculum development and (he went on to argue) 'action through examination syllabuses is the cheapest approach'.

We believe this is a case to be taken seriously. The implications for curriculum change at 16–19 are very far-reaching indeed. Is the analysis borne out by existing practice? In so far as it is, what should their overall policy be, as they undertake these new responsibilities?

There are two aspects to be considered in depth. The first concerns the role of teachers. In both kinds of change the new foundations seem to come from them. The board has to ascertain the aims of teachers of the subject in order to (re)formulate the examination objectives. There may be some idealisation here of existing practice, but the ideal is worth stating, we take it, and sets a standard for the future. In that case, how can teachers' aims be formulated and made available to the boards? We have found that in discussion with colleagues teachers may modify and extend their sense of realisable aims; indeed this has been one of the main purposes of our conferences and workshops over the past three years. Moreover, both in totally new subjects and in new developments of the old, these aims may be tentative and exploratory for a time, open to change as teachers share their experiences and realise more of the possibilities in the new course. How are teachers to formulate provisional aims, communicate them to examiners and advisory panels, and still leave room for joint reformulation at a later stage?

Questions like these arise because of the positive role assigned to teachers — a role that has rarely been provided for in the past. The second aspect for deeper study is the positive role asserted for the boards. The responsibility for assisting teachers with new or revised syllabuses seems to fall largely or entirely on them. Is this wise? And if they are to advise on 'appropriate practical work', 'materials' and 'teaching strategies', where are these ideas to be drawn from? It seems that the examination boards may be facing a choice of two paths, one involving them in a much more complex educational role, the other taking them straight to an authoritative position over content and teaching.

These are matters for major policy decisions, based on detailed study of the actual relations of teachers and the boards. In the sections that follow we will offer evidence from our own experience of positive relations developing and open to further extension, and suggest the factors that may limit them or render them negative.

3.5   Introducing New Subjects: the Interlocking Roles of Teachers and the Boards

In drawing on the project's experience of joint work with the boards, we want to use first-hand observation to take the analysis further. Because our experience is necessarily limited, our main concern is to suggest a series of questions that could be vitally important to teachers and the boards, as curriculum development continues at 16–19.

To begin with we shall consider the introduction of a completely new subject (type 2) at A level. In this case, a group of 'interested educationalists', experienced teachers in FE in the main, put forward a proposal for a syllabus in communication studies. The AEB took up the proposal, which was amended and finally ratified in the summer of 1976. AEB 'centres' were then informed and invited to meetings in five regional centres to discuss the syllabus with representatives of the newly appointed Advisory Panel, the chief examiner and the moderator.

At this initial phase, with a new syllabus area designed by a small group, what role could the teachers take? For most of the time, they wanted to elicit from the board the exact demands made, first by the examination, and secondly by the syllabus. They expected authoritative answers: indeed, when the panel showed signs of tentativeness or a willingness to negotiate over details as the syllabus was implemented, there was possibly as much uneasiness as satisfaction. The implicit response to a mode 1 syllabus was that something already cut-and-dried existed and the principal task of the teacher was to find out what that was.

In this phase, then, the board held all the initiatives. The teachers' role was very dependent, excited perhaps, but also — because of the importance of A level to the student — anxious in the face of so wide-ranging and novel a task. Their emphasis was heavily on the externally defined examination demands, rather than the potential opportunities the syllabus offered. However tentative and exploratory the Advisory Panel were, they were being read as authorities. And yet, the educational success of the new subject was bound to depend, in the long run, on the teachers' initiatives in planning and developing the course.

How can an examination board shift the initiative to teachers?

Given the almost inevitable dependency that is set up in the circumstances we observed, it has a very difficult task — supposing it is aware that it exists. It is almost essential in the next stage to publish a recommended book list, and in the light of questions at the initial meetings to prepare detailed notes for guidance. In these respects, the board keeps the initiative. But somehow, in planning a course, teachers have surely got to take on an independent role, unless, that is, their work week by week is simply to be modelled on the specimen papers or on the treatment offered by recommended books (supposing they exist for such a new subject).

The development of new 'courses', new programmes of work, is the responsibility and prerogative of teachers, not examining boards. If the board intervenes directly or indirectly in this process, the course outlines, approaches and materials that result are likely to be seen as authoritative. They will not need to be imposed: they will simply tend to be adopted. (There is enough evidence of this happening with established courses, from the sales of textbooks by chief examiners.) There seems to be only one solution: some independent agency is needed whose effective role is to encourage the teachers to begin to take the initiative, first in course design, and finally (following Mr Vickerman's model) in the active revision of syllabuses. Otherwise his question 'What are the aims of teachers of the subject?' becomes 'What did the board indicate the aims were to be?'

In the case under discussion, by agreement with the AEB and the Panel, our project team acted as such an agency for the second phase. With a nationally available syllabus this was not altogether easy. Ideally, regular regional or local meetings are needed, running through the two years of the course in the case of an A level. The second best — adopted in this case — is to convene planning conferences in two (or more) major centres.

The primary aim of such conferences is to draw out teachers' existing experience and resources, to pool these experiences, and from that starting point to produce and analytically describe a range of potential approaches to the course itself. That is to say, teachers must feel they have something to offer, colleagues (not authorities) they can learn from and practical ways of planning ahead. At the same time, they want to see alternatives worth considering in depth at their leisure, and to have the stimulus to strengthen and extend their own resources. In the case of communication studies there was a particular need to draw in specialisms besides English, and yet to seek for some overall integration of the rather baffling variety of elements.

This is quite a complex task in itself. In addition, the conferences must necessarily set up an exchange between the teachers and the board's representatives, and on our observations this inevitably involves some reversion to the dependent role. For example, it was only by unusual tact and determination that the AEB avoided the trap at this stage of accepting teachers' demands for a short-list of three or four textbooks and/or a list of the concepts to be covered; in the end, however, teachers did seem to recognise that in an exploratory phase of defining a new subject both of these steps could be against their own interests.

In a third phase, the successes and failures of the initial course have to be exchanged and sifted, and ideas for the most unfamiliar areas discussed in some depth. In communication studies we were able to follow teachers' suggestions and base the second summer conference on presentations by student groups, drawing on their work during the first two terms. This produced a fuller and more graphic account of work in progress than teachers' summaries could have done, and emphasised the adult role offered to students by an A-level course worth its salt.

In the first conferences to discuss their actual courses, teachers can feel very exposed — and no doubt censor themselves accordingly — if there is any sense of an authoritative observer looking on at their work. By the later conferences, on the other hand, confidence has grown and teachers are more familiar with each other's work. There is a strong sense of joint achievements and with it a good opportunity for the development 'agency' to hand over its organising role to regional committees, formal or informal. In the case of communication studies, this happened at the end of the second summer conference.

This handing over, and the continued existence of teacher-organised groups, is essential. First, it probably takes three to five years for any department to feel that, given the staff and resources available, it has fully exploited the possibilities of a new syllabus. Secondly, about the same period will probably be needed by the board to weigh up the full potential of the system of assessment. These two things are not independent, of course. A clearer sense of the aims actually being realised by teachers is a better foundation for assessment; an assessment grounded on a clear sense of the realisable aims is a better incentive to teaching and learning. Thus, in communication studies, for example, the moderating team are seeing the full range of course work projects submitted for assessment, and on that basis have been able to offer critical advice, sharpening teachers' awareness of students' potential achievement in this section; similarly, teachers' comments on the demands of the specimen essay paper already have been helpful to the examiners. What seems to be called for, then, is a collaborative dialogue between teachers and examiners. At some point, we feel, the existence of an external agency could get in the way of such collaboration.

How can genuine collaboration be set up? This again is not as simple as it might seem. One natural focus is a joint discussion after the assessment has been made each year. But consider the two sides more closely. The examining team will have given many hours to the design of the new 'papers', the scrutiny of course and examination work from a range of different departments, and the evaluation of the whole process. Will groups of teachers have had the opportunity to meet and discuss the available evidence with something approaching this thoroughness? Will they have tested their individual judgement against that of a range of different departments, discovering where there is firm common ground? If not, the two sides cannot speak on equal terms. For both these reasons, then, it is an important part of curriculum development to ensure that teachers have support for regional meetings, in order to consider the way the system of assessment is currently working and the possibility of making constructive suggestions for the future. More important, teachers can help the examiners realise how the assessment system is having positive and negative feedback into actual courses, and thus set up a joint discussion of the best ways of increasing the first effect and eliminating the second.

In this section, then, we have considered some of the key development questions that may arise when a new subject is made nationally available by a board. Naturally we are not assuming that these are the only questions. For instance, we have not discussed the provision of in-service support, so that teachers can develop a better theoretical perspective, or strengthen their practical expertise in a new subject. What we have pursued is a central theme that calls for further discussion nationally, we believe. The theme is the relationship between the teachers organising the new courses, and the examiners and panel organising the system of qualification. Is this to be a collaborative enterprise, or not? Is the power and responsibility to be shared, or not? Without the existence of some independent agency to assist the teachers we believe that boards inevitably run the risk of assuming power, consciously or unconsciously, and relegating teachers to a dependent role in curriculum development.

We have indicated some critical points in each phase where initiative should pass to the teachers, or be shared by the two sides, working on equal terms as colleagues in an educational venture. This sharing of the initiative will depend on conscious provision, much of it neglected or not even seriously considered in the past.

If our analysis is worth serious consideration, there are lessons for the immediate future. As a Schools Council team, we are much more aware than we were three years ago of the role of the boards in curriculum development. Each of the four changes described in section 3.4 offers an opportunity for collaborative learning; if we had our time again, we would be better equipped to define what teams such as ours had to offer the boards. Similarly we can see that other groups, not necessarily full-time development teams, could act as the 'independent agency', provided that they were responsible to a steering committee capable of reviewing the whole process, teaching and learning as well as assessing.

Our main immediate concern is for vocational teachers of communication, who have been carrying through a complex national restructuring of their courses, largely without direct support of this kind. Where strong teacher-organised groups already existed, as in West Yorkshire, they seem to have taken this in their stride. Here and elsewhere, the colleges of education (techs) have given some valuable support to teacher groups. In Inner London the LEA had already available a strong team of teacher advisers in communication. Nevertheless, in various regions we have met a strong feeling among FE teachers that the initiative lay entirely at the centre, and that their role was essentially subservient to it. It seems that a pattern of regional support agencies needs to be urgently considered, with a clear policy of restoring the initiative to the teachers.

Wherever schools or colleges feel threatened or pressurised by mode 1 examination changes, such feelings are a poor foundation for the essential task of designing new courses to exploit the improvements and extensions offered in the syllabus. With a new subject teachers can opt in to teaching it; with revisions of existing subjects, they find it hard to opt out. And yet one must acknowledge that many English syllabuses or examinations do need improving, as the available theory of language and learning and the available evidence of potential achievements continues to challenge past theory and practice. Let us look more carefully, then, at what may be required when changes are introduced into an existing subject with deeply rooted traditions in teaching and examining.

3.6   Changes in Traditional Subjects and Methods of Assessment: the Teacher's Task

For our main example in this section we consider work going on in a pilot scheme to modify the syllabus and assessment in A-level literature. In this case the proposal for a mode I was put forward, rather as a last resort, when half a dozen local groups of teachers reported in our first year that they had had their mode III proposals turned down. The project team called a conference to discuss the next step, and elicited the fact that three basic changes were common ground among all groups. Following a proposal from the teachers, we wrote on their behalf to the English A-Level Committee, asking if the boards were prepared to mount a mode 1 incorporating the proposed changes. Finally, the AEB agreed to do so; the new syllabus was circulated to AEB centres and via the project to English advisers and all groups we knew to be interested. In the event it was largely existing AEB centres that took up the proposal, and indeed for all the departments concerned this was effectively an externally produced syllabus.

The strategy adopted for the pilot experiment was to set up four regional consortia of teachers, in three cases with the direct support of LEA English advisers. In those three consortia, provision was made both for a one-day meeting each term with a regional 'moderator' appointed by the board, and (by agreement) for additional development meetings co-ordinated by members of the project team. Thus we have had the opportunity both to attend the moderators' meetings and, together with the teachers, advisers and the moderator in each of the three consortia, to plan further practical workshops during the first year of the course. In addition, we asked one department in each consortium if we might attend some of their internal meetings and, with their help, document something of the process of translating the syllabus into a programme of work. In what follows we shall be generalising on a mass of observations made by all three members of the team.

First, what happened in terms of the initiative? In the initial meeting of each consortium we observed once again the dependent relationship: the teacher asks the question, the board secretary or moderator provides the answer. But this time there was a difference in scale: teachers numbered between twelve and twenty and board representatives one or two. Moreover, the moderators knew that they wanted to set up a working relationship with the group; we observed more than one of them in the initial meetings not being content to provide the answer, but instead inviting the teachers to consider what they were broadly hoping for from the new syllabus, or — where the rules were not already established — to discuss what they would find sensible.

The initial anxieties were naturally about the demands of the assessment system, especially at this included a folder of course work pieces and a long essay on a subject of the student's own choice (novel ideas at this level). With a mode III syllabus the teachers might have had more experience and confidence in trying out the necessary approaches beforehand; with a mode 1 some of them had simply noted a new opportunity and hoped to match it. Essentially, then, many were feeling their way, trying to find out how far the new provisions would affect — or even determine — their planning of the course. Imagining a new two-year programme is no easy task, and any uncertainty is liable to turn what seemed new opportunities into new constraints. We observed the ebb and flow in these feelings throughout the first sessions. How far would the alternative syllabus make radically different demands on their teaching and the students' learning?

Surprisingly enough, then, teachers may feel more exposed in a safe area that suddenly becomes uncertain than in an entirely open area like communication studies, where almost everyone counts as a beginner. In appearance, the syllabus was simply extending the range of reading and inviting a wider range of writing than one usually gets at A level. What, it may be asked, had the teachers to worry about?

The difference can be summed up if we analyse the contrast between two kinds of written task. On a mass examination model, the texts are set, and all candidates are offered the same questions. Teacher and student have little responsibility for text, and none for topic and title. Their joint role is reduced to answering an external demand. Effectively the board takes over the responsibility for deciding not simply the texts worth studying but the kinds of written treatment that are considered of value. This has long been the sole model used to assess English literature at A level, and all teachers have grown up familiar with its constraints. Many of us, therefore, adopted one or more elements of it in much of our teaching. Consider, by way of contrast, the provision for a long essay on a subject of the student's choice. With guidance, a student must decide which texts to read, which to select for treatment in the essay, what approach to adopt and what the topic and title are to be. Finally, there is the decision which draft is good enough to submit. Stated in this form, the model of the written task has swung to the opposite extreme. There are new tasks for the teachers, and new questions about their responsibility. What guidance, criticism and advice should they be offering? What, in these circumstances, with an individual student in mind, do they judge to be texts potentially worth studying, and a written treatment of potential value? Internal values and internal judgements actually do count — right up to the point where the final draft is sent to the moderator.

We have used the long essay here to indicate a polar contrast with the set question, but for each of the selected pieces in the folder of course work the same issues of guidance, criticism and advice may be felt.

Thus, the effect of the alternative syllabus was to give teachers a share of the responsibility for defining one of the essentials of the 'subject' — the range of written work that counts as worthwhile. Since their previous share had been nil, and they still remained subject to external judgement too, they were bound to need the opportunity for collaborative discussion with the moderator (on equal terms), and preferably support from some external agency. For the underlying questions go beyond judgements on a final written product; indeed they start, not with assessing, but with teaching and learning — with the problem of deciding for any given student whether the guidance, criticism and advice offered is the best a teacher can give.

It is not difficult to demonstrate that this sets up the demand for a kind of in-service education. Few English teachers till very recently had publicly discussed the question: what are the range and sequence of activities that might contribute to a (major) independent piece of written work? To give an adequate answer one must look behind the writing task to the kinds of talk, drama and reading aloud that maybe first helped the student to come to terms with more difficult texts, possibly with rather alien cultural assumptions. One must look for the moments when students began to take real satisfaction in the discoveries they had made, and actually *wanted* to articulate them. And from that point, one needs to study the processes of articulation, through the stages of notes, tutorial discussion and written drafts that progressively defined the task. Teachers who have studied these things closely, especially as a group, have something very positive to contribute in discussions with a sympathetic and open-minded moderator. (For the moderator, too, is learning and may be as uncertain about the potential of certain texts and topics as the teacher is.)

What has been said here about the long essay and the other pieces of writing for the folder could equally well have been said about the communication studies 'project', of course. The same problems were being faced: it was simply a matter of priorities that tended to make them a minor issue in the first year. The new literature syllabus, on the other hand, rests heavily on existing content, but seeks to modify the aims and the mode of assessment; changes in teaching and learning are therefore much more likely to be faced early on. If the teachers have in-service support at this stage, they can tackle the problems explicitly, jointly and experimentally in the opening year(s) of the course. Without it, they are quite likely to carry over much more than they suspect of the existing examination model for writing.

We found evidence to support this negative finding in a series of seminars the project team were invited to join and jointly run with a group of Leicestershire schools. The group was originally established almost a decade ago, and successfully negotiated with the JMB a literature A level with a course work element. In our early meetings we looked closely at the kinds of literature questions found in traditional A-level papers and considered their suitability for course work: many were felt to be totally unsuitable. However, in exercises to produce alternative, 'course work' questions, both the Leicestershire group and project team members found themselves sometimes reduced to blushes. It was these failures that taught us all to look again, more fundamentally, at the way the whole written task built up, and the stages of formulation that led through to a written piece addressed to a wider audience. This was a confident group, no less experienced than our own team, and yet over several years that challenge had not altogether been met. Equally, our experience showed that, given the opportunity to study the evidence and the stimulus of interested colleagues from outside, the group themselves had the critical power and teacherly insight needed to face it.

It might be suggested that usually the moderators were best placed to offer such support. In the AEB experiment they have certainly recognised the problem and in several of the consortia, rather than introduce early pressure for assessable written products, emphasised the opportunities for exploratory writing and discussion in the first year of the course. In general, however, while we feel that the moderators' sympathetic understanding of teaching problems is vital, we would not recommend that moderators should normally be expected to take responsibility for in-service support, for two reasons.

The first, drawn from our observation, is that every moderator and examiner working with a small group of teachers in this way has a complex role already. Their initial role, working as a teacher, is to ensure that internal assessments by each department in the consortia are related to a common sense of standards, built up and articulated among the members. In so far as the material evidence is new, this demands very careful guidance in sifting opinion, attitude and implicit or explicit criteria, if teachers are genuinely to learn. Probably, to some degree, the moderators have to learn with them, too. Their final role, however, is as the authoritative judges against which to match the departmental assessments. There are already bound to be some occasions when the three roles — teacher, colleague, judge — become confused in teachers' minds, as we have observed. Adding the responsibility for advice on teaching and learning could be asking too much, and place the moderator in a difficult position.

In general, teachers need to feel free to modify or reject the ideas about teaching and learning offered in in-service workshops. And while the board's meetings will naturally be statutory, there are many advantages when the supporting workshops are organised on a voluntary basis, in consultation with the consortium. The teachers may vary a good deal in their actual practice and those who come need to feel that their individual approach to teaching and learning is being stimulated and extended. In these circumstances, then, we believe an independent agency has a much simpler role than the moderator or examiner.

We should emphasise the opportunity this leaves for teacher initiative, too. Thus our team were particularly glad when two independent A-level literature groups — in Leicestershire and Sheffield — backed by their English advisers, invited us to help in organising seminars and workshops. Both groups were originally inspired by the local NATE branch, and pointed to the value of the voluntary professional association in curriculum development.

There is a second reason for advocating independent in-service support. This is simply that the moderator, examiners and advisory panel may also welcome an opportunity for collaborative learning rather than being stuck with a directive role. If they are, indeed, to explore the variety of new things that the changes inaugurated by the board make possible they will be freer to do so, and to raise their own questions, in independently organised workshops.

To sum up on our second case: new syllabuses and examinations that modify familiar areas may well set up the demand for changes in teaching and learning. This will especially be true when the method of assessment gives the teacher some responsibility for deciding the potential value of 'course work' tasks proposed by the student. Without in-service support most teachers will tend unwittingly to hold on to methods and assumptions drawn from the external examination 'question'.

In our view, therefore, the notion that curriculum and examination development can go on independently of in-service education is a fallacy. Syllabus and examination development of all four types outlined in section 3.4 will call for an important element of continuing professional education, sometimes on the central issues of teaching and learning. This implies that LEAs will need resources to finance and organise the continuing education of teachers working in curriculum and examination development. If schools and colleges are to benefit fully from the in-service expansion promised first by Margaret Thatcher and, more recently, by Shirley Williams, this is an important sector where increased resources can be of long-term benefit.

Both our previous arguments and those in this section suggest why these underlying extensions of teachers' responsibilities should be supported by independent agencies rather than the examination board. Thus our experience and observations lead us to the conclusion that the process of 'curriculum and examination' development calls for special kinds of collaboration between three parties: the inaugurating board, the teachers involved and in-service agencies. When the board chooses to work through regional consortia there are strong and manifest gains in the effective collaboration that is possible: this is clear from a comparison of our first case and our second. An additional advantage is that the consortia form training grounds for teachers (or, better, departments) learning to take their part in a 'public examination'.

There is a further question, however. If it is true that the process of 'examination' development frequently includes the demand for changes in teaching and learning, in order to exploit changes in the potential material for assessment, who is to monitor this whole process? Examining boards are equipped to monitor the approaches to assessment, and to do so with increasing delicacy. But implicit changes in teaching and learning seem to run beyond their brief and their current expertise.

Thus, when a 'syllabus' invites teachers to produce new kinds of evidence of a student's achievements, drawn from course work conditions, *some body* is needed to consider what independent support needs to be made available, and preferably to review the provision during the experimental period, to ensure that the opportunities for greater teacher responsibility have been realised in practice. In the case under review the effective decisions were taken in discussions between the board, the LEA English advisers and the project team. This is entirely *ad hoc*. Does not a new and less temporary relationship between the parties need to be thought out?

3.7   Teachers' Roles in Syllabus and Examination Design

So far we have been considering mode 1 syllabuses, one already available nationally, the other in a pilot stage. Both new syllabuses had this in common: although they were proposed by a group of teachers and taken up by a national (GCE) board, the task of interpreting them in practice fell to teachers who had not been involved in the initial framing of the proposal. On our observation this inevitably tends to leave the initiative in the early phase largely or entirely in the hands of the board. However, with co-operation between the board and an independent 'development' team, it is possible to restore the initiative to teachers as they collaboratively plan the course, and on that basis to set up a constructive discussion between teachers and the board, so that both can contribute to and strengthen each other's work. Thus, on this model, teachers do have an active role at a later stage both in the framing of 'papers' and in the periodical revision of the syllabus and examination.

However, it will be obvious from the outline that, while this model may represent the way things worked out in practice, it is neither the only possibility nor the ideal. The difficulty about such 'externally designed' examination syllabuses is that, not having considered all the alternative paths that were rejected, nor felt the implicit hopes that underlay the planning, a newcomer building the bridge between 'syllabus' and 'course' has to start at both ends. By contrast the participating teacher has an insider's understanding of the syllabus: making it is often an important contribution to his or her professional education. So the base for one end of the bridge is already secure, and in addition there will be at least inklings and possibly considerable practical experience of the kind of course this syllabus was intended to make possible and reward.

Thus in examination development and recurrent revision (an equally important concept) the ideal is to draw more teachers into the process of discussing alternatives and relating syllabus and assessment aims to the kind of course they would like to envisage. And thus Mr Vickerman's valuable definition of the board's role: start with 'What are the aims of teachers of the subject?' Manifestly, a critical discussion and sifting of those aims is one of the best possible preparations for teaching the course. Equally, *What are the best ways of assessing those aims?* is a question that helps teachers to realise where they may have been toeing the line to external standards without considering whether there were not other, or broader, values they wanted to see recognised in English 16–19. For the sake of all concerned, then, it seems worth trying to draw teachers who want to assert new aims in their teaching into the preliminary stages of designing an appropriate examination syllabus. How is this to be done?

There is, of course, one simple answer, adopted by TEC for the general studies and communication element of all its courses: offer no mode 1, and ask instead for mode II or mode III syllabuses. The fact that a group of employers of critical importance to the national economy did not, in the event, insist on national syllabuses in communication ought to make us pause for thought. Although TEC expected consultation with technical colleagues and with local industry, they left the initiative with general studies and communication teachers, locally or regionally. However, if we are anxious to preserve the initiative for teachers of English and communication, we have also to recall that TEC were not in a position to provide any detailed support to local groups or departments as they worked on these syllabuses and systems of assessment. And when the syllabuses were validated there was no national network of in-service support for teachers as they turned to the more arduous and complex job of translating each syllabus into a new course. These drawbacks, already clear when the project organised a national seminar on communication in TEC with the Association for Liberal Education in 1976, mean that a detailed evaluation of this basic approach cannot usefully be made as yet.

What are the alternatives in between? In reviewing this question, we have finally come to the conclusion that the answer depends not on the mode of syllabus, as we had earlier thought, but on the actual relations between teachers and the boards. Indeed, there was a more fundamental question: when it comes to the public examination of students' work, what kind of dialogue is permitted, or encouraged, between teachers with initiatives to offer and representatives of the board?

The answer varies enormously in current practice at 16–19, but there is a fundamental difference in the position of boards serving a given region and those with national coverage. We shall therefore look at each in turn.

Within a board, the detailed validation of English and communication examination syllabuses falls to the subject panel or committee. Their constitution and remit is therefore crucial. How are the members related to the departments the board serves? In the case of a regional board, many may be direct representatives. Thus, in the East Midlands REB for instance, each English department is represented on a local subject panel, and each of the thirteen local panels appoints a member to the regional subject panel. It is the practice of the regional panel to send out 'discussion documents on objectives, content, schemes of assessment, etc.' for comment by all thirteen local panels. Part of the remit of local panels is to 'ensure that syllabuses and examinations respond to changes in the curriculum'.

This pattern was set up in the 1970s because, in the words of the secretary, Mr D. J. Ramsden, 'it became clear that the close relationship between curriculum and assessment that many claimed for CSE was far from satisfactory'. A structure such as this, therefore, seeks to relate the two as intimately as possible. Let us consider some of its potentialities. A department with initiatives to propose can try them out first in the local and then in the regional panel. If they are accepted for discussion they will be sent out to each of the local panels; at the same time it is possible for the regional panel to make comments and suggestions — and to invite local panels to see what they think.

Such a two-way flow of ideas at the formative stage of a new examination syllabus would be a valuable gain. It would allow different kinds of expertise to be drawn in, and more tentative drafts to be submitted for exploratory discussion. Other departments who might be interested would be alerted at an early phase and could make constructive contributions.

When a new syllabus is launched, the regional structure allows for development work translating it into new courses to be planned ahead with the LEA English advisers. Students' work can be exchanged, collected and presented without much difficulty, and regional 'guidelines' for the syllabus drawn up in workshop conferences for the participating teachers and (other) panel representatives. Finally, there is provision for recurrent revision of each syllabus and examination as the local panels fulfil their responsibility to ensure that these keep in step with changes in the actual curriculum.

Thus, a structure on these lines enables a regional board to escape from the either/or logic of our earlier analysis. Initiatives from a regional English panel are *necessarily* initiatives from some of the departments they represent. There are checks and balances to ensure that neither individual members of the regional panel nor an examining team can take up a dominant role in curriculum development unchallenged. Revision of syllabus and examination is the responsibility of the grass-roots panels, so that participating departments from the start are invited to take a constructive share in collaboration with the regional panel.

So much for the general structure and its potential. In fact, as a project team we stumbled into this analysis, not from studying constitutions and terms of reference, but simply from observing the *élan* of some teachers in the SREB English/Communication Panel while jointly selecting some CEE course work folders for publication. It struck us that in this case the panel and some of the participating departments were the same people, and that the consequences for what one meant by 'teachers' and 'the board' merited closer analysis. Unfortunately, the postponement from year to year of any national decision on CEE and 17+ provision has meant that the project was unable to assist with any widespread development at this level: thus we are not in a position to report from a participant-observer role on the way democratic regional possibilities work out in practice.

Boards with a national coverage are in a different position — and in many ways a more difficult one. On the face of it their English committees or panels are very similar, most of the members being teachers from schools or colleges served by the board. However, national coverage prevents the establishment of anything analogous to a local 'panel'. Thus, in their case there is no regular two-way channel, arming committee members with proposals and detailed comments from the grass-roots to take to the board meetings, and giving them the opportunity to discuss the board's proposals and comments with a local network of departmental colleagues.

This relative disadvantage to panel members holds equally for teachers who want to propose new initiatives. They have no direct and natural contact with a local member of the board's panel, and no local group associated with the board in which to air their early ideas and receive criticism, advice and further suggestions.

When a board has a national coverage, we can see no immediate way of avoiding this fundamental problem. The position is very fairly summed up by the JMB: 'a system of regional representation could not . . . be used unless the regions were so relatively few in number and, as a result, so large in size as to preclude the establishment of a genuine community of interest among the teachers in each region' (1976 Report). In their initial role, this must have seemed much less of a handicap to national boards. But they now have an emerging, 'active' role as development agencies. This imposes new responsibilities, among them the need to foster initiatives from teachers whose work and aims challenge the limitations in existing objectives of English and communication examination syllabuses. In a period when, we have argued, a new overall structure of choices needs to be developed at 16–19, how are such initiatives to be encouraged? How, in the longer term, can an English committee in the board be given a sense of genuine dialogue with the departments they serve?

We make no pretence of having found a complete answer in the course of our three years' work with teachers and boards. The best we can offer at this stage is a brief review of the main opportunities, and the procedures we have observed in one or other of them. For convenience, the opportunities for dialogue can be grouped under three headings:

(a) while local groups of teachers are preparing examination syllabuses that modify or extend the existing English curriculum or methods of assessment, or both;

(b) when new subjects or alternative syllabuses are in their initial period of use;

(c) when existing syllabuses come up for revision, or an extension of the range of provision is under discussion — for example, through the report of the English Steering Group for N & F.

The first case is probably the most difficult to provide for adequately. A local group of teachers who would like to propose changes in syllabus or assessment, to meet their aims in teaching literature, for instance, may have had no face-to-face contact with the board. Without a local panel to take soundings in, they may have little idea what support they can expect. They will probably be unfamiliar with the board's procedures for considering proposals for change. Teachers working in such relative isolation are at their weakest.

One answer, of course, is self-help. Thus a strong group of Sheffield schools who decided to prepare a literature proposal to the JMB invited not only the local university professors of English literature and language, but also a former chief examiner, to discuss their preliminary ideas. In Avon, the secretary of a similar group circulated all board secretaries to ask whether they would be interested to consider a proposal for an alternative syllabus in literature. (One replied affirmatively.) However, as we shall see, initiatives such as these are no replacement for direct contact with the board's English committee. In only one case that we observed was a board able to help a group at this exploratory stage of their thinking. Teachers from a Hackney school were looking for some way of matching the A-level syllabus to their multi-cultural sixth form: an opportunity to discuss with the schools liaison officer for the London Board radically changed their understanding of the scope and complexity of their task. We have met many other groups in our three years for whom such early advice would have been valuable.

Without it, what happens? Of five mode III A level syllabuses that we know to have been submitted to English committees, four were effectively rejected at the first meeting between teachers and the committee. We believe that committees would prefer not to be placed in this position for the one occasion when they can talk direct to schools served by the board. If we are right, some system of earlier liaison such as London offered would certainly be a help.

With the remaining group, that in Sheffield, the proposal was not immediately accepted but a dialogue did begin. A working party from the committee met group representatives and probed various sections of the submission, raising questions and offering suggestions. Both sides had then to report back, and a further meeting was arranged. Thus a further obstacle arises in the way of constructive dialogue. Committees formed of serving teachers who meet once a term are bound to slow up the process of negotiations and discussion, unless they delegate full powers to their working party. If discusssions on a new syllabus take a year, under the board's provisions possibly a third of the committee members may have changed. If two years, two-thirds. Yet we know of more than one alternative A level in English that it took between two and three years to design and win acceptance for. We are not clear what would be the best way of resolving this difficulty.

Currently, our first heading seems to offer the greatest problems for the boards, whatever goodwill there may be. With the remaining two there is stronger evidence that the problems are not intractable. Thus, some years ago the Cambridge Board took the first steps to introduce a new type of 'open book' question in O-level literature, and since that time has held an annual meeting with participating departments to review the value of the idea and of the kind of work it enabled. As a result, what started as a single national conference has become three 'regional' conferences, drawing in the much larger group of schools now taking part and, because of the positive response in discussions each year, the 'open book' question has become an original kind of open book paper. In this case, we note, the chief examiner and the secretary to the English committee have had an important role in the dialogue.

Experience in this case suggests that when the board is positively interested in a new form of assessment, and sees a possible opportunity to improve the quality of evidence available for 'examination', it is of great help to have an exchange with teachers so that, as they progressively realise the potential of the new approach, they can explicitly adapt their teaching to exploit it fully. An annual meeting may fall short of the ideal, but by focusing on the examination questions and possibilities for the course in the new academic year, it can be of immediate service to both the examiners and the teachers.

Here and elsewhere under our second heading, however, the boards seem to take the development aspect of their work more diffidently and less seriously than one might expect. Knowing the uneasiness there has been about the examination of literature, for instance, since its inception, any method of assessment which may change the quality of the evidence a student can offer for examination deserves careful and public scrutiny by the English committee, and discussion with all the teachers served by the board. Surprisingly, we have seen little evidence to date of English committees promoting conferences to discuss the results of innovations they have supported.

Finally, if we dare say it, the best stimulus to teachers' initiative may come from suggestions and questions tentatively offered by the English committees themselves. A method used in the past by the JMB has been to circulate a written questionnaire to a sample of schools, enabling them to indicate their interest in various aspects of English not currently covered at A level. This is a useful start, but for two-way communication spoken language is naturally more flexible and penetrating than written. If we are right in believing that the range of provision in English syllabuses at 18+ needs careful consideration nationally, such questionnaires should lead to (regional?) conferences in which the potential aims of interested schools and colleges can be discussed in depth. Drawing on our own experience here, a one-day conference of teacher and adviser representatives, broken into groups to look at various existing models for a 'language' element or syllabus at A level, can produce very detailed and constructive indications of the kinds of aims different departments have in mind for the wider range of students staying on to 18+. We wonder if such conferences, would not form the best basis for syllabus revision and new proposals.

If they were tried, there would be a different starting point for groups of teachers wishing to take the initiative, or for the English committee trying to meet the need themselves — or possibly for joint working parties bridging the gap between the two?

3.8   Co-ordinating Developments in Course, Syllabus and Examination

So far we have focused on the individual board as an agent in curriculum development, and thus on the lines of communication between the English panel, or committee, and the wide range of departments they serve. We

have not considered differences in interest and aim among those departments, nor common interests and aims among the boards.

It is safe to predict that, given the scale of recent changes at 16–19,
radical differences will emerge both between departments and between
boards. Currently there is a major split in the profession between those who
see English as a unified subject, those committed to a language/literature
division, and those now defining courses in terms of communication. There
is a further division between teachers who see oracy, the media and verbal
communication as essential parts of English and those who see them at best
as extras, like the Mock Turtle's washing. And cutting across both divisions
there are teachers who believe that, without a selected sample of course
work, English examining is invalid, and those who remain satisfied with the
evidence in examination papers. For the moment, we are not concerned to
analyse or adjudicate in these disputes, but simply to point to the fact that
very deep divisions do exist in English and communication alone. As a
result every subject committee and board faces complex decisions. Here are
teachers with manifestly different aims and objectives: should one or more
schools of thought be provided for, or some compromise attempted, or
what?

Similarly, in setting up new qualifications at 17+, or a revised structure
of qualifications at 18+, there are divisions externally and internally
between those who call for academic or vocational specialism from 16, those
who want to delay it, and those who want both opportunities to be open.
How is an individual board to reach a decision which to provide for in its
syllabuses?

In a given field like English and communication these are extremely
intractable questions, especially for committees that meet perhaps once a
term on a single day. It seems to be in their common interest that a national
discussion should be organised and a serious review of the alternative
answers undertaken. Some conflicts are in principle reducible: they persist
for lack of a thorough analysis of available evidence. The relative value of
selected course work and set papers of various kinds probably belongs in
this category. Thus CSE and GCE boards have now had over a decade of
examination developments along both these lines and with thousands of
candidates double-entered at 16+, there must be no shortage of compara-
tive material in English simply awaiting inspection. A minimum of co-
operation between boards should make this possible.

Other conflicts are not reducible in this way, and behind them may lie the
essential forces in historical change. As new technology shifts the balance of
power among the modes of communication, and specific institutions such
as the television authorities begin to take a dominant role in culture and
society, arguments about 'English' and the curriculum take on a new
significance. Essentially they concern the role of the schools, colleges and

HE within a society in which they are only one 'educational' force, and not always the most compelling.

As things stand, the subject committee of an individual board, and the local or regional group of enterprising teachers, have to take all these conflicts on their shoulders in relative isolation. No central forum exists, even for a major area like English and communication, where the main issues can be regularly and seriously discussed, the necessary evidence called for and guidance on policy produced.

Thus, the teachers dealing with English and communication in — let us say for the sake of coverage — a tertiary college may have to deal with and negotiate syllabuses variously called English, language and communication. For one board these syllabuses may contain minimal aims plus a list of the examination paper questions; for another examining body they may consist of a brief list of objectives; for a third, the serried ranks of behavioural objectives set out on Grönland lines. The system of assessment may prohibit the inclusion of course work, or allow it to count for 100 per cent of the final mark; may reject multiple-choice questions or insist on a multiple-choice paper — in 'communication' — counting for 50 per cent of the marks; may demand traditional essay and comprehension, or replace them by case studies and projects . . . The teachers may be excluded from assessment in one case, and given the major responsibility for it (without training) in others.

On the intellectual plane, it is the kind of treatment with which Pavlov produced neuroses in his experimental dogs. And it is very natural, therefore, to seek refuge from these facts in a worldly cynicism or simply to feel outraged. The question is, what is to be done?

Essentially, a set of decisions started in 1918 and continuing into the 1970s have delegated responsibility for 16–19 curricula and examinations to a progressively wider range of individual boards, institutes and councils. What has not been provided for is any wider forum to which they feel responsible, and where the best of the decisions they take severally and independently can be critically sifted and integrated.

Behind this, probably, lies the unwritten assumption that consensus exists on the main directions for education and on educational 'standards'. If so, it is false, and manifestly so. Without a consensus, there seem to be two likely roads: domination by an elite answer, or a rational and democratic discussion to determine the points of agreement and of difference.

In the final issue, it is the DES that must take responsibility for providing such a forum — for ensuring that the voices in it are representative, and that it is capable of producing guidelines, based on a critical analysis of the experience of the different delegated bodies.

That there will remain differences has to be accepted, we believe. The three years of the project have brought us into joint work with teachers from very different backgrounds: direct grant and public schools, multi-racial inner urban comprehensives, tertiaries in small industrial towns, sixth form colleges in the commuter belt, and FE colleges on the coalfields. The drive and roots for education may have things in common, but socially and culturally there are great differences in emphasis, aspirations and attitudes. If these did not affect the teaching of English and communication something fundamental would be wrong.

It is for this reason that we have argued consistently in this report for some pluralism in the aims, syllabuses and material sampled for assessment, especially as the majority of an age group increasingly has to be taken into account.

Equally consistently, we would argue for the direct discussion of 'standards'. Among teachers of English and communication it *is* possible to assume some common awareness of the effect and quality with which language is used. Indeed, in our experience over many workshops, when groups of teachers are asked to respond acutely and discriminatingly to actual samples of language in use, they are seen at their best. This is where the 'examination' of English and communication begins, and this — not syllabuses or examination marks — is the final court of appeal in all arguments about standards, or the positive and negative effects of examining.

However, a broader consensus about the effect and quality of language in use is not incompatible with differences over the weight to be given to particular uses. Some teachers lean towards imagination, some to reason; some to reflection, some to social action; some to practice, some to analysis. All are affected by the social and cultural life of the students they teach, and the specific aspirations they have for them. It is these differences of emphasis that need to be allowed for in the syllabuses for the next generation of students.

3.9   The Immediate Tasks Ahead

In the final stages of the project there have been two central tasks. The first was to produce this report, a diagnosis based on our three years' work with colleagues. The second was to draw together the people who have been responsible for different strands of development work in a given region, and to discuss plans for the next five years. The development of a subject such as English and communication — and perhaps many others? — depends in the first place on small face-to-face groups planning and exchanging practical ideas. In the current climate, however, it is extremely rare for any one LEA to have groups tackling each of the main development problems at 17+ and 18 +. Thus, to achieve a co-ordinated view of 16–19 work and the possibilities of further development, regional meetings are essential as a second stage. Within a region spanning Tyneside to Cleveland, for instance, or Avon to Devon, active departments and groups may well be able to cover all the main potential areas discussed in Part 2. Across a region groups are strong enough to stimulate each other and close enough to meet at regular intervals to take stock of the position overall.

The next five years, it is already clear, are an interim stage. Whatever is decided nationally about 16+, CEE and N & F will not be fully implemented until the mid-1980s. Meanwhile, in order to meet the actual needs of students, broader qualifications have to be found at 17+, and a broader range of courses defined at 18+. How is this to be done within the current provision?

At 17+ there are three main kinds of opportunity for interim development work. The oldest are the reformed O levels that followed the 1964 Lockwood Report. Especially in the north, these have become the basis for a partnership among groups of participating schools and colleges, permitting a regular discussion not only of standards but also of the range of work to aim for, and the most promising approaches. In some regions — but not all — the CEE has laid a similar basis for development groups. More recently, the City and Guilds Foundation courses have opened the way for a broader vocationally-oriented course to 17+, with discussion among participating departments. None of these may yet be an ideal solution, but each gives scope for a maturer role for students and for stronger practical experience with spoken and written English. An exchange across a region can already draw on a variety of students' work and begin to illustrate the choices available in planning 17+ courses.

At 18+ the opportunities for development are more restricted. However, four major regions already have large groups working on 'alternative literature' syllabuses (with the AEB and the JMB) and the Cambridge Board's recent initiative offers further scope for local or regional groups. In addition, in almost every region there are now active departments starting on the communication studies A level. Regional working parties have formed in London, the South-West and the North, and it is of long-term importance that some of their members are equally involved in developing the new BEC courses. As regards English at A level, national working parties have now begun to formulate proposals for 1980.

Once again, if teachers and advisers are to appreciate the significance of these choices at 18+, and their potential links with 17+ courses, regional discussions and working groups form the next stage.

However, if activities stop there the prospects are bleak. What Part 3 has tried to indicate is the interdependence of teachers, the examining bodies and other enabling agencies. Thus, if regional groups of teachers and advisers are formulating integrated policies for English and communication 16–19, it is vital that parallel — and linked — discussions should be mounted among those with national responsibility for curriculum and qualifications.

There are two main groups who can promote such discussions, the first voluntary, the second statutory. The two main voluntary associations, the NATE and the ALE, are already making an essential contribution locally and regionally; almost every group we have worked with over the past three years has gained insight, drive and direction from their members. Moreover, the two associations are already linked by joint membership in NATE's 16+ Committee, which is currently producing a series of guidance and discussion documents on the major issues at 16–19. During the next decade these two voluntary associations will offer the major forum for teachers to define their position nationally: it is a big responsibility.

Among the examining bodies, and in particular their English/communication panels or committees, there is no similar provision or opportunity for joint discussion. This seriously weakens the ability of teacher and other delegates to take a national view of new demands on the system and the developments needed. This is a significant and rather frightening gap. Who is to take responsibility for bridging it? On the schools' side, this falls to the Schools Council and, in the particular case, to its English Committee. Overall, however, it is the DES that needs to foster and enable an integrated view.

The problems we have discussed at 16–19, and the potential solutions, are beyond a single board. But every board could make a contribution if there was some co-ordinated policy in view, simply by calling on and responding to the initiative of different regional groups. Indeed many different examining bodies have already contributions to offer, as our report indicates. What limits or fritters away the effect of their enterprise is first their relative isolation, and secondly the resulting sense that 'experimental' programmes are not a matter of deeply serious national concern. With actual and potential 16–19 students in mind, we believe they are. There is the responsibility and challenge to all of us when we think of the new generation that now extends through into the twenty-first century.

Appendix
Notes, Sources, Acknowledgements

Part 1

1.1

Sources: *15 to 18: A Report of the Central Advisory Council* (the Crowther Report), 1959, pp. 407, 409

Early Leaving: A Report of the Central Advisory Council, 1954, pp. 8, 9

The Certificate of Secondary Education (the Beloe Report), SSEC, 1962, p. 9

So far as the figures for students 16–19 are concerned, there are many traps for the unwary reader in the annual *Statistics of Education* for England and Wales. During the project we have noted major errors in the national press, and especially among political critics of education. This note is therefore a warning about the mistaken claims and accusations that will be made unless the *Statistics* are read critically. It also points to the flaws and gaps in these statistics, and thus the need for the DES urgently to reconsider the basis on which they are collected.

(a) It is important to know each year the number of students staying on in full-time education for courses beyond the fifth form, whether on one-year courses or two-year courses.

Surprisingly enough, this total is not given in the annual *Statistics*. However, it can be estimated from the figures available. Thus 1976, Vol. 1, p. 35 clearly shows how many pupils were staying on in school for a sixth year, beyond the statutory leaving age, and what courses they were following. In January 1976 the overall total staying for a sixth year was 201,000. What we need next is a parallel table for FE. Unfortunately, no such table exists. All that is given in *Statistics* is a table of full-time students who were *aged 16 on 31 December 1975* (1975, Vol. 3, p. 4). However, by 31 December roughly a third of those who left school the previous summer have reached the age of 17. This is why the 'schools' table we referred to sensibly quotes the age on 31 August 1975. So the two tables are not comparable.

Nevertheless, it is still possible to estimate the total who left school in the summer of 1975 and went on to full-time courses in FE. We do know that about a third of those who moved from the fifth form into full-time FE had reached the age of 17 by 31 December. Thus the total of 16-year-olds at that date represents roughly two-thirds of the total group who moved to FE from the fifth form. Thus we can estimate that in all about 105,000 FE students were doing a year in full-time education beyond the fifth form.

Given this figure, we can then estimate those engaged in a second year's full-time education beyond the fifth form. Since the results do not appear in *Statistics* it is worth tabling them here;

Students staying on in full-time education

	Schools	FE	Age Group
Staying a year beyond the fifth form in full-time education	201,000	est. 105,000	41%
Staying two years beyond the fifth form	126,000	est. 55,000	25%

It is not possible to make a direct comparison with 1951, as the earlier statistics are much cruder. This is why we have hade to base our elementary contrast in the text on the numbers aged 17 on 1 January in 1951 and 1976. As we have now pointed out, some of these will be in their first year beyond the fifth form, some in their second. Thus, the figures are simply a crude guide to 'staying on'.

(b) Next it is important to know the examination entries and achievements of students, ideally at two points: first as they leave the fifth form, and secondly by the time they have reached the age of 19.

Once again, the annual *Statistics of Education* fail to provide the answers. They do give the numbers *entering* O level who were aged 16 on 1 September following (1976, Vol. 2, p. 39). Unfortunately, from our point of view these are rather rough indicators as both in 1951 and 1976 they include a small, but unspecified, number of candidates from outside England and Wales. However, they do offer a crude estimate of the proportion of the fifth form using the examination in each of these years.

The overall O-level results of 16-year-old candidates are not available.

For those leaving *school* each year there are many tables analysing cumulative examination achievements. However, these are rendered almost useless for our purposes by the fact that 13.6 per cent leave for FE courses (1976, Vol. 2, p. 5), hoping no doubt to add to their achievements, but no attempt is made to survey FE leavers' achievements on a similar basis or to co-ordinate the overall achievements of the schools-FE system at 16–19.

The results are tantalising, to say the least. Thus we know (1976, Vol. 2, p. ix) that 36 per cent of *school* 'leavers' gained O-level English grades A–C, or CSE grade 1, and the same year the number of FE students starting one-year GCE courses was:

37,000 full-time
28,000 part-time day
149,000 evening only
———————
214,000 students in all
———————

It would be interesting to know how many of these were under 19 and — for instance — added a similar O-level grade in English to their tally. Indeed it is hard to see why their results should be ignored, when those in schools are treated to such a detailed scrutiny. Surely the DES does not actually intend to be unequal in its treatment of these two overlapping systems?

Clearly, because of these gaps it is difficult to give more than crude estimates of the examination achievements of students 16–19. The best we can do, in the circumstances, is to make clear some of the main dangers that readers of the annual *Statistics* should be alerted to.

1.2
Sources: The Crowther Report, p. 265
Tenth Report of the House of Commons Select Committee on Expenditure, *The Attainments of the School Leaver*, Vol. 1, 1977, pp. liv, xxiii
The Examining of English Language (the Lockwood Report), 1964, pp. 9–13
Times Educational Supplement, 2 September 1977, p. 6
The Reliability of GCE O-level Examinations in English Language, E. A. Hewitt, JMB, 1967
The 1968 CSE Monitoring Experiment, Desmond L. Nuttall, Schools Council Working Paper 34, Evans/Methuen Educational, 1971
Studies in Examining at 16+: English, Terry Brown, ND, Institute of Education, University of Durham
An Analysis of Examination Standards, P.E. Roe, YREB, 1976
The Work of the Joint Matriculation Board, R. Christopher, JMB, 1969
Criticisms from various Black Papers
Statistics of Education, Vol. 2, 1976

The quotation from John Mitchell comes from an article specially written for the project newsletter and based on his Diploma work at Leeds University. Coventry LEA worked in the same field during 1977 when two teachers on part-secondment took evidence from training officers in the engineering industry and examined the actual communication demands met by apprentices. We were grateful to the authority for letting us see this report in an interim form. It offers a very useful first analysis of the actual demands being met, the help received from training officers and FE courses, and the earlier guidance that schools might give, (including, for example, the ability to use indexing and cataloguing systems, which in industry are often very complex; experience in solving problems by discussion; and experience in distinguishing between the forms of writing required for different tasks).

We were given further valuable help in this field by Dr John Gardner, Principal of Leigh (Tertiary) College, and Bryan Lee and Gordon Hodgeon, the English advisers for Rotherham and Cleveland. Among the findings of their several working parties we might mention:

(a) 'Considerable uncertainty about the aims and objectives of the CSE examination.'
'Few of the employers knew that there were different modes and that the school-based mode III was subject to a process of validation. CSE grade 1 was accepted as an O-level equivalent, but the employers saw little value in the lower grades and many employers had introduced their own admission tests.'

(b) 'Some employers wanted the school to develop vocational courses to the exclusion of what were seen as the peripheral subjects, e.g. the humanities and the aesthetic. Other employers preferred a good general education with emphasis on the social role.'

(c) 'Analysis of language used by young employees and trainees suggests that those uses which are most obvious (such as writing, which offers preserved evidence of the activity) are not necessarily the most important uses, and those skills which are most obvious (such as those which give mechanical accuracy) are not necessarily the most important skills.'
A major implication of their evidence is the need 'to encourage schools and employers to develop new practices in teaching of students and training of employees in language use'.

1.3

Sources: *The Attainments of the School Leaver*, Vol. 1, p. xxxi
A Language for Life (the Bullock Report), 1975, pp. 150, 120, 119
Cleveland Schools/Industry Liaison Working Group, *Final Report*, 1976–7

1.4

Sources: *The Teaching of English in England* (the Newbolt Report), 1921, pp. 71, 310, 312
The Bullock Report, pp. 224, 322, 548

1.5

Sources: *The Attainments of the School Leaver*, Vol. 1., p. xiv

The Crowther Report, pp. 284, 303
Language Performance (a 'discussion document') APU, 1978
One-Year Courses in Colleges and Sixth Forms, D. Vincent and J. Dean, NFER, 1977, Table 11
Schools Council 18+ Research Programme: Report of the English Steering Group, 1977, pp. 3–4 (our italics in the text)

Part 2

2.1

Source: *Language and Education,* Fred Flower, Longmans, 1966

In 1978 the AEB A level in communications studies had been accepted for entrance purposes by over twenty universities (including Cambridge) and not accepted by five (including Oxford).

In 1978 over 60,000 candidates were double-entered for CSE and GCE (Shirley Williams, *TES,* November 1978).

2.2

Sources: *The Teaching of English in England* (the Newbolt Report), p. 301
Curriculum and Examinations in Secondary Schools (the Norwood Report), 1943, pp. 33, 93, 94
The Crowther Report, p. 126

2.4

Sources: Quotations from Dryden, Pope, Johnson and Hazlitt
The Newbolt Report, p. 280
The English Association, quoted from the Newbolt Report, p. 303

For the work on which this section is based we are particularly indebted to the following groups and their English advisers:

(a) the Leicestershire Alternative A Level (JMB) group, who have invited us each term to discuss the potentialities of their course work element;
(b) the Northern, Avon and Devon consortia of the AEB Alternative A Level, with whom we have organised a programme of development meetings;
(c) the Sheffield Alternative A Level group, who invited us to all the planning meetings for their proposal (now accepted by JMB), and for whom we have organised workshops;
(d) the NATE 16+ Committee and the groups of teachers who have joined the project's commission at successive NATE conferences 1976–8.

We have also had the active co-operation of the moderators for the four AEB consortia, the chief examiner, Dr Peter Buckroyd, and Malcolm Fain, the AEB secretary responsible for this area.

For examples of students' work and comments we are indebted to students and teachers at Wyggeston School, Beauchamp School and Exeter (Tertiary) College.

In addition we have drawn heavily on an article (in our booklet series) by Richard Gill of Wyggeston School, Leicester, and quoted from an article in *Use of English* (Spring 1978) by Peter Phillips and Alan Child of Don Valley High School and a report to the Nottingham ATO by Vic Taylor of Christ the King Comprehensive School, Nottinghamshire.

2.5

Sources: The Newbolt Report, pp. 10, 294, 358

Quotations from students are selected from the survey carried out by the project in 1977 with the help of participating departments.

We should like to acknowledge the steady encouragement we have received from the AEB and its Communication Studies Panel, particularly from Marion Strudwick, John Gardner, Jim Keegan and John Mitchell. In addition we have drawn throughout this section on two main sources:

(a) the ideas put forward by teachers in the London and Huddersfield conferences organised by the project in 1977 and 1978, and more fully reported in our pamphlet series;

(b) the N & F commissioned group, convened by John Gardner, for which the project acted as observer.

2.6

Source: The Crowther Report, p. 270

In reviewing the proposals we have borne in mind the points made by teachers at a delegate conference called by the project in April 1978. The work is being followed up (Autumn 1978) in a northern and a southern working party.

For the anthology pieces we are indebted to: Lawnswood School, Leeds; Queen Mary's College, Basingstoke; Swanhurst School, Birmingham; Netherstowe Comprehensive School, Lichfield; Oldham Technical College; Filton Technical College; and the Schools Council Writing Research Unit (for the first and last two pieces).

2.7

We are indebted for much of this discussion to continuing contact during the project with the Cheshire working party convened by Geoffrey Thornton. Their work has been published by the authority under the title *Communication and Response*, 1978.

2.8

For this section we have drawn on three sources:

(a) a series of workshops organised jointly with Marjorie Holt of Bolton College of Education (Technical), with the advice of Ken Hastings, HMI;

(b) a parallel series organised jointly with Eddie Webb and Geoff Stanton of Garnett College, with advice from Paul Clark (ILEA advisory teacher) and James O'Connor, HMI;

(c) the West Yorkshire FE group, who invited us throughout our three years to their regular meetings.

In all, about thirty colleges were represented in this work.

The briefing for the photography students was drawn up by Martin Broome, then at Kitson College, Leeds.

The Vale of Belvoir project undertaken by South-East Derbyshire College is reported in detail in our booklet series.

2.9

This section and the next are based on a joint schools-FE conference organised by the project with the help of Emrys Evans, University of Birmingham. This was fully reported in our discussion paper series.

2.10

Source: *One-Year Courses in Colleges and Sixth Forms,* p. 93

The CEE students quoted were interviewed at Haggerston School, ILEA, and we are much indebted to their teacher, Jane Leggett, who wrote one of our original booklets describing this work.

Junior's work was drawn from Northumberland Park School, Haringey, and we are indebted to his communication teacher, Sue Crump, for this and further detailed analysis of the pilot foundation courses for City and Guilds.

The CEE/A-level course was organised by Joan Markham and Virginia Graham of Swanshurst School, Birmingham, and we are grateful to both them and their colleagues for continuing help throughout our three years. Swanshurst was one of several departments represented in NATE's Birmingham-Worcester group which has monitored one-year courses throughout the period of our project and produced the valuable reports both in our discussion paper series and in the *TES* (24 November 1978).

2.11

Sources: 'Examinations at 18+', *Schools Council Examinations Bulletin* 38, pp. 5–6

One-Year Courses in Colleges and Sixth Forms Vincent and Dean, *NFER*, 1977

Part 3

3.3

Source: The Newbolt Report, p. 280

3.7

The quotations from Mr D. J. Ramsden are drawn from a paper given to the Schools Council conference on 'Curriculum-Examinations Interaction', 1 December 1977.

For their critical advice and encouragement throughout the project we should like to thank the following:

Margaret Gill	Lecturer, Rusden State College, Victoria, Imperial Relations Trust Research Fellow and member of the project team September 1975–January 1977
Maurice Plaskow	Curriculum Officer, Schools Council

Members of the Consultative Committee:

Fred Flower, MBE	Principal, Kingsway-Princeton College, London (Committee Chairman)
James Britton	Formerly Professor, Goldsmiths' College, University of London
Stephen Brook	Goldsmiths' College, University of London
Angela Dale	St John's College of FE, Manchester
Dr Alyn Davies	Principal, Bretton Hall College of HE
Martin Davies	Lecturer in English and Education, University of Stirling
Emrys Evans	Lecturer in Education, University of Birmingham School of Education
Ann Gray	Head of English Department, Wakefield Girls' High School
Ted Hopkin	Head of English, Liberal Arts Department, Exeter (Tertiary) College
John Love	Deputy Head, Llantarnam Comprehensive School, Cwmbran
Graham Martin	Professor of English Literature, Open University
Geoffrey Melling	HMI (member until appointment as Director, FE Curriculum Review and Development Unit)
Ian Morgan	Vice-Principal, W. R. Tuson College, Preston
Dennis Roberts	Headmaster, Park House School, Sheffield
David Short	HMI (from 1977)
Don Taylor	Headmaster, Durrants School, Rickmansworth, Herts.
Geoffrey Thornton	Inspector for English, ILEA
Alice Wakefield	Deputy Head, Brune Park School, Gosport, Hants.

Finally, this report would not have been produced without the care and persistence under fire of our joint secretaries, Mollie Dixon and Hilda Walters.